Igbo Syntax

The Structure and Rules that Govern Igbo Phrases and Well-formed Sentences

Elisha O. Ogbonna

Igbo Syntax: *The Structure and Rules that Govern Igbo Phrases and Well-formed Sentences*

by Elisha O. Ogbonna

This book is written to provide educational and Igbo language learning information for linguistic and advanced learners.

Copyright © May 2024 by Elisha O. Ogbonna

All rights reserved. No part of this book may be reproduced, transmitted, or distributed in any form by any means, including, but not limited to, recording, photocopying, or taking screenshots of parts of the book, without prior written permission from the author or the publisher. Brief quotations for noncommercial purposes, such as book reviews, permitted by Fair Use of the Canada Copyright Law, are allowed without written permissions, as long as such quotations do not cause damage to the book's commercial value.

ISBN:
978-1-7781320-0-1 (Hardcover)
978-1-7777461-9-3 (Paperback)
978-1-7781320-1-8 (eBook)

Produced by:

Prinoelio Press
For Igbo Learning Hub
E-mail: Igbolearninghub@gmail.com
https://www.Igbo learninghub.com

Table of Contents

Introduction to Syntax (*Okwu Mmalite Amụmàmụ Mmebe Ahịrịokwu*)   7

CHAPTER 1   11

The Basic Units of Igbo Syntax   11
    1.1 Words (Mkpụrụokwu)   11
    1.2 Clitics (Nsokwunye)   12
    1.3 Proclitics (Nsokwunye kemkpọaha):   13
    1.4 Enclitics (Ọdabere/Nsokwunye Kengwaa):   14
    Exercise   16

CHAPTER 2   17

Word Order Typology (Ụdị nke Usorookwu)   17
    2.1 What is Word Order?   17
    2.2 Parts of Word Order   17
    2.3 Types of Word Groups   18
    2.4 Topological classification of Igbo sentence   19
    2.5 Hierarchical Structure of Igbo Sentence   21
    Exercise   32

CHAPTER 3   33

Word Classes/Syntactic Category (*Ụdị na Nhazị Okwu*)   33
    3.1 Noun (Mkpọaha/Aha)   35
    3.2 Verbs (Ngwaa)   38
    3.3 Adjective (Nkọwaha)   41
    3.4 Adverb (Nkwuwa)   42
    3.5 Preposition (Mbuuzo)   42
    3.6 Determiners *(Nkwuso)*:   43
    3.7 Conjunction (Njikọ)   45
    3.8 Inflectional Elements *(Mgbanwe/inflekshọn)*:   46
    3.9 Complementizer *(Mmeju)*:   47
    Exercise   49

CHAPTER 4   51

The Lexicon (*Usoro Okwu*)   51
    4.1 Syntax and Lexicon Items   52
    4.2 Criteria for Noun classification   56
    4.3 Common Classes of Noun   59
    4.4 Subcategorization, Selection, and Construction of Nouns   61
    4.5 Construction: 62
    4.6 Criteria for verbs classification   63
    4.7 Serial Verb Construction   80
    4.8 Individual Verbs, Complements, and Adjuncts   84
    Exercise   90

CHAPTER 5   91

Phrasal Categories (*Ọdịdị nke Nkebiokwu Igbo*)   91
    5.1 Noun Phrase (Nkebiokwu keaha)   92
    5.2 Adjective Phrases (Nkebiokwu kenkọwaaha):   93
    5.3 Adverbial Phrases (Nkebiokwu kenkwuwa):   94
    5.4 Prepositional Phrase (Nkebiokwu kembuụzọ)   95
    5.5 Infinitive Phrase (Nkebiokwu kemfinitiivu)   95
    5.6 Gerund Phrase (Nkebiokwukejerondu)   97
    5.7 Demonstrative Phrases (Nkebiokwu kenruaka)   99
    5.8 Collective Phrases (Nkebiokwu kemkpokọta)   100
    5.9 Interrogative Phrase (Nkebiokwu kenjụajụjụ)   100
    5.10 Possessive Phrases (Nkebiokwu kennọchinke)   101
    5.11 Number Phrases (Nkebiokwu keọnụọgụgụ)   102
    Exercise   104

CHAPTER 6   105

Igbo Phrase Structure Rules (*Iwu Nhazi Nkebiokwu Igbo*)   105
    6.1 Phrase structure rules   105
    6.2 Surface structure: 112
    6.3 Phrase tree structures   114
    Exercise   116

CHAPTER 7   117

Transformational Grammar (Mgbanwe Ụtọasụsụ)   117
    7.1 Movement Rule in transformative Grammar (Iwu kemgbanwe ọnọdụ)   117

7.2 Deletion Rule in Transformative Grammar (Iwu nke Mwepu): 122
7.3 Insertion for Question Formation (Ntinye ke mmebe ajụjụ): 126
Exercise 128

CHAPTER 8   129

Grammatical Functions (Ọrụ Ụtọasụsụ Igbo)   129
   8.1 Subject: 130
   8.2 Verb: 131
   8.3 Object: 134
   8.4 Complement: 136
   8.5 Adverbial: 138
   Exercise 148

CHAPTER 9   149

Heads and Modifiers (Ọdịdị Ụtọasụsụ nke Nkebiahịrị Igbo)   149
   9.1 Heads, Modifiers, and Meanings 149
   9.2 Complements and Adjuncts: Enhancing Structure 151
   9.3 Clauses: Building Blocks of Communication 153
   9.4 Projection from Lexical Heads to Phrases 154
   Exercise 160

CHAPTER 10   161

Constituent Structure (Ndoko Akụrụngwa)   161
   10.1 Definition of Constituent structure: 161
   10.2 Types of Constituents: 164
   10.3 Tests for Constituents: 165
   Exercise 176

CHAPTER 11   177

   11.1 The Grammatical Nature of Igbo Clauses: 177
   11.2 Main/Independent Clause 178
   11.3 Subordinate/Dependent Clause 181
   Exercise 189

CHAPTER 12   191

Cleft Sentence in Igbo Grammar (Nkewaa *Ahịrịokwu dị n'asụsụ Igbo*)   191
   12.1 The syntax of clefts clauses 191

12.2 Cleft Construction:	192
12.3 The cleft pronoun in Igbo:	195
12.4 kinds of cleft constructions in Igbo:	197
12.5 Igbo copular clauses	200
Exercise	204

CHAPTER 13 — 205

The Structure and Formation of Igbo Sentence (*Nhazi na Mmebe Ahịrịokwu Igbo*) — 205

13.1 A sentence—grammatical unit:	205
13.2 Types of Sentences based on SUBJ-PRED construction.	205
13.3 Types of Sentences based on Structures.	212
Exercise	217
About the Author	218
Other Books	219
INDEX	224

Introduction to Syntax (Okwu Mmalite *Amụmàmụ Mmebe Ahịrịokwu*)

Understanding the Foundation: Syntax in Language
In the realm of linguistics and communication, syntax serves as the fundamental framework that governs how words and phrases are organized to create meaningful sentences. It is akin to the structural foundation of a building, providing coherence and order to language. This book delves into the intricate world of Igbo syntax, providing comprehensive insights and examples to enhance your understanding.

What is Syntax?
Syntax is the arrangement of words and phrases to create well-structured and meaningful sentences. It encompasses the rules and principles that guide the formation of sentences in a language. A proper grasp of syntax is essential for effective communication and clear expression of ideas.

In linguistics, syntax is the study of how words and morphemes combine to form larger units such as phrases and sentences. It refers to the rules governing how words combine to form phrases, clauses, and sentences. It can also be defined as the arrangement of words in sentences, clauses, and phrases, and the study of the formation of sentences and the relationship of their component. In spoken and written language, syntax refers to the set of rules that determine the arrangement of words in a sentence.

Since syntax deals with rules governing the arrangement of words in a sentence, it is considered as the part of linguistics that focuses on the level of the sentence. It is concerned with the meanings of words in the arrangement and combination with each other to form phrases or sentences. As a result, it focuses on the resultant differences in meaning occasioned by the changes or rearrangements of word order through the addition or subtraction of words from sentences or simply the changes in the form of sentences.

Syntax also deals with how related different types of sentences are with one another including detailed examination of the elements or structure of ambiguous sentences.

Linguistic typology, a field of linguistics that studies and classifies languages according to their structural features, attempts to classify languages on two main features:

According to high-order principles of language morphology.
According to the language syntax (arrangement of words in a sentence).

This field of linguistics aims to describe and explain the common properties and the structural diversity of the world's languages and make sets of generalizations across these languages irrespective of what family of language they belong to.

The Role of Syntax in Communication
Syntax plays a pivotal role in conveying intended meanings and facilitating effective communication. It ensures that sentences are constructed logically, allowing ideas to flow seamlessly and readers or listeners to comprehend the message without ambiguity.

Syntax Components and Their Functions
To grasp the nuances of syntax, let's break down its key components and explore their functions within sentences.

1. Word Order
The order in which words appear in a sentence greatly impacts its meaning. Different languages follow distinct word orders, and even a slight rearrangement can alter the message conveyed.

Example 1: Igbo (Subject-Verb-Object)
Ọ na-agụ akwụkwọ.   Ọ *(isiahịrị)* na-agụ *(ngwaa)* akwụkwọ *(nnara)*.
She (subject) reads (verb) a book (object).

*Akwụkwọ na-agụ Ọ.   *Akwụkwọ *(nnara)* na-agụ *(ngwaa)* Ọ *(isiahịrị)*.
**A book (object) reads (verb) she (subject).*

2. Parts of Speech
Each word in a sentence belongs to a specific part of speech (e.g., nouns (Mkpọaha/Aha), verbs (ngwaa), adjectives (Nkọwaha), adverbs (Nkwuwa)), and their arrangement influences the sentence's structure.

Example 2: Noun-Adjective Order in Igbo
Ose (mkpọaha) uhie (nkọwaha) na-ekpo ọkụ.
The red (adjective) pepper (noun) is hot.
[Adjective-Noun in English]

Ose (mkpọaha) na-acha uhie uhie (nkọwaha) na-ekpo ọkụ
The pepper (noun) is red (adjective) and delicious.
[Adjective-Noun in English]

3. Phrases and Clauses
Phrases and clauses are essential building blocks of sentences, contributing to their complexity and depth.

Example 3: Noun Phrase (Nkebiokwu keaha) and Adjective Clause (Nkebiokwu kenkọwaaha)
Akwụkwọ ahụ (Mkpọaha) Jọn tụrụ aro (Nkebiokwu kenkọwaaha) na-adọrọ mmasị
The book (noun) that John recommended (adjective clause) is fascinating.

Akwụkwọ ahụ (Mkpọaha) na-adọrọ mmasị, Jọn tụkwara aro (Nkebiokwu kenkọwaaha) ya.
The book (noun) is fascinating, and John recommended (adjective clause) it.

4. Sentence Types
Different sentence types (*declarative* (ahịrịnkwụsà), *interrogative* (ahịrịajụjụ), *imperative* (ahịrịntimiwu), *exclamatory* (ahịrịmkpu) *optative* (ahịrịnchọ)) have distinct syntax patterns that convey specific functions.
Example 4: Interrogative and Declarative Sentences

a. Ihe nkiri ahụ ọ masịrị gị?
Did *(auxiliary verb)* you *(subject)* enjoy *(main verb)* the movie? (interrogative)

b. Ihe nkiri ahụ *(isiahịrị)* masịrị *(ngwaa)* gị *(nnara)*.
You *(subject)* enjoyed *(main verb)* the movie. (declarative)

Application of syntax
1. Creative Writing
In creative writing, syntax plays a vital role in setting the tone and rhythm of the narrative.

Example 5:
Ìhè ọnwa gbara egwu *(nkebiokwukengwaa)* site n'alaka *(nkebiokwukeaha)* ndị na-akwaghari, na-eme kwa onyinyo mara mma *(nkebiokwukengwaa)* n'ala ọhịa ahụ.
The moonlight danced *(verb phrase)* through the swaying branches *(noun phrase)*, casting enchanting shadows *(verb phrase)* on the forest floor.

2. Public Speaking
Effective public speakers utilize syntax to emphasize key points and engage their audience.

Example 6:
Site na-ijikọta ọnụ, anyị nwere ike *(nkebiokwukengwaa)* ịkpalite mgbanwe, kpalie olile anya *(nkebiokwukengwaa)*, ma mee ka ọdịnihu dị mma *(nkebiokwukengwaa)* maka ọgbọ ndị na-abịa.
"Together, we can (verb phrase) ignite change, inspire hope (verb phrase), and shape a brighter future (verb phrase) for generations to come."

3. Formal Writing
In formal writing, syntax ensures clarity and precision, making complex ideas more accessible.

Example 7:
Site na nchọcha ziri ezi *(nkebiokwukembuụzọ)*, usoro ntụcha zuru oke *(nkebiokwukenkọwaha)*, na nkọwa nke ntụgharị uche *(nkebiokwukenkọwaha)*, ihe ọmụmụ ahụ na-enye ihè *(nkebiokwuke(ngwaa)* kemgbagwoju anya nke mgbanwe dị na omume ọha mmadụ.
Through meticulous research *(prepositional phrase)*, comprehensive analysis *(adjective phrase)*, and thoughtful interpretation *(adjective phrase)*, the study illuminates *(verb)* the intricate dynamics of social behavior.

4. Everyday Conversation
Even in casual conversations, syntax influences how messages are conveyed and received.

Example 8:
Dịka Ị kwuru *(nkebiokwukembuụzọ)*, anyị kwesịrị ịgbalịsi ike *(isingwaa)* mgbe niile maka uto nke onwe na nkwalite na-aga n'ihu *(nkebiokwukeaha)*.
"Just like (prepositional phrase) you said, we should (modal verb) always strive (main verb) for personal growth and continuous improvement (noun phrase)."

5. Academic Discourse
Syntax is crucial in academic discourse, aiding in the presentation of complex arguments and concepts.

Example 9:
Njatule a *(nkebiokwukeaha)* na-akwado nke ọma *(nkebiokwukengwaa)* echiche ahụ, na-enye ihe akaebe gbara ọkpụrụkpụ *(nkebiokwukengwaa)* maka atụtụ atụrụ aro ya.
 The empirical data (noun phrase) vividly substantiates (verb phrase) the hypothesis, providing compelling evidence (verb phrase) for the proposed theory.

Chapter 1
The Basic Units of Igbo Syntax

There are several ways of classifying languages. Three of the many ways that languages can be classified are phonological, structural, and syntactical classifications. When language is categorized based on: segmental and suprasegmental parameters, it is called *phonological classification*. When language is classified based on the internal structure of the words, it is referred to as *structural classification* and when language is categorized based on their word order and relationship between their head and modifiers, it is referred to as *syntactic classification*.

In Igbo language, syntax forms the backbone of linguistic structure. Understanding the fundamental components is of great important to unraveling the intricacies of Igbo communication.

1.1 Words (Mkpụrụokwu)

At the heart of Igbo syntax are words – the building blocks of expression. Nouns, verbs, adjectives, and more come together to create meaning and convey ideas. In the context of language and linguistics, the term "word" refers to a fundamental unit of speech and writing that carries meaning. It is a discrete entity that represents a specific concept, object, action, or idea. A word is the building block of sentences and forms the basis of communication.

Structure of a Word: A word is composed of one or more sounds (phonemes) and is typically represented by a sequence of letters in written form. It often consists of a combination of vowels and consonants that come together to create a recognizable sound pattern.

For example, in English, the word "cat" is made up of three phonemes: /k/ - /æ/ - /t/. In Igbo language, "cat" is called "nwamba" and it is made up of five phonemes /nw/ - /a/ - /m/ - /b/ - /a/.

Morphology and Meaning: Words possess both form and meaning. Morphology is the study of the structure and formation of words. It examines how words are built from smaller units called morphemes, which are the smallest grammatical units that carry meaning. For instance, the word "unhappiness" consists of three morphemes: "un-" (a prefix indicating negation), "happy" (a root word), and "-ness" (a suffix indicating a state or quality).

Generally, most Igbo verbs come with affixes or other nominals as part of their complex e.g.

bá (*enter*)	bárà (*entered*)	bátà (*enter into*)
cha (*cut*)	chara (*cut* [pst])	chapụ (*cut out*)
chọ (*look for*)	chọrọ (*searched*)	chọta (*find*)
gwá (*tell*)	gwárá (*told*)	gwátụrụ (*share info*)
ma (*know*)	mara (*knew*)	maka (*because*)
ri (*eat*)	riri (*ate*)	rịpụ/gbapụ (*escape*)
zi (*inform*)	ziri (*informed*)	zipu (*send (a person)*)

Word Usage: Words are combined in various ways to create meaningful sentences, enabling us to convey complex ideas, share experiences, and interact with one another. The arrangement of words and their relationships within sentences, known as syntax, determines the structure and meaning of a sentence.

A word is a fundamental linguistic unit that serves as the core element of communication, encompassing both form and meaning. Understanding the role of words is essential for comprehending language and expressing ideas effectively.

1.2 Clitics (Nsokwunye)

Clitics, though small in form, play a significant role in Igbo sentences. These elements attach to words, subtly inflecting their meanings and contributing to the overall syntax. In linguistics, the term "clitic" refers to a type of linguistic element that functions similarly to a word but is dependent on another nearby word (usually a more prominent one) for its full meaning. Clitics are unique in that they do not typically stand alone as independent meaningful words. They either attach themselves or stand alone to other words to take on grammatical or syntactic roles within a sentence of some language.

For examples:
Onye (kwa) ka I na-cho?   *Who is (that/particularly) is s/he looking for?*
Gini buzi ihe O mere?   *What did s/he (finally/at the end) do?*

Types of Clitics:
In general, there are three types of Clitics, namely: proclitics, mesoclitics and enclitics. Mesoclitics do not apply to the Igbo language. Mesoclitics are clitics that appear within a word, often between the root and an affix, and are not part of Igbo language's grammatical structure.

So, in Igbo language, the two types of clitics that exist are mainly proclitics and enclitics. They play a significant role in conveying Igbo grammatical information as would reveal below.

1.3 Proclitics (Nsokwunye kemkpọaha):

These are clitics that come after a noun or pronoun in a sentence. They are linguistic elements that do not typically stand alone as meaningful independent words but rather become closely connected to the word that they follow. Proclitics are standalone elements and do not attach to the noun or pronoun that they follow. They play a significant role in language by conveying grammatical, syntactic, or semantic information within a sentence. Examples of Igbo proclitics are: kwa, kwanu, zi, ga, kwu, sọ, nwa, cha.

Examples with nouns (mkpọaha) in a sentence:

1. **Onye (kwa) ka I na-cho?**
   Who is (in particular) is s/he looking for?

2. **E jidela nwoke nu gburu mmadụ.**
   That man that killed someone has been apprehended.

3. **Ije nwa anyị gbara izu ya enweghịzị isi**
   That (Our) proposed/planned trip has been aborted.

4. **Mmiri kwu ka o nyeghi unu.**
   He could not even afford water for you (people).

5. **Ngajị cha ka Uche enweghị.**
   Uche could not (at least) afford a spoon.

6. **Nne m zụtara efere ga ụnyahụ.**
   My mom bought assorted dishes/plates yesterday.

7. **Ọ zụtara anụ rị tupu m mata.**
   S/he already bought the meat before I knew it

Examples with Pronouns (Nnọchiaha) and the subject of a sentence using: kwanu, zi, kwu, kwa, sọ, kwu and cha.

1. **Gini kwanu ka O mere?**
   What (exactly/in particulaar) did s/he do?

2. **Gini zi ka O mere?**
   What (in the end/in particulaar) did s/he do?

3. **Onye kwu gwara gị na anọ m n'ụlọ ọrụ?**
   Who (exactly) told you I'm at work?

4. **Ọ kwa Uche na Eze ka Ị kpọrọ?**
   It was Uche and Eze that you invited/called?

5. **Hapu ya sọ, Achoghị m ka O soro anyị ga ebe ahụ**
   Let him/her be; I don't want hime/her to accompany us to that location/place.

6. **Ha cha ka Ọ kpọchiri n'ụlọ nkpọrọ.**
   They were all locked up in a prison/cell.

7. **M kwu ka Ọ kpọrọ asị.**
   S/he hates (even) me as well.

1.4 Enclitics (Ọdabere/Nsokwunye Kengwaa):
These are clitics that attach to the end of a word. An "enclitic" is a type of clitic that attaches to the end of a word or a phrase. Enclitics are linguistic elements that do not typically stand alone as independent words but rather become closely connected to the word that precedes them. Enclitics play a significant role in language by conveying grammatical, syntactic, or semantic information within a sentence.

Significance of Enclitics:
Enclitics are essential for understanding the structure and grammar of a language. They contribute to word order, verb conjugation, and overall sentence formation. By attaching themselves to other words, enclitics convey specific grammatical or syntactic information, allowing speakers to communicate efficiently and convey nuanced meanings. The study of enclitics is crucial for comprehending how languages use these small linguistic elements to convey important details while maintaining the coherence and clarity of sentences.

Here are Examples of Igbo enclitics: *cha, nno, nụ, si, zi, ri, ga, kwu, kwa, kwanụ and nwa*.

Igbo | English
1. **Ha bụ*nụ* ụmụ akwụkwọ.** | *They are typical/regular students.*
2. **Ị bụ*nno* onye ara.** | *You're acting crazy.*
3. **Ị bụ*zị* ụmụaka?** | *(Why) is your behavior childlike?*
4. **Ego ndi a bu*cha* nke gi.** | *All of this money belongs to you.*
5. **Bịanụ ọsịsọ.** | *You (all) should come immediately*

6. **Ọ bụcha ihe merenụ.** *It was part of all that happened.*
7. **Anyi zi ka o ruoro Ị banye.** *It's our turn to go in.*

Clitics are distinct from full-fledged words in that they rely on neighboring words to provide context and meaning. They either stand alone as in the case of proclitics or attach themselves to other words (as in the case of enclitics), Clitics can appear in various positions within a sentence, but their function is crucial for conveying complete ideas. Their usage varies across languages, and understanding clitics is vital for analyzing syntax, sentence structure, and the overall flow of communication.

Exercise

1. What are the three main ways languages can be classified, and how does each classification method differ?
2. What is the significance of understanding the basic units of Igbo syntax?
3. How are words defined in the context of language and linguistics?
4. Explain the structure of a word and provide examples from both English and Igbo languages.
5. What is morphology, and how does it relate to the study of words?
6. Can you illustrate how morphology contributes to the meaning of words using examples from Igbo verbs?
7. How are words used to convey meaning within a sentence, and what role does syntax play?
8. Define clitics and explain their role in Igbo sentences.
9. What distinguishes proclitics from enclitics in Igbo language?
10. Provide examples of proclitics used with both nouns and pronouns in Igbo sentences.
11. How do enclitics contribute to the structure and grammar of Igbo sentences?
12. Discuss the significance of enclitics in conveying grammatical and syntactic information.
13. Can you explain the difference between proclitics and enclitics, and how they function within Igbo syntax?
14. What types of clitics exist in general, and which ones are applicable to Igbo language?
15. How do clitics contribute to the coherence and clarity of Igbo sentences?
16. Provide examples of enclitics used in Igbo sentences and explain their functions.
17. In what ways do clitics differ from full-fledged words, and how does this impact sentence structure?
18. Why is understanding clitics crucial for analyzing Igbo syntax?
19. How do clitics vary in their usage across different languages?
20. Can you summarize the importance of studying clitics in relation to language analysis and communication?

Chapter 2
Word Order Typology (Ụdị nke Usorookwu)

2.1 What is Word Order?
Human languages can be classified in many ways. Syntactically, languages can be classified either on the basis of their word order or the relationship between heads and modifier. In linguistics, word order is a term that is used to define the order of the syntactic constituents of a language. Word order simply refers to the standard arrangement of words in a **phrase, clause, or sentence**.

In general, word order is how words are arranged in a sentence. It is the arrangement of the functional elements within a sentence. It does not mean literal arrangement of words. A sentence, at its most basic level, has three parts: the subject, the object and the verb. Sentences can certainly be more complicated, with adjectives, adverbs, prepositional phrases and more, but it's these three parts that decide word order.

For example: The words "Ọ hụrụ m (*He saw me*)" can't be rearranged as "Ọ m hụrụ (*He me saw*)," "hụrụ m Ọ (*Saw me he*)" or any other order.

When words are translated into another language, it would not necessary need to be done word-by-word unless the word order in that language is the same otherwise the whole sentence would need to be restructured.

2.2 Parts of Word Order

Subject
The subject is the person, place or thing that's performing an action. In English, the subject is the noun or noun phrase that appears before the verb. In "Ọ hụrụ m (*He saw me*)," the subject is "Ọ (*He*)." In "Enugwu mara mma (*Enugu is beautiful*)," the subject is "Enugu." In "Obi na Ada gara ahịa (*Obi and Ada went to the market*)," the subject is "Obi and Ada." There can also be multiple subjects in a sentence.

Verb
This is the action word in the sentence. In "Ọ hụrụ m (*S/he saw me,*)" the verb is "hụrụ (*saw*)." There can be more than one verb per sentence. In "Abịara m, ahụkwara m wee merie (*I came, I saw and I conquered*)," you have "bịara (*came*)," "hụkwara (*saw*)" and "merie (*conquered*)."

Object
The object is the noun to which the action is being done. In "Ọ hụrụ m (*He saw me*)," the object is "m (*me*)." At its simplest, the object is the noun that appears after the verb. Unlike the other two parts of word order, a sentence doesn't require an object. You can just say "Ọ bịara (*He came*)," where there's no object at all. Object can be either direct or indirect object.

The direct object is the person, place or thing that the action is being done to, and the indirect object is the person, place or thing the action is being done for. In the sentence "Enyere m Amaka onyinye (I gave Amaka a gift)," the direct object is "onyinye (*a gift)*" because it's the thing being given, and the indirect object is "Amaka" because the present is for her.

2.3 Types of Word Groups
The three parts of Word groups are:
1. Nkebiokwu   *(Phrase/ Frez)*
2. Nkebiahiri   *(clause/Klozu)*
3. Ahiriokwu   *(sentence)*

Phrase (Nkebiokwu): A phrase is a group of words that function as a single unit in a sentence, but do not contain both a subject and a verb. In other words, a phrase does not express a complete thought and cannot stand alone as a sentence. There are several types of phrases, including: Noun Phrase, Verb Phrase, Adjective Phrase, Adverb Phrase, Prepositional Phrase and so on.

Phrases play a crucial role in constructing sentences and conveying meaning in a language. They can be used to add detail and specificity, express relationships between words and ideas, and convey tone and attitude. Understanding phrases is essential for analyzing and understanding the structure and meaning of sentences.

Clause (Nkebiahịrị): A clause is a group of words that contain both a subject and a verb and express a complete thought. In other words, a clause can stand alone as a sentence or be part of a larger sentence.
There are two main types of clauses: independent clauses and dependent clauses.

Independent Clause: An independent clause is a complete sentence and can stand alone as a sentence. It expresses a complete thought and includes a subject and a verb.

For example,
- "Ọ na-abụ abụ mara mma."   "*She sings beautifully.*"

Dependent Clause: A dependent clause is not a complete sentence, as it cannot stand alone. It relies on an independent clause to form a complete thought. Dependent clauses typically begin with subordinating conjunctions, such as "N'ihi na" *(because)*, "Kemgbe" *(since),*" n'agbanyeghị" *(although)*, and "mgbe" *(when)*.

For example,
N'ihi na ọ na-abụ abụ mara mma
"*Because she sings beautifully.*"

Sentence (Ahịrịokwu): A sentence can contain one or more independent and dependent clauses, forming complex sentences. The way in which clauses are combined can greatly impact the meaning and structure of a sentence, making the understanding of clauses an essential part of linguistic analysis.

For examples:
1. Biko, ị nwere ike inye m nnu?
Can you please pass me the salt?

2. Ọ na-ekwukarị eziokwu, n'agbanyeghị otú o si sie ike.
He always tells the truth, no matter how difficult it is.

3. Ọ na-enwe mmasị ịgba egwu na mmiri ozuzo.
She loves to dance in the rain.

4. Nwamba ahụ chụpụrụ òké gburugburu ụlọ ahụ.
The cat chased the mouse around the room.

5. Eluigwe bụ ọmarịcha ndò na-acha anụnụ anụnụ.
The sky is a beautiful shade of blue.

2.4 Topological classification of Igbo sentence
A sentence is a grammatical unit that conveys a complete thought and consists of one or more words. It typically has a subject and a predicate, where the subject is what the sentence is about and the predicate tells something about the subject. The structure of a sentence can vary based on the language, but generally a sentence has a specific order of elements.

The formation of a sentence also depends on various grammatical rules such as word order, agreement, and tense, which govern the way words are used and combined to create grammatically correct sentences.

Igbo is a tonal language spoken in southeastern Nigeria. The structure and formation of Igbo sentences follow specific rules and patterns. In Igbo, a basic sentence typically consists of a subject, verb, and object. The subject and verb are usually marked for tense and aspect, indicating when an action took place or its completion status. The subject and object are typically noun phrases, while the verb is the main predicate of the sentence.

In terms of syntax, subject (*isiahịrị*), verb (*ngwaa*) and object (*nnara*) (SVO) is one of the parameters for the topological classification of Igbo. Igbo language uses the SVO pattern in which the subject precedes the the verb and object. The simplest way to establish the fact thst Igbo language fall under the SVO word order pattern is through the analysis of Igbo declarative sentences.

S	/V/	O	
Ada	/zụrụ-PST/	Uwe Mwụda.	Ada zụtara Uwe Mwụda
Ada	*/buy-PST/*	*a skirt .*	*Ada bought a skirt*
Eze	/gba-PST/	bọọlụ.	Eze gbara bọọlụ.
Eze	*/kick-PST/*	*a ball.*	*Eze kicked a ball.*
Obi	/ri-PST/	nri	Obi riri nri.
Obi	*/eat-PST/*	*food.*	*Obi ate food.*
Emeka	/hụ-PST/	nwanyị ahụ.	Emeka hụrụ nwanyị ahụ.
Emeka	*/see-PST/*	*the woman.*	*Emeka saw the woman.*

It is important to note that occasionally Igbo word order may come in the form of Verb, Subject and Object (VSO). This is only possible when an adverb precedes the sentence. VSO word order is limited on the condition that an adverb must be used in the sentence. Remember that in a sentence adverbs are moveable. The can can either be at the beginning of a sentence or be moved to the end of a sentence. For example:

Ọ /bịa-PST/ ụnyaahụ   Ọ   bịara   ụnyaahụ
Yesterday, he/she /come-PST/.   *Yesterday, he/she came.*

Ọ /bịa-PST/ ụnyaahụ   Ọ bịara ụnyaahụ
He/she /come-PST/ yesterday.   *He/she came yesterday.*

2.5 Hierarchical Structure of Igbo Sentence

The hierarchical structure of Igbo sentence plays a central role in Igbo language learning and speaking. The hierarchical structure of Igbo sentence shows the sequential sentence structure and the hierarchical process of Igbo phrase, clause and sentence that are fundamental to the comprehension, production, and acquisition of Igbo language. When Igbo sentences are analyzed as hierarchically structured sentence: words are grouped into phrases (or 'constituents'), which are grouped into higher-level phrases (or clause), and so on until a complete sentence is formed.

The particular analysis that is assigned to a given sentence depends on the details of the syntactic category of the words in the sentence and the order in which they occur. The relevancy of the hierarchical structure plays a key role in descriptions of how listeners (recipient) cognitive system may treat a sentence along the lines in which words are combined into components that have a linear order but no further part/whole structure or beyond.

Igbo sentences can also be modified by the use of adverbials, prepositions, and other particles to add additional information or to convey a specific meaning. For example, adverbials can be used to indicate time or location, while prepositions can be used to show relationships between nouns or pronouns.

In terms of sentence formation, Igbo sentences can be simple, compound, or complex. Simple sentences consist of a single clause, while compound sentences consist of two or more clauses connected by a conjunction. Complex sentences consist of one main clause and one or more subordinate clauses, with the subordinate clauses providing additional information about the main clause.

It's important to note that the structure and formation of Igbo sentences can be influenced by various factors such as tone, word order, and context. Additionally, there are regional variations in the way Igbo sentences are formed and structured, which can impact how the language is used in different areas.

A. Subject-Verb-Object (SVO):

This is where the subject performs the action indicated by the verb and the object receives the action. The sentence structure is one of the most basic and fundamental structures in Igbo grammar. It is composed of three essential elements: the subject, the verb, and the object. The subject is the noun or pronoun that performs the action described by the verb.

The verb is the action word that describes what the subject is doing. The object is the noun or pronoun that receives the action described by the verb. This structure is called Subject-Verb-Object (SVO) because the subject is listed first, followed by the verb, and finally the object. This structure is used in many simple sentences in Igbo language and is easy to understand and construct.

Examples of SVO sentences are:

"Ọ na-abụ abụ/Ọ na-agụ egwu."   *"She sings a song".*

The sentence "She sings a song" can be analyzed as follows:

a) Isiahịrị (IA): "**Ọ**"   Subject (S): *"She"*
b) Ngwaa (N): "**na-abụ**"/"**na-agụ**"   Verb (V): *"sings"*
c) Nnara (Nnr): "**abụ**"/"**egwu**"   Direct Object (DO): *"a song"*

This sentence follows an SVO (Subject-Verb-Object) structure. "She" is the subject, "sings" is the verb, and "a song" is the direct object, specifying what she is singing.

Anyị riri garri.   *We ate garri.*

The sentence "We ate garri" can be translated to English as:

a) Isiahịrị (IA):: " **Anyị** "   Subject (S): *"We"*
b) Ngwaa (N): " **riri** "   Verb (V): *"ate"*
c) Nnara (Nnr): "**garri**"   Direct Object (DO): *"garri"*

In English, this sentence follows an SVO (Subject-Verb-Object) structure. "We" is the subject, "ate" is the verb, and "garri" is the direct object, specifying what was eaten.

Ha na-agụ akwụkwọ.   *They read books.*

The sentence "They read books" is already in English. Here's the breakdown:

a) Isiahịrị (IA): "**Ha**   Subject (S): *"They"*
b) Ngwaa (N): "**na-agụ**"   Verb (V): *"read"*
c) Nnara (Nnr): "**akwụkwọ**"   Direct Object (DO): *"books"*

This sentence follows an SVO (Subject-Verb-Object) structure. "They" is the subject, "read" is the verb, and "books" is the direct object, specifying what they are reading.

Ọ na-ede akwụkwọ ozi.　　　　*She writes letters.*

The sentence "She writes letters" is already in English. Here's the breakdown:

a) Isiahịrị (IA): "**Ọ**"　　　　Subject (S): *"She"*
b) Ngwaa (N): "**na-ede**"　　　　Verb (V): *"writes"*
c) Nnara (Nnr): "**akwụkwọ ozi**"　　　　Direct Object (DO): *"letters"*

This sentence follows an SVO (Subject-Verb-Object) structure. "She" is the subject, "writes" is the verb, and "letters" is the direct object, specifying what she is writing.

Ndị mmadụ na-ekiri ihe nkiri.　　　　*People watch movies.*

The sentence "People watch movies" is already in English. Here's the breakdown:

a) Isiahịrị (IA): "**Ndị mmadụ**"　　　　Subject (S): *"People"*
b) Ngwaa (N): "**na-ekiri**"　　　　Verb (V): *"watch"*
c) Nnara (Nnr): "**ihe nkiri**"　　　　Direct Object (DO): *"movies"*

This sentence follows an SVO (Subject-Verb-Object) structure. "People" is the subject, "watch" is the verb, and "movies" is the direct object, specifying what people are watching.

Nne m na-eko achịcha Bekee.　　　　*Mom bakes bread.*

The sentence "Mom bakes bread" is already in English. Here's the breakdown:

a) Isiahịrị (IA): "**Nne m**"　　　　Subject (S): *"Mom"*
b) Ngwaa (N): "**na-eko**"　　　　Verb (V): *"bakes"*
c) Nnara (Nnr): "**achịcha Bekee**"　　　　Direct Object (DO): *"bread"*

This sentence follows an SVO (Subject-Verb-Object) structure. "Mom" is the subject, "bakes" is the verb, and "bread" is the direct object, specifying what Mom is baking.

Anyị na-ewu ụlọ ájá.　　　　*We build sandcastles.*

The sentence "We build sandcastles" is already in English. Here's the breakdown:

a) Isiahịrị (IA): "**Anyị**"　　　　Subject (S): *"We"*

b) Ngwaa (N): "**na-ewu**" Verb (V): *"build"*
c) Nnara (Nnr): "**ụlọ ájá**" Direct Object (DO): *"sandcastles"*

This sentence follows an SVO (Subject-Verb-Object) structure. "We" is the subject, "build" is the verb, and "sandcastles" is the object, specifying what we are building.

As shown in the above examples, Igbo word order is similar to that of English language. It is in the order of Subject – Verb – Object. In the Igbo sentence; "Ọ hụrụ m" translated in English as: "He saw me." As can be seen in the above example, Igbo language uses SVO. Other languages that use SVO are Chinese, French, Igbo, Italian, Norwegian, Polish, Swahili, Swedish and Yoruba. Example of S-V-O word order in Igbo language:

More examples:

	Igbo	English	Order
1.	O nyere m aka.	*He helped me.*	S-V-O
2.	Ha gara Ụlọ akwụkwọ.	*They went to school.*	S-V-O
3.	Ọ na-arụ n'ụlọ ọgwụ.	*She works at the hospital.*	S-V-O
4.	O bi n'Ọnịcha.	*He lives in Onitsha.*	S-V-O
5.	Nweke bịara Ụnyahụ.	*Nweke came yesterday.*	S-V-O
6.	Nneka bụ onye nkuzi.	*Nneka is a teacher.*	S-V-O

B. Subject-Verb-Indirect Object-Direct Object (SVIO):

In this structure, the sentence includes both an indirect object and a direct object, which receive the action described by the verb. In the Subject-Verb-Indirect Object-Direct Object (SVIO) structure, the subject performs the action indicated by the verb and both the indirect object and the direct object receive the action. The indirect object typically indicates the person or entity to whom or for whom the action is being performed, while the direct object is the thing or person directly affected by the action. An example of an SVIO sentence is "She gave her friend a gift." In this sentence, "She" is the subject, "gave" is the verb, "her friend" is the indirect object, and "a gift" is the direct object.

Examples:

O nyere nwanne ya nwaanyị akwụkwọ. *He handed his sister a book.*

The sentence "He handed his sister a book" is already in English. Here's the breakdown:

a) Isiahịrị (IA): "**O**" Subject (S): *"He"*
b) Ngwaa (N): "**nyere**" Verb (V): *"handed"*

    c) Nnapụta (Npt): "**nwanne ya**"   Indirect Object (IO): *"his sister"*
    d) Nnara (Nnr): "**akwụkwọ**"   Direct Object (DO): *"a book"*

This sentence follows an SIOV (Subject-Indirect Object-Verb-Direct Object) structure. "He" is the subject, "handed" is the verb, "his sister" is the indirect object, and "a book" is the direct object, specifying what he handed to his sister.

Ha zigara ndị mụrụ ha akwụkwọ ozi.   *They sent their parents a postcard.*

The sentence "They sent their parents a postcard" is already in English. Here's the breakdown:
    a) Isiahịrị (IA): "**Ha**"   Subject (S): *"They"*
    b) Ngwaa (N): "**zigara**t"   Verb (V): *"sent"*
    c) Nnapụta (Npt): "**ndị mụrụ ha**"   Indirect Object (IO): *"their parents"*
    d) Nnara (Nnr): "**akwụkwọ ozi**"   Direct Object (DO): *"a postcard"*

This sentence follows an SIOV (Subject-Indirect Object-Verb-Direct Object) structure. "They" is the subject, "sent" is the verb, "their parents" is the indirect object, and "a postcard" is the direct object, specifying what they sent.

O siere ezinụlọ ya nri dị ụtọ.   *She cooked her family a delicious meal.*

The sentence "She cooked her family a delicious meal" is already in English. Here's the breakdown:
    a) Isiahịrị (IA): "**O**"   Subject (S): *"She"*
    b) Ngwaa (N): "**siere**"   Verb (V): *"cooked"*
    c) Nnapụta (Npt): "**ezinụlọ ya**"   Indirect Object (IO): *"her family"*
    d) Nnara (Nnr): "**nri dị ụtọ**"   Direct Object (DO): *"a delicious meal"*

This sentence follows an SIOV (Subject-Indirect Object-Verb-Direct Object) structure. "She" is the subject, "cooked" is the verb, "her family" is the indirect object, and "a delicious meal" is the direct object, specifying what she cooked.

Ha nyere ndị agbata obi ha enyemaka.   *They offered the neighbors some help.*

The sentence "They offered the neighbors some help" is already in English. Here's the breakdown:
    a) Isiahịrị (IA): "**Ha**"   Subject (S): *"They"*
    b) Ngwaa (N): "**nyere**"   Verb (V): *"offered."*
    c) Nnara (Nnr): " **ndị agbata obi ha** "   Direct Object (DO): *"the neighbors"*
    d) Nnapụta (Npt): "**enyemaka**"   Indirect Object (IO): *"some help"*

This sentence follows an SVO (Subject-Verb-Object) structure. "They" is the subject, "offered" is the verb, "the neighbors" is the direct object, and "some help" is the indirect object, specifying what they offered.

Mama m kwakọbara m nri ehihie dị mma.   *Mom packed me a healthy lunch.*

The sentence "Mom packed me a healthy lunch" is already in English. Here's the breakdown:
   a) Isiahịrị (IA): "**Mama m**"   Subject (S): *"Mom"*
   b) Ngwaa (N): "**kwakọbara**"   Verb (V): *"packed"*
   c) Nnapụta (Npt): "**m**"   Indirect Object (IO): *"me"*
   d) Nnara (Nnr): "**nri ehihie dị mma**"   Direct Object (DO): *"a healthy lunch"*

This sentence follows an SIOV (Subject-Indirect Object-Verb-Direct Object) structure. "Mom" is the subject, "packed" is the verb, "me" is the indirect object, and "a healthy lunch" is the direct object, specifying what Mom packed.

O gosiri ndị enyi ya ngwa ọhụrụ ya.   *He showed his friends his new gadget.*

The sentence "He showed his friends his new gadget" is already in English. Here's the breakdown:
   a) Isiahịrị (IA): "**O**"   Subject (S): *"He"*
   b) Ngwaa (N): "**gosiri**"   Verb (V): *"showed"*
   c) Nnapụta (Npt): "**ndị enyi ya**"   Indirect Object (IO): *"his friends"*
   d) Nnara (Nnr): "**ngwa ọhụrụ ya**"   Direct Object (DO): *"his new gadget"*

This sentence follows an SIOV (Subject-Indirect Object-Verb-Direct Object) structure. "He" is the subject, "showed" is the verb, "his friends" is the indirect object, and "his new gadget" is the direct object, specifying what he showed.

C. Subject-Verb-Object-Complement (SVOC):
In this structure, the sentence includes both an object and a complement, which provide additional information about the object. In an SVOC sentence structure, the complement provides additional information about the object. It can be a noun, adjective, or clause that gives more detail about the object. The complement is typically linked to the object by a linking verb such as "to be" or "to seem". Here are examples of sentences with the subject-verb-object-complement (SVOC) structure:

Ọ nwere ya na ezigbo enyi ya. *She considers him her best friend.*

In the sentence "She considers him her best friend":
    a) Isiahịrị (IA): "**Ọ**"   Subject (S): *"She"*
    b) Ngwaa (N): "**nwere**"   Verb (V): *"considers"*
    c) Nnara (Nnr): "**ya**"   Object (O): *"him"*
    d) Mmeju (M): "**na ezigbo enyi ya.**"   Object Complement (OC): *"her best friend."*

This sentence can be analyzed as an SVO (Subject-Verb-Object) construction with an object complement. "She" is the subject, "considers" is the verb, "him" is the direct object, and "her best friend" acts as the object complement, specifying the role or identity of the direct object "him."

Mkpọtụ ahụ kpasuru ya iwe.   *The noise drove him mad.*

In the sentence "The noise drove him mad":
    a) Isiahịrị (IA): "**Mkpọtụ ahụ**"   Subject (S): *"The noise"*
    b) Ngwaa (N): "**kpasuru**"   Verb (V): *"drove"*
    c) Nnara (Nnr): "**ya**"   Direct Object (DO): *"him"*
    d) Mmeju (M): "**iwe**"   Object Complement (OC): *"mad"*

This sentence can be analyzed as an SVO (Subject-Verb-Object) construction with an object complement. "The noise" is the subject, "drove" is the verb, "him" is the direct object, and "mad" acts as the object complement, describing the state to which he was driven.

Anyị hụrụ na ụlọ ahụ tọgbọrọ chakoo.   *We found the house empty.*

In the sentence "We found the house empty":
    a) Isiahịrị (IA): "**Anyị**"   Subject (S): *"We"*
    b) Ngwaa (N): "**hụrụ**"   Verb (V): *"found"*
    c) Nnara (Nnr): "**ụlọ ahụ**"   Direct Object (DO): *"the house"*
    d) Mmeju (M): "**tọgbọrọ chakoo**"   Object Complement (OC): *"empty"*

This sentence can be analyzed as an SVO (Subject-Verb-Object) construction with an object complement. "We" is the subject, "found" is the verb, "the house" is the direct object, and "empty" acts as the object complement, describing the state of the house.

Echere m na atụmatụ ahụ enweghị amamihe.   *I thought the plan unwise.*

In the sentence "I thought the plan unwise":

a) Isiahịrị (IA): "**E**" Subject (S): *"I"*
b) Ngwaa (N): "**chere**" Verb (V): *"thought"*
c) Nnara (Nnr): "**na atụmatụ ahụ**" Direct Object (DO): *"the plan"*
d) Mmeju (M): "**enweghị amamihe**" Object Complement (OC): *"unwise"*

This sentence can be analyzed as an SVO (Subject-Verb-Object) construction with an object complement. "I" is the subject, "thought" is the verb, "the plan" is the direct object, and "unwise" acts as the object complement, expressing the opinion or judgment about the plan.

Igbo: Anyị na-ewere okwu ahụ dị ka ihe dị mkpa.
English: We consider the matter very important.

In the sentence "We consider the matter very important":
a) Isiahịrị (IA): "**Anyị**" Subject (S): *"We"*
b) Ngwaa (N): "**na-ewere**" Verb (V): *"consider."*
c) Nnara (Nnr): "**okwu ahụ**" Direct Object (DO): *"the matter"*
d) Mmeju (M): "**(dị ka) ihe dị mkpa**" Object Complement (OC): *"very important."*

This sentence can be analyzed as an SVO (Subject-Verb-Object) construction with an object complement. "We" is the subject, "consider" is the verb, "the matter" is the direct object, and "very important" acts as the object complement, describing the level of importance attributed to the matter.

Remember that in SVOC sentences, the object complement provides additional information about the direct object and completes the meaning of the sentence.

D. Subject-Verb-Adjective (SVA):
In this structure, the sentence only includes a subject, verb, and adjective, and describes a quality or attribute of the subject. In the Subject-Verb-Adjective (SVA) structure, the sentence is composed of only three elements: a subject, a verb, and an adjective. The adjective modifies or describes the subject, providing information about its quality or attribute. An example of an SVA sentence is "The sky is blue." In this sentence, the subject is "the sky," the verb is "is," and the adjective is "blue," which describes the sky's color. This sentence structure is commonly used to make simple, straightforward statements about the qualities or attributes of a subject.

Example:
Mmekọrịta ahụ malitere ịka njọ ka oge na-aga. *The relationship became strained over time.*

The sentence "The relationship became strained over time". Here's the breakdown:

Isiahịrị (IA): "**Mmekọrịta ahụ**" Subject (S): *"The relationship"*
Ngwaa (N): "**malitere**" Verb (V): *"became"*
Nkọwaha (Nk): "**ịka njọ**" Adjective (A): *"strained"*
Nkebiokwu Kenkwuwa (NKnkw): "**ka oge na-aga**" Adverbial Phrase (AdvP): *"over time"*

This sentence follows an SVA (Subject-Verb-Adjective) structure with an adverbial phrase. "The relationship" is the subject, "became" is the verb, "strained" is the adjective describing the condition of the relationship, and "over time" is the adverbial phrase providing information about the duration or process of the change.

Nsogbu mgbakọ na mwepụ a na-egosi ihe ịma aka.
The math problem proves challenging.

The sentence "The math problem proves challenging" can be analyzed as follows:
  a) Isiahịrị (IA): "**Nsogbu mgbakọ na mwepụ a**" Subject (S): *"The math problem"*
  b) Ngwaa (N): "**na-egosi**" Verb (V): *"proves"*
  c) Nkọwaha (Nk): "**ihe ịma aka**" Adjective (A): *"challenging"*

This sentence follows an SVC (Subject-Verb-Complement) structure. The subject is "The math problem," the verb is "proves," and the adjective "challenging" acts as the complement, describing the nature of the math problem.

Ụgbọala ahụ yiri nke ọhụrụ. *The car seems brand new.*

In the sentence "The car seems brand new":
  a) Isiahịrị (IA): "**Ụgbọala ahụ**" Subject (S): *"The car"*
  b) Ngwaa (N): "**yiri**" Verb (V): *"seems"*
  c) Nkọwaha (Nk): "**nke ọhụrụ**" Adjective (A): *"brand new"*

This sentence can be analyzed as an SVC (Subject-Verb-Complement) construction. "The car" serves as the subject, "seems" is the verb, and "brand new" acts as the complement, describing the condition or state of the car.

Okwu ahụ na-eme ka ekwenye. *The speech is persuasive.*

In the sentence "The speech is persuasive":

a) Isiahịrị (IA): "**Okwu ahụ**" Subject (S): *"The speech"*
b) Ngwaa (N): "**na-eme**" Verb (V): *"is"*
c) Nkọwaha (Nk): "**ekwenye**" Adjectives (A): *"persuasive"*

This sentence can be analyzed as an SVA (Subject-Verb-Adjective) construction. "The speech" is the subject, "is" is the verb, and the adjectives "persuasive" describe the quality of the speech.

E. Subject-Verb-Adverb (SVAdv):

In this structure, the sentence only includes a subject, verb, and adverb, and describes the manner or extent of the action described by the verb. Subject-Verb-Adverb (SVAdv) is a basic sentence structure in which the subject performs the action described by the verb, and the adverb modifies the verb by providing information about the manner or extent of the action.

This sentence structure is common in English and other languages. For example, "She sings beautifully" is an SVAdv sentence, with "She" being the subject, "sings" being the verb, and "beautifully" being the adverb that describes the manner of the action. The subject-verb-adverb structure is simple and straightforward, and it allows for efficient and clear communication of ideas.

For examples:

Ụgbọala ahụ kwụsịrị na mberede. *The car stopped suddenly.*

In the sentence "The car stopped suddenly":
a) Isiahịrị (IA): "**Ụgbọala ahụ**" Subject (S): *"The car"*
b) Ngwaa (N): "**kwụsịrị**" Verb (V): *"stopped"*
c) Nkwuwa (Nkw): "**na mberede**" Adverb (Adv): *"suddenly"*

This sentence follows an SVA (Subject-Verb-Adverb) structure. "The car" is the subject, "stopped" is the verb, and "suddenly" is an adverb modifying the action of stopping.

Ọ na-ekwu nwayọ nwayọ. *He speaks softly.*

In the sentence "He speaks softly":
a) Isiahịrị (IA): "**Ọ**" Subject (S): *"He"*
b) Ngwaa (N): "**na-ekwu**" Verb (V): *"speaks"*
c) Nkwuwa (Nkw): "**nwayọ nwayọ**" Adverb (Adv): *"softly"*

This sentence follows an SVA (Subject-Verb-Adverb) structure. "He" is the subject, "speaks" is the verb, and "softly" is an adverb modifying the manner in which he speaks.

Ha rutere n'ikpeazụ. *They arrived finally.*

In the sentence "They arrived finally":
  a) Isiahịrị (IA): "**Ha**"   Subject (S): "*They*"
  b) Ngwaa (N): "**rutere**"   Verb (V): *"arrived"*
  c) Nkwuwa (Nkw): "**n'ikpeazụ**"   Adverb (Adv): *"finally"*

This sentence follows an SVA (Subject-Verb-Adverb) structure. "They" is the subject, "arrived" is the verb, and "finally" is an adverb modifying the timing of their arrival.

Anyị ga-aga echi. *We'll go tomorrow.*

The sentence "We'll go tomorrow" can be analyzed as follows:
  Isiahịrị (IA): "**Anyị**"   Subject (S): "*We*"
  Enyemaka Ngwaa (EN): "**ga**"   Modal Verb (MV): *"will"*
  Isi ngwaa (IS): "**aga**"   Main Verb (V): *"go"*
  Nkwuwa (Nkw): "**echi**"   Adverb (Adv): *"tomorrow"*

This sentence follows a subject + modal verb + main verb + adverb (S + MV + V + Adv) structure. "We" is the subject, "will" is the modal verb indicating future tense, "go" is the main verb, and "tomorrow" is the adverb specifying when the action will take place.

The sentence expresses the intention or plan that "we" will undertake the action of going on the day following the current one, which is "tomorrow."

Exercise

1. What is word order, and why is it important in linguistic analysis?
2. How does word order affect the structure of sentences in human languages?
3. What are the three basic parts of a sentence, and how do they determine word order?
4. Can you explain the difference between a subject, a verb, and an object in a sentence?
5. Provide examples of different word orders found in languages around the world.
6. What role do phrases, clauses, and sentences play in determining word order?
7. How do languages like Igbo and English utilize subject-verb-object (SVO) word order?
8. Explain the significance of hierarchical structure in understanding sentence formation.
9. What are the main types of clauses, and how do they contribute to sentence structure?
10. How does word order vary in languages that use subject-verb-indirect object-direct object (SVIOD) structure?
11. Give 5 examples of sentences with subject-verb-object-complement (SVOC) structure?
12. What distinguishes subject-verb-adjective (SVA) sentences from other sentence structures?
13. How does word order affect the meaning and interpretation of a sentence?
14. Discuss the role of adverbs and adverbial phrases in influencing word order.
15. Why is it important to study word order typology in linguistics?
16. How do languages with different word order patterns handle translation and interpretation?
17. Provide examples of how word order can change emphasis and nuance in a sentence.
18. What are some common word order patterns found in world languages?
19. How do syntactic categories such as noun phrases and verb phrases contribute to word order?
20. Can you analyze the word order of sentences in different languages and identify their syntactic structures?

Chapter 3

Word Classes/Syntactic Category (*Ụdị na Nhazị Okwu*)

Syntactic Category refers to the grammatical classification of words based on their role in a sentence. In linguistic theory, the main categories of words include nouns, verbs, adjectives, adverbs, prepositions, pronouns, conjunctions and interjections.

Distribution of Word Classes refers to the way in which these different categories of words are used within a language or a particular text. The distribution of different word classes can vary depending on factors such as the context, genre, and purpose of the text.

For example, in written Igbo, nouns tend to be the most frequently occurring word class, followed by verbs, adjectives, and adverbs.
For example:

- a) Anọ m na nwute. *I am sad.*
- b) Obi dị m ụtọ. *I am happy (joyful).*
- c) Ọ na-abịa echi, *He is coming tomorrow.*
- d) Ọ na-eme nke ọma *He is doing well.*

This distribution can change, however, in different genres of writing, such as poetry or advertising, where the frequency of certain word classes may be shifted to create a desired effect. Additionally, the distribution of word classes may vary cross-linguistically, with some languages placing a greater emphasis on verbs, for instance, while others place more importance on adjectives.

The study of the syntactic categories and distribution of word classes is an important aspect of linguistic analysis, as it helps to shed light on the grammar and structure of a language and can also reveal cultural and societal attitudes and values.

There are two views of the taxonomy of word classes. They are conventional/traditional view and structuralist view. Generally, words are placed into classes based on what they mean and how they are used in a sentence.

According to conventional view word classes can syntactically be grouped into: Open class elements or closed class elements.

Open categories are considered open because new words can be added to the class over time. Thus, these categories are open to new members. These categories are sometimes also called lexical categories or content words because these categories are the ones that do most of the lexical semantic work in a sentence: they convey most of the meaning of a sentence. Open class element include: Nouns, verbs, adjectives and adverbs.

Closed class elements are limited in number with numeral which may be viewed as unlimited. Closed categories are considered closed because they contain a small number of words; new items are very rarely added. This class elements inclue prepositions, articles (which does not exist in Igbo grammar), pronouns, conjunctions, auxiliaries, and Numerals.

Structuralist view like conventional words does group words into open and closed elements but with slight changes and the introduction of determiners and inflectional elements. Part of the pronoun (e.g. I, me … become part of the noun while my, this … moves to determiners). Numerals like one, some … become part of the determiners as well. As a result, pronouns and numerals are not given a class under the structuralist category.

The differences that exist between conventional and structuralist views can be summarized in the following table:

Conventional/Traditional		*Structuralist view*	
Open	**Closed**	**Open**	**Closed**
Nouns	Prepositions	Nouns	Determiners
Verbs	Pronouns	Verbs	Conjunctions
Adjectives	Articles	Adjectives	Inflectional
Adverbs	Conjunction	Adverbs	Complementizers
	Auxiliaries		
	Numerals		

The following descriptions are based on the structuralist approach to syntactic category of word classes.

Open Class Elements

Nouns: cat, dog, house, man, woman, boy etc. and I, me etc (pronouns)
Verbs: play, love, hate, like, etc.
Adjectives: long, short, big, small, bigger, shorter, etc.
Adverbs: quick, fast, well, etc.

Closed Class Elements

Nkwuso *(Determiners)*: a, the, this, my, one, some
Njikọ *(Conjunctions)*: and, or, if
Mgbanwe/inflekshọn *(Inflectional)*: do, has, will,
Mmeju *(Complementizers)*: who, that

DESCRIPTION OF STRUCTURALIST ELEMENTS

OPEN CLASS ELEMENTS

3.1 Noun (Mkpọaha/Aha)

A noun is the name of a person, place, thing, or idea. Examples

English	*Igbo*
Classroom	Klaasị
Train	Ụgbọ oloko
Food	nri
Dog	Nkịta
Forest	Ọhịa
Table	Okpokoro
Joy	Ọṅụ

Pronoun (*Nnochiaha*): In their syntactic distribution, pronouns do the job that noun phrases do and can substitute them. However, English language pronoun rarely appears with determinant 'the', but it can replace an entire noun phrase. Based on syntactic function, some pronouns can become part of the larger category of nouns, remembering that they're a special case. They include I, me, you, we, us, they, them, he, him, she, her, it

Igbo pronouns, unlike English language, are not gendered as a result the same pronouns are used for male, female and inanimate beings. There are four singular pronouns (i, ị, o, and ọ) and two impersonal pronouns (a and e).

Igbo language does not distinguish between subject and object pronouns as it is with English (e.g.

he vs. him) but person (first, second, and third singular and plural subjects) is distinguished as you would see in the examples below. Pronouns can also be marked for demonstrative or possession.

Every Igbo pronoun stands alone in a sentence. They do not join to verb or noun except they are in prefixed form, as in the case of first-person impersonal singular and third person impersonal plural pronouns. The following are examples of standalone and prefixed forms of Igbo pronouns:

First person singular	*Igbo*
I went to the market.	Ejere m ahịa.
I asked a question.	Ajụrụ m ajụjụ.

2nd person singular	*Igbo*
You made my day.	Ị mere taa ụbọchịoma nye m.
You are kind.	Ị bụ ezigbo mmadụ.

3rd person singular	*Igbo*
She is so beautiful	Ọ maka/ ọ mara ezigbo mma
He is handsome	Ọ maka/ ọ mara ezigbo mma
It is so beautiful	Ọ mara ezigbo mma

3rd person plural	*Igbo*
They did the dishes	Asara efere.
They cooked food	Esiri nri

The following are various types of pronouns.
a. Subject Pronoun (Nnochiaha) is a word that takes place of a noun in a sentence. It functions as and acts as a substitute for a noun or nouns. Examples: I, you, it, they, we, he, she.

Subject

English	Igbo	Plural	Igbo
I/me	*m, mụ*	We	*anyị*
You	*Ị, gị*	You	*unu*
He/she/it	*O*	They	*ha*
He/she/it	*Ọ*	They	*ha*

b. Personal Pronoun (Nnochionye): this type of pronoun refers to the speaker or the person spoken to, or to a person or things whose identity is clear, usually because they have already been mentioned. It includes all the subject pronouns and object pronouns. For example:

Subject

English	Igbo	Plural	Igbo
I/me	m, mụ	We	anyị
You	Ị, gị	You	unu
He/she/it	O	They	ha
He/she/it	Ọ	They	ha
He/she/it	ya	They	ha

Object

Me	m/mụ	Us	anyi
You	gị	You	unu
Him/her/it	ya	them	ha

c. *Impersonal pronoun (Nnochimpesin)*: Also known as impersonal pronoun, impersonal pronoun is used in a sentence to show non-specific beings, objects, or places. This can be used to represent countable noun or uncountable nouns; e.g. it (a, e). The two impersonal pronouns in Igbo language are a and e.

d. *Reflexive Pronoun (Nnochionwe/Nnochinkowa)*: This type of pronoun is used in a sentence to refer to subject of the sentence. It is preceded by adverb, adjective, pronoun, or noun to which it refers, so long as that antecedent is located within the same clause. They end with the suffix 'self' (onwe); e.g. myself, yourself, himself, herself, oneself, itself, ourselves, yourselves, and themselves.

Examples:

English	*Igbo*	*English*	*Igbo*
Myself	onwe/ Munwà	*Yourself*	onwe gi/ Ginwà
Himself	onwe ya	*Herself*	onwe ya
Oneself	onwe ya	*Itself*	onwe ya
Ourselves	onwe anyi/ Anyịnwà	*Yourselves*	onwe unu
Themselves	onwe ha		

e. *Emphatic Pronoun (Nnochionweonye)*: This type of pronoun is used in a sentence to explain the action done by a noun without anyone's help. Examples of emphatic pronouns are the same form as reflexive pronouns. However, the difference between emphatic pronoun and reflexive pronoun is that reflexive pronoun acts as direct or indirect object in a sentence while emphatic pronouns are essentially unnecessary. For example:

1. I went to the hospital myself. (Reflexive pronoun)

E jere m ụlọ-ọgwụ na nke onwe m.

2. The doctor himself treated me. (Emphatic pronoun)
   Dọkịta na onwe ya lekọtara anya.

The word "myself" in the first sentence serves to reinforce that it was the subject (i.e. the president) that performed the action. Please note that emphatic pronoun can be removed from a sentence and the meaning of the sentence would still remain intact.

3.2 Verbs (Ngwaa)

a. *Infinitive Verbs (Isingwaa)*: This is a verb form that functions as a noun or is used with auxiliary verbs, and that names the action or state without specifying the subject. In Igbo language, the letter "ị" and "I" plus the root verb comprise the infinitive form of verb.

Examples:

English	Igbo root verb	English	Igbo root verb
to be	ịbu/ịdị	to bring	iweta
to buy	ịzụta	to call	ịkpọ
to chew	ịta	to come	ịbịa
to cook	isi nri	to cry	ibe akwa
to dance	ịgba egwu	to do	ime
to drink	ịṅu	to eat	iri (nri)
to enter	ịbanye/ịbata	to find/look	ịchọ/chọta
to follow	isoro	to forget	ichefu
to fry	ighe	to get	inweta
to give	inye	to go	ịga
to have/own	inwe	to hear	ịnụ
to hold	ijide	to know	ịma
to laugh	ịchi (chi a)	to learn	ịmụta
to leave	ịhapụ	to listen	ige ntị
to look	ile (anya)	to mark	ịka (akara)
to get out	ịpụta	to play	igwu egwu
to pray	ikpe ekpere	to read	ịgụ
to remember	icheta	to run	ịgba ọsọ
to say	ikwu (okwu)	to see	ịhụ
to sell	ire (ahịa)	to bathe	ịsa ahụ
to sing	ịguọ abụ/ ịbụọ abụ	to sit	ịnọdu
to sleep	ịrahụ (ura)	to speak	ịsụ

to stand	iguzo/ikuli	*to stay*	ino
to swallow	ilo	*to take*	iwere
to teach	ikuzi	*to tell*	igwa
to think	iche echiche	*to throw*	itu
to touch	imetu	*to understand*	ighota
to wait	ichere	*to walk*	iga ije
to wash	isa	*to wear*	iyi
to work	iru	*to write*	ide

b. *Linking Verbs (njiko ngwaa)*: This type of verb that connects a noun or a pronoun with a word that identifies or describes it; e.g. is, am, are, etc.
Examples:

English	*Igbo*
is	bu
am	bu
are	bu

C. *Modal verb:* Modal verbs are a kind of auxiliary verb that communicate various relationships to reality or truth by signifying capacity, permission, necessity, possibility, and other associated ideas. They are employed to change a sentence's primary verb. In Igbo language, four different types of modal verbs have been identified. They are:

Periphrastic (verb + NP) verbal structures: (like nwé íké (*can*), kwe mee (*could*), and ike kwe (*perhaps, may/might*). For example:

1. E**nwere** m *ike* ikpo piano.   (*I can play the piano.*)
2. O **nwere ike** igwu mmiri mgbe o ka di obere. (*She could swim when she was younger.*)
3. O buru na o ga-e**kwe** gi **mee**, nyere ndi mmadu aka. (*If you would, help other people.*)
4. **Ikekwe** mmiri ga-ezo echi.   (***Perhaps** it will rain tomorrow.*)
5. I **nwere ike** ibiri akwukwo m.   (*You **may** borrow my book.*)
6. O **nwere ike** isonyere anyi iri nri abali. (*She **might** join us for dinner.*)

Capability modal verb: This is a modal verb that is used to express ability or capacity of someone. When used in interrogative expression, it questions for clarity the someone ability either directly or politely. e.g. nwu (*able*).

1. Ada aga-enwe*nwu* ike ibia hu m?   *Would Ada be able to come and see me?*
2. O ga-enwe*nwu* ike ibia hu m.   *He/she would be able to come and see me.*

3. Kalu nwe*nwu* ike ịrụcha ọrụ ahụ n'oge. (*Kalu is capable of finishing the task on time.*)

Compulsion modal verb: The term "compulsion" describes a situation in which someone is compelled to act, usually against their will. It can also be used to describe an overwhelming desire or inclination to carry out specific actions. E.g. rírí (*must/have to*).

1. Eze ga-erichariri nri ya.   *Eze must finish his food.*
2. Amaka ga-azariri ekwentị ahụ.   *Amaka has to answer the phone.*

Obligatory modal verbs: It refers to something that someone is expected to perform. An obligation is when someone has a responsibility or duty to carry out a specific action. e.g. kwesi (*should/ought to/suppose to*).

For examples:

1. Ị kwesịrị irubere ndị mụrụ gị isi.
   "You are supposed to respect your parents."

2. Anyị kwesịrị iyibe eriri oche anyị n'oge mfepu ụgbọ elu.
   "We ought to keep our seat belts on during the flight."

3. O kwesiri inyefee ihe omume ụlọ ya n'ụtụtụ Fraịde.
   "He should turn in his homework on Friday morning."

4. Ihe nkiri a kwesịrị ịmalite n'elekere asaa nke abalị.
   "The movie is supposed to start at 7 p.m."

Verb conjugations:

In linguistics, conjugation is the creation of derived forms of a verb from its principal parts by inflection. For instance, in English language, the verb break can be conjugated to form the words break, breaks, broke, broken and breaking to differentiate present, present continuous, past and past perfect tense respectively.

Verbs conjugate to demonstrate tense changes. In Igbo language, verbs do differentiate between present and past using affixes. Suffixes are added to Igbo verbs to describe the tense and quality of the verb. For examples:

1. -tara/-tere   *action in the past*   O metara ya
2. -la/-le   *completed action*   O mela ya

3. -ri   *past completed action*   O melari ya
4. -go   *already completed action*   O mego ya
5. -lu   *to intensify an action*   O melu ya

3.3 Adjective (Nkọwaha)

An adjective is a word that describes or gives more information about a noun or pronoun. It tells you what kind, how many, or which one. Unlike English language where adjectives precede nouns, in Igbo language adjective can either precede or follow the noun.

There are few adjectives in Igbo. Instead, verb suffixes are used to describe actions. The following are examples of adjectives:

Igbo	English	Igbo	English	Igbo	English
ala	*low*	ọsịsọ	*fast*	chakoo	*empty*
elu	*high*	iwe	*angry*	ihere	*shy*
nsọ	*holy/sacred*	anya	*far*	obi ụtọ/aṅụrị	*happy*
obi ọjọọ	*sad*	ọcha	*bright*	ọcha	*clean*
ocha	*light*	oji	*dark*	ogologo	*long*
ntakịrị	*short*	ohu/ohuru	*new*	ochie	*old*
ọjọọ	*ugly*	ọjọọ	*bad*	ọkụ	*hot*
oyi	*cold*	ọma/mma	*beautiful*	ọma	*good*
siri ike	*hard*	dara ọnụ	*expensive*	ukwu	*big*
nta	*small*	ụtọ	*sweet*	ilu	*bitter*

Demonstrative adjectives: these are words used to modify a noun so that we know which specific person, place, or thing is mentioned. Examples of demonstrative adjectives in Igbo language are: ahụ (that). Nke a (this), ndị ahụ (those), ndị a (these). In Igbo language, demonstrative adjectives follow the noun they are modifying. For example:

Igbo   **English**
1. Nye m kalama ahụ   *Give me that bottle.*
2. Achọrọ m akwụkwọ ndị ahụ   *I want those books.*
3. Ọ chọrọ izute ya ụbọchị ahụ   *He wanted to meet her that day.*
4. Mango ndị a na-ere ure   *These mangoes are rotting.*
5. Apụghị ichefu ihe ahụ mere   *I can't forget that incident.*
6. Ụmụ ntakịrị ndị ahụ were iwe   *Those children were angry.*
7. Mkpịsị odide ahụ bụ nke m   *This pen belongs to me.*
8. Ụlọ ahụ nwere ụlọ-ahịa   *That building has a shop.*

3.4 Adverb (Nkwuwa)

An adverb is a word that describes a verb, adjective, or another adverb by giving more information about how or when something happens. It tells how, when, where, or to what extent, e.g. loudly, slowly, quickly, finally, always, tomorrow. Examples of Igbo adverbs are:

Igbo	English	Igbo	English
ma ncha	*Never*	tara akpụ	*Rarely*
mgbe ụfọdụ	*Sometimes*	mgbe niīle	*Usually*
mgbe niīle	*Always*	nkeọma	*Very*

	Igbo	English
a)	Ọ na-agụ egwu n'olu dara ụda	*She sings loudly.*
b)	Ọ gbara ọsọ ngwa ngwa	*He/she ran quickly.*
c)	Ọ kwuru okwu n'olu dị jụụ	*He/she spoke softly.*
d)	Eze kwara ụkwara n'olu dara ụda	*Eze coughed loudly.*
e)	Ọ na-afụ Ọja nke oma.	*He plays the flute beautifully.*
f)	Ha riri achịcha bekee n'anyaukwu	*They ate the cake greedily.*

Interrogative adverbs are used to ask a question. In Igbo, a question can only be initiated by either an interrogative or a personal pronoun. Following interrogatives are commonly used:

Igbo	*English*	*Igbo*	*English*
Kedụ	*how, when, where, which?*	ebee	*where, which place?*
olee	*how much, how many?*	onye	*Who?*
gịnị/ọ gịnị?	*What?*	kedụ?	*How?*
maka gịnị?	*Why?*		

CLOSED CLASS ELEMENTS

3.5 Preposition (Mbuuzo)

Preposition is part of the conventional or traditional approach to syntactic category. However, because of its important role in Igbo word order, it is necessary to have good understanding of its form and function in Igbo language. The rest of the descriptions are structuralist descriptions.

A preposition is a word that describes a relationship between a noun or pronoun and another word in a sentence, e.g. at, on, in, across, besides, during, for, of, to, with, throughout etc. It goes before a noun or pronoun to specify a place, position or time. In Igbo, there is only one preposition "na". When preceding a vowel, it drops its vowel sound and letter and takes on the tone of noun that follows it. It is written as n'.
Examples:

Igbo	English	Igbo	English
na	*and*	n'okpuru	*under*
tupu	*before*	n'ikpeazụ	*after*
n'ime	*inside*	n'ihe/n'ilo	*outside*
na	*with*	mana	*but*
maka	*for*	si	*from*
je	*to*	ime	*in*

Examples:
a) Ọ dị n'elu akwa ndina.   *it is on top of the bed.*
b) Ọ dị n'okpuru akwa ndina.   *it is under the bed.*
c) Ọ dị n'ime akpati   *it is inside the box.*
d) Ọ dị n' akụkụ akwa ndina.   *it is beside the bed.*
e) Ọ nọ n'ụlọ.   *he/she n is in the house.*
f) Ọ dị n'elu aja.   *it is on sand.*

In combination with a noun, it can specify the location of the preposition in more detail:

Noun	**Mkpoaha**	**Preposition**	**Mbuuzo**
top	elu	*in, at, on*	na (common)
top	elu	*up*	n'enu
underside	okpuru	*under, below*	n'okpuru
interior	ime	*inside*	n'ime
edge	ọnụnụ	*on top of*	n'onunu
beside	n'akụkụ		

3.6 Determiners *(Nkwuso)*:

These are a nominal syntactic category distinct both from adjectives and nouns, despite the close affinity among them. They are commonly understood to comprise the word classes of article, demonstrative, and quantifier, as well as some possessives and some nominal agreement markers. It is defined as a word, phrase, or affix that occurs together with a noun or noun phrase and serves to express the reference of that noun or noun phrase in the context. Nkwuso *(Determiners)* are used with nouns to clarify the noun. Common English determiners are 'a', 'the', 'some', 'this', and 'each'.

Possessive determiner (Nnochinke): This type of pronoun is used in a sentence to show that something belongs to someone, e.g. my, our, your, his, her, its and theirs. There exists an independent form of each of the above possessive pronouns and they are: mine, ours, yours, his, hers, its, and theirs. For example:

English	Igbo	English	Igbo
mine	nke m	Yours	nke gị
His	nke ya	Her	nke ya
Our/ours	nke anyị	Their/theirs	nke ha

Demonstrative determiner (Nnochingosi): This type of pronoun is used in a sentence to point out specific things. There are only four demonstrative pronouns, and they are: this, that, these and those. Examples in Igbo language are as follows:

English	Igbo	English	Igbo
This	ihe a	That	ihe ahụ
These	ihe ndị a	Those	ihe dị ahụ

Plurality: In terms of count or number, a noun can be either singular noun or plural noun. Singular noun is a term that is used to refer to one person, place, thing, or idea. Plural nouns, on the other hand, is used to refer to more than one person, place, thing, or idea.

In English language, plural is marked with 's' or 'es' for singular noun ending in a consonant and vowel respectively. For nouns that end with y makes the plural by dropping the y and adding-ies. Examples: penny becomes pennies. Spy becomes spies and baby becomes babies. Plurals might not be marked at all or might be marked incorrectly. *I want two sandwiches/I want two sandwiches.

In Igbo language, plural is marked with a prefix /ọtụtụ/, /ndị/, /ụmụ/. /ọtụtụ/ is an Igbo plural marker word that is translated to /many/ in English language. The word 'many' is used as an Nkwuso *(a determiner)* or pronoun indicative of quantity that describes a plural noun and tells us that there is a large number of that noun, as in these examples:

English	**Igbo**
She worked for hours.	Ọ rụrụ ọrụ ọtụtụ awa (oge).
We bought cups.	Anyị zụtara ọtụtụ iko.

It is important to note that English language has definite (the) and indefinite (a, an) articles. There is no article in Igbo language. For examples:

English	**Igbo**	**Literal translation**
I have a dog.	Enwere m Nkịta.	*I have dog.*

I am a student.   Abụ m nwa akwụkwọ   **I am student.*

More examples:

Ọtụtụ ndị mmadụ nọ n'ahịa.   *"Many people are in the market."*
Lots of *PL* person   be *PP* market

Ụmụ ntakịrị na-egwuri egwu n'èzí.   *"Little children are playing outside."*
PL   child   *Aux*   verb play outside.

Ndị obodo ahụ nọ na nzukọ.   *"The villagers are in a meeting."*
PL village *DET* be *PP* gathering.

Ọ   zụtara ụgbọ ala ndị   a.   *"She bought these cars."*
She/He buy-*PST* car   *PL*   *DET*

E   mere uwe ndị ahụ n'Aba.   *"Those clothes were made in Aba."*
IND   made cloth *PL* that *PP* Aba

Ewu ndị a na-abawanye ụba.   *"These goats are increasing in numbers."*
Goat *PL DET Aux* increase many.

3.7 Conjunction (Njikọ)

Conjunction: The conjunction is a small but important closed word class. It is sometimes called a "joining word" (from the Latin conjunctio: "the act of joining"). A conjunction is a word that is used to connect words, phrases, and clauses. A coordinating conjunction connects words, phrases, and clauses of equal importance. The main coordinating conjunctions are and, or, and but. Examples in Igbo language are as follows:

Igbo	*English*	*Igbo*	*English*
kama	*instead of*	mgbe ahụ	*then*
mana	*but*	maka	*as, so*
otu	*as, that*	na	*and, that*
ma ọ bụ	*or*	ọzọkwa	*moreover*

Example in sentences:

Igbo   *English*

a) Achọrọ m Ji kama Garri — *I want Yam instead of Garri.*
b) Maka na ọ dịmma, ka m jïrï rie ya — *As this is good, I enjoyed it.*
c) Ọ dị mma otu osi buru izu ụka. — *It is good, as it is the weekend.*
d) Ihe a mara mma mana ọdị oke ọnụ — *This is good, but expensive.*
e) Mụ na gị na-eje ahịa — *You and I are going to shop.*

3.8 Inflectional Elements *(Mgbanwe/inflekshọn):*

Inflection, formerly flection or accidence, in linguistics, is used to refer to the change in the form of a word (in English, usually the addition of endings) to mark such distinctions as tense, person, number, gender, mood, voice, and case. The change of form that words undergo to mark such distinctions as those of case, gender, number, tense, person, mood, or voice can be affected witverbsh auxiliaries such as: is, was, are, were, be, do, has, will. These are commonly known as helping verb.

c. *Auxiliary Verbs (Enyemaka ngwaa)*: This is a verb that changes or helps another verb, e.g. am, is, are, was, were, be, been, will, has, have, had, do, does, did. In Igbo language, auxiliary verbs often complement verb form to express an action in simple, continuous, or future tense. When an auxiliary verb is complementing a simple participle, the auxiliary verb is joined to the complement with a hyphen. This is especially the case when the infinitive accompanying starts with a vowel. The hyphen is used to differentiate/separate the auxiliary verb which is a form of prefix of the simple participle from main verb.

For example:

Igbo	*English*
a) Ben gà-enweta ụgbọ ala.	*Ben will catch the bus*
b) Eze nà-àbia ebe a.	*Eze is coming here*
c) Ngọzị ga-àbịa	*Ngọzị will come*
d) Ọ ga-àbịa	*He/She will come*
e) Eze na-abịa	*Eze is coming*
f) Ọ na-abịa	*He/She is coming*

However, when the auxiliary verb takes on the suffix of negation, it is written separately from the complement without a hyphen and as a one word with the suffix.

For example:

Igbo	*English*
a) Ngọzị agaghị àbịa.	*Ngọzị will not come.*

b) Ọ gaghị àbịa. *He/She will not come.*
c) Eze anaghị abịa. *Eze is not coming.*
d) Ọ naghị abịa. *He/She is not coming.*

3.9 Complementizer *(Mmeju)*:

Complementizers are words that, in traditional terms, introduce a complement clause of a sentence. The function of complementizers is to mark the status of mood of a sentence: whether the event is non-real or is real, whether it is true or false. A complementizer or complementizer is a functional category (part of speech) that includes those words that can be used to turn a clause into the subject or object of a sentence. They are comprised of subordinate conjunctions, relative pronouns, and relative adverbs. Examples of complementizers are after, although, as long as, as soon as, as such, because, before, by the time that, if, sinces, once, since, so that, until, when and while. The words "that," "if," and "to" are the most popularly utilized complementizers in the English language.

Igbo	*English*	*Igbo*	*English*
Mgbe, emecha, gasịrị	*after*	ọ bụ ezie na	*although*
dị ka ogologo oge	*as long as*	ozugbo	*as soon as*
dị ka ndị dị otú ahụ	*as such*	n'ihi na	*because*
tupu	*before*	site na oge na	*by the time that*
ma ọ bụrụ na	*if*	n'ihe dị ka	*inasmuch as*
otu ugboro	*once*	kemgbe	*since*
ka o were	*so that*	ruo mgbe	*until*
mgbe	*when*	mgbe	*while*

Examples in sentences:

1. N'agbanyeghị na ike gwụrụ ya, ụra abịaghị.
   Although she was exhausted, sleep didn't come.

2. Ozugbo m bịara, ọ na-apụ.
   As soon as, I came she was leaving.

3. Ọ sara ahụ mgbe egwuregwu ahụ gasịrị.
   He took a shower after the game.

4. Mgbe m chechara echiche, ekpebiri m ịla ezumike nká.
   After much thought, I have decided to retire.

5. Aga m aga na nri mgbe ezumike

I will go on a diet after the holidays.

6. O riri nri ehihie wee pụọ obere oge ka e mesịrị
   He ate lunch and left just after.

7. Ahụbeghị m ya kemgbe ụnyaahụ
   I haven't seen him since yesterday

8. Eribeghị m nri kemgbe nri ụtụtụ.
   I haven't eaten since breakfast.

9. Ekwentị ahụ kụrụ mgbe m na-asa efere.
   The phone rang while I was doing the dishes.

10. Ọ rụsiri ọrụ ike ka o wee gafee ule ahụ.
    She worked hard so that she would pass the test.

11. Aga m eji ụgbọ ala aga ka m nwee ike iburu ibu karịa.
    I'll go by car so that I can take more luggage.

12. Eri kwala nri, tupu m gawa.
    Do not eat until I go.

Exercise

1. What are the main syntactic categories of word classes, and how are they defined?
2. How does the distribution of word classes vary in different genres of writing, and what factors influence this variation?
3. Explain the difference between open class elements and closed class elements in conventional/traditional views of word class taxonomy.
4. How does the structuralist view differ from the conventional/traditional view in terms of categorizing word classes?
5. Provide examples of open class elements and closed class elements in Igbo language.
6. Describe the structuralist approach to the syntactic category of nouns in Igbo language.
7. What are pronouns, and how do they function syntactically in Igbo language?
8. Explain the difference between subject pronouns, personal pronouns, and impersonal pronouns in Igbo.
9. How are reflexive pronouns used in Igbo, and what distinguishes them from emphatic pronouns?
10. Provide examples of different types of verbs in Igbo, including infinitive verbs, linking verbs, and modal verbs.
11. What suffixes are added to Igbo verbs to describe tense changes, and how are they used?
12. Describe the syntactic category of adjectives in Igbo and how they differ from adjectives in English.
13. What are demonstrative adjectives, and how are they used in Igbo to modify nouns?
14. Explain the role of adverbs in Igbo language, providing examples of their usage.
15. How do interrogative adverbs function in Igbo, and what are some common interrogative adverbs?
16. Describe the role of prepositions in Igbo language and provide examples of their usage.
17. What are determiners, and how do they clarify the reference of nouns in Igbo sentences?
18. Explain possessive determiners and demonstrative determiners in Igbo, providing examples.
19. Describe the concept of plurality in Igbo nouns and how it is expressed.
20. What is the function of conjunctions in Igbo language, and what are some common examples of conjunctions used in Igbo sentences?

Chapter 4

The Lexicon (*Usoro Okwu*)

The Lexicon

The "lexicon" is a fundamental and integral component of language that serves as a comprehensive repository of words, phrases, and lexical units. It encompasses the entirety of a language's vocabulary, encompassing every conceivable term, expression, and linguistic element that speakers employ to communicate. For examples:

Igbo	**English**	**Igbo**	**English**
Akpụokwu	*epigram*	Edensibịa/Ejiamaatụ	*reference*
Eserese	*diagram*	Mwetuokwu/Mgbudaokwu	*Anticlimax*
Nhagideokwu	*antithesis*	Nkọwaokwu	*dictionary*
Nsokwunye	*enclitic*	Nkwuma	*euphemism*
Nsona	*hyponymy*	Olumba/olundi	*dialect*
Ọnọniisi	*superordinate*	Ụkabụilu	*anecdotes*
Ụmiedemede	*abstract*		

In practical terms, the lexicon encompasses not only individual words but also idiomatic expressions, compound words, specialized terminology, and even words that hold cultural or historical significance. It serves as a dynamic reservoir that continually expands and adapts to reflect the evolving nature of human communication. For examples:

a) Agwo noro ibe ya — *fraud that defrauds fraudsters.*
b) Aka ntụtụ — *Pickpocket/Poacher*
c) Atụmatụ sayensị asụsụ — *Linguistic theories*
d) Atụtụ mmụta nsinogbe — *behaviourist theory*
e) Atụtụ njirimee — *Use theory*
f) Echiche ngụnyere — *entailment*
g) Ndakọrịta ụdaume — *vowel harmony*
h) Ngwa nchọcha — *data*

i) Nkọwaaha mkpọkọta	*indefinite pronoun*
j) Nkọwaaha nrụaka	*demonstrative pronoun*
k) Nnyocha mmebere okwu	*componential analysis*
l) Ntuleghari agụmagụ	*literature review*
m) Okwu ndịna	*hyponymy*

In computational linguistics, a lexicon is also used to refer to a database or a list of words and their attributes, which can be used in natural language processing tasks such as language modeling, text classification, and information retrieval.

Vocabulary refers to the set of words used by an individual or in a particular language, subject area, or text. It refers to the stock of words that a person knows and uses in their daily communication, as well as their understanding of the meanings and usage of those words. Vocabulary is an essential aspect of language ability, as it determines an individual's ability to express their thoughts and ideas clearly and effectively.

Vocabulary can be divided into two types: oral vocabulary, which includes the words an individual uses when speaking, and reading vocabulary, which includes the words an individual recognizes when reading. The size of an individual's vocabulary is determined by the number of words they know and use, and it is a crucial factor in language development and academic success.

In the context of education, building a rich vocabulary is a crucial aspect of language learning and literacy development. Teachers often use a variety of strategies to help students expand their vocabulary, such as teaching new words, providing opportunities for students to use new words in context, and encouraging students to read widely and to learn words from a variety of sources.

The lexicon is pivotal to language understanding and production. It enables individuals to decipher meanings, create sentences, and convey intentions effectively. Lexical units are equipped with intricate layers of semantics, encompassing not only denotative meanings but also connotations, nuances, and cultural associations.

4.1 Syntax and Lexicon Items

Lexicon items encompass nouns, verbs, adjectives, adverbs, and countless other linguistic components that allow us to articulate thoughts, emotions, and ideas. These individual building blocks are the vehicles through which meaning is conveyed and shared.

In linguistic terms, a lexicon is also known as a mental dictionary, as it refers to the set of words and their meanings that are stored in an individual's memory. The lexicon of a language is constantly changing, as new words are added, and old words fall out of use.

Consider lexicon items as the colors on an artist's palette. Just as an artist carefully selects and blends colors to create a masterpiece, language users strategically choose lexicon items to construct eloquent sentences. Each lexicon item brings with it a specific semantic realm, evoking feelings, imagery, and concepts that shape the essence of communication.

A lexicon typically includes information about the pronunciation, definition, grammatical properties, and usage of each word. It may also include information about the word's history, etymology, and its relationships to other words. The lexicon is a fundamental component of a language, as it provides the building blocks for creating meaningful sentences and expressing ideas.

Syntax and lexicon items complement each other in a manner reminiscent of a musical symphony. Just as different instruments harmonize to produce a melodious composition, syntax and lexicon items harmoniously merge to create coherent and impactful language. This synergy enables language users to convey not only information but also emotions, intentions, and vivid mental images.

Common types of lexical items/blocks

Lexical items, also known as linguistic units, encompass a wide array of linguistic elements that form the fundamental building blocks of language. These elements serve as the foundation for communication and can be categorized into several common types, each with its distinct characteristics and examples.

Words: These are the basic units of language and can stand alone as meaningful entities. Examples include "Nwamba *(cat)*", "akwụkwọ *(book)*" and "osisi *(tree)*."

Parts of Words (Affixes): These are the smaller components within words that contribute to their meaning or grammatical function. Examples include the prefixes (Ngaaniihu) "o-" in "odee *(writer/author)*," the infixes (Nnoṇaetiti) "-r-" in "akaraka *(fate/destiny)*", the suffix (Nsonaazu) "-ra" in "dara *(fell)*," and so on.

Phrasal Verbs: These are verbs combined with one or more particles or prepositions to create unique meanings. Examples include "baa n'ime *(get in)*", "n'agbanyeghị *(in spite)*" and "gbadaa *(get down)*."

Multiword Expressions: These are fixed combinations of words that convey a specific meaning beyond the sum of their individual parts. Examples include "ọcha ka ọ maka *(make believe)*" and "nwoke n'ihe (manliness)."

Collocations: These are word pairs or groups of words that frequently occur together due to linguistic convention. Examples include Àmàmíhé/Àkọ *(Wisdom)*, Akọ na uche *(intelligence)*, Ezi na ụlọ/Ezinụlọ **(Family)**, Isi njedebe *(The end)* and so on.

Institutionalized Utterances: These are common phrases or expressions used in specific social or institutional contexts. Examples include "ị nata oriri *(holy communion)*," "I bu ọnụ *(fasting)*," "I ri ji *(new yam festival)*," "ị kwụ ụgwọ isi *(dowry)*," and "agbam akwụkwọ *(wedding)*, ị gba akwụkwọ *(lawsuit)*" and so on.

Idioms: These are figurative expressions where the meaning cannot be deduced from the individual words. Examples include Okorobịa ọnụ-ntụ (*chronic bachelor)*, Ntụkwụba ọnụ (*disdain)*, Akpataghị akụ *(Destitution)*, ịkwụ ụdọ (*to commit suicide)* and so on.

Sayings/Proverbs: These are culturally ingrained expressions that convey wisdom or common beliefs. Examples include Ihe ka-nte *(overwhelming/enormous)*, Mmiri riri enyi *(overwhelming/enormous)*, anya nlefe/nlefe anya *(disrespect; impertinent)*, ntị ike *(stubbornly disobedient)*, gbuo ya nkenke *(shorten/summarize)*.

Neologisms (Newly Coined Words): Neologisms, which are newly coined words or terms, represent a fascinating phenomenon in language evolution. These lexical innovations often emerge to encapsulate emerging concepts, adapt to changing technologies, or simply reflect shifts in cultural and societal trends. They enrich our vocabulary by providing succinct expressions for novel ideas, technologies, or experiences. For examples:

Coined word	**Translation**	**Meaning/Usage**
Akpatịokwu	*Chattering box*	Radio
Asambodo	*Asambodo*	Certificate
Ekwentị	*Ear Gong*	Handset
Mahadum	*know it all*	University
Ogbunigwe	*kills in multitude*	Bomb
Ọkada	*loud noise (bike)*	Motocycle
Okooko	*Flower*	Flower
Onyoonyo	*item for viewing*	Television
Ọzutaakụ	*Wealth buyer*	Stock broker

Slang and colloquialisms: Slang and colloquialisms are intriguing facets of language, often characterized by their informality and connection to specific social or cultural groups. These linguistic phenomena add color, nuance, and a sense of identity to communication. They are not typically found in formal writing or academic discourse but are prevalent in everyday conversation, pop culture, and subcultures. Let's delve deeper into these linguistic expressions:

Slang: Slang consists of informal words, phrases, or expressions that deviate from standard language usage. It often evolves quickly and may be regional or associated with specific groups. Slang can serve various purposes, including emphasizing solidarity within a group, concealing meaning from outsiders, or simply injecting humor and creativity into speech.

Colloquialisms: Colloquialisms are informal expressions or words commonly used in everyday spoken language. Unlike slang, colloquialisms are generally accepted by society and are not as likely to be seen as unconventional or rebellious. They can vary by region and may not always align with formal written language. Colloquialisms often capture the essence of local culture and may not be easily understood by speakers from other regions.

Both slang and colloquialisms play essential roles in communication. They reflect the dynamic nature of language, adapt to evolving social contexts, and help people express themselves with familiarity and authenticity. While they may not be suitable for all situations, they enrich language by allowing speakers to connect on a more personal and relatable level.

Examples of Igbo Slang and Colloquialisms:

a) Anịkịrịja — *An old noisy bicycle*
b) Bọchaa — *Escape/Get out immediately*
c) Gbachaa m — *Give me a share (money)*
d) Oko — *An old person*
e) Okongwu — *An old person*
f) Owu ite — *bankrupt/poverty-stricken*
g) Paakuul — *Cool down/relax*
h) Sụlịa — *To play football well*

Sentence Frames and Heads: These are structures that serve as templates for constructing sentences. Examples include "Ọ bụghị ihe… dịka Ị na-eche *(That is not as...as you think)*" and "Ihe merenu bụ na… *(The problem or issue was..)*."

Text Frames: These are recurring patterns or templates in written discourse that facilitate organization and coherence. Examples include " N'akwụkwọ nyocha a anyị na-enyocha ...," "Nke mbụ ...," "Nke abụọ ...," na "N'ikpeazụ .... *(In this paper we explore...,*" "*First...,*" "*Second...,*" *and* "*Lastly...).*"

Noun-modifier semantic relations: this is the idea of noun-modifier semantic relationships. In such relationships, certain combinations of words exhibit a standardized interpretation. For example, consider the phrase "ọnụ ụtọ (*literal meaning*: sweet mouth versus *actual meaning* flattery)." In this case, it is conventionally understood to denote using the mouth to say flattery words rather than a mouth characterized by sweetness or sweetness or mouth.

This example underscores the fundamental role of established linguistic patterns and associations in conveying meaning with precision and clarity in language. They showcase the diversity of lexical units within the lexicon, ranging from everyday words and idiomatic expressions to specialized terminology and cultural references. The lexicon serves as a rich resource that empowers language users to communicate effectively, convey nuances, and navigate the intricate tapestry of language.

4.2 Criteria for Noun classification

Within the lexicon, nouns emerge as a prominent category, representing entities, objects, places, or concepts. Nouns provide the foundational structure upon which sentences are constructed, and they often undergo various grammatical modifications to convey nuances of meaning. The classification of Igbo nouns into different classes helps linguists categorize and analyze their usage patterns, leading to a deeper understanding of how nouns function within sentences.

Nouns in Igbo linguistics can be classified into different categories or classes based on various criteria. Here are some of the main criteria used for classifying nouns:

1. Semantic Criteria:

Common Nouns: Refer to general, everyday entities. Examples:
"Nkịta *(dog)*"   (referring to a general type of domesticated animal)
"Ụgbọ ala *(car)*"   (referring to a common mode of transportation)
"Ụlọ *(house)*"   (referring to a typical dwelling)

Proper Nouns: Refer to specific, unique individuals or places. Examples:
"Jọn *(John)*"   (referring to a specific person)
"Ogbunike Cave"   (referring to a unique landmark)
"Ibeto Cement"   (referring to a specific brand)

Concrete Nouns: Refer to tangible, physical objects. Examples:
"Osisi *(tree)*"   (referring to a physical plant with leaves and branches)
"Oroma *(Orange)*"   (referring to a tangible fruit)
"Ugwu *(mountain)*"   (referring to a physical geographical feature)

Abstract Nouns: Refer to intangible concepts, emotions, or qualities. Examples:

"Ịhụnanya *(love)*" (referring to the abstract concept of affection)
"nnwere onwe *(freedom)*" (referring to the intangible state of being free)
"obi ụtọ *(happiness)*" (referring to the emotional quality of joy)

These examples demonstrate how nouns can be categorized based on their semantic characteristics. Common nouns are general and refer to everyday things, while proper nouns specify unique individuals or places. Concrete nouns represent tangible, physical objects, while abstract nouns represent intangible concepts, emotions, or qualities.

2. Grammatical Criteria:

Countable Nouns (Count Nouns): Can be counted as discrete units. Examples:
"Akwụkwá *(book)*" (You can count individual books: one book, two books, three books, etc).
"Nwamba (cat)" (You can count individual cats: one cat, two cats, three cats, etc).
"Ụgbọ ala (car)" (You can count individual cars: one car, two cars, three cars, etc).

Uncountable Nouns (Mass Nouns): Cannot be counted individually. Examples:
"Mmiri *(water)*" (You cannot count individual units of water in the same way you count discrete objects).
"Ihe ọmụma *(knowledge)*" (You cannot count knowledge as individual units).
"Aja *(sand)*" (Sand, in general, is not counted as individual grains in everyday language).

Collective Nouns: Refer to groups or collections of individuals or things. Examples:
"òtù *(team)*" (referring to a group of players or individuals working together)
"ìgwè *(herd)*" (referring to a collection of animals, such as cattle or sheep)
"Ezinụlọ *(family)*" (referring to a group of related individuals living together)

Compound Nouns: are formed by combining two or more words. Examples:
Èké + m̀má Èkém̀má *(good market day)* (formed by combining "Èké *(market day)*" and m̀má *(good)*")
Àdá + Ézè Àdáèzè *(princess)* (formed by combining Àdá *(first daughter)*" and "Ézè *(king)*")
Ífé + Ómá Íféómá *(Goodies/Good thing)* (formed by combining "Ífé *(thing/entity)*" and "Ómá *(good)*")

Gender-specific Nouns: Categorized by gender in some languages. Examples:
"Nwoke" *(man)* and "Nwanyị" *(woman)* are gender-specific nouns.
"Okeokpa" *(Rooster)* and "Nnekwu" *(Hen)* are gender-specific nouns.
"Ọkụkọ" (chicken) are gender-neutral noun.

"Ewu" (goat) are gender-neutral noun.

These examples illustrate how nouns can be categorized based on various grammatical criteria, including countability, collectiveness, compounding, and gender-specificity.

3. Animate vs. Inanimate Criteria:
Animate Nouns: Refer to living beings or things with qualities of living beings. Examples:
"Nkịta *(dog)*" (referring to a living and breathing animal)
"Mmadụ *(human)*" (referring to a species characterized by consciousness and the ability to reason)
"Osisi *(tree)*" (though not a living being in the same way animals are, it has qualities of a living entity, such as growth)

Inanimate Nouns: Refer to non-living objects or things. Examples:
"Oche *(chair)*" (referring to a piece of furniture, which is not alive)
"nkume *(rock)*" (referring to a solid, non-living object)
"Efere (plate)" (referring to a kitchen utensil, which lacks consciousness)

These examples demonstrate the distinction between animate nouns, which typically refer to living beings or things with qualities of living beings, and inanimate nouns, which refer to non-living objects or things.

4. Morphological Criteria:
Agent Nouns: are formed by adding prefix "o/ọ" and two verb roots together. Example with Noun agent (Ahaomee/Omee):

Prefix (nganiihu)	*Two verb roots* (Isingwaa abụọ)	*Noun Agent* (Ahaomee/Omee)	*Meaning* (Ihe ọ pụtata)
O	de + e	ode	*writer*
O	me + e	omee	*doer*
Ọ	gba + a	ọgbaa	*shooter*
Ọ	kụ + ụ	ọkụụ	*planter/sower*
O	je + e	ojee	*traveler/goer*

Verbal Nouns (Gerunds): Nouns formed by adding prefix "o/ọ", a verb root and infinitive together. Examples:

Prefix (nganiihu)	Verb root (Isingwaa)	Infinitives (Mfinitivu)	Gerund (Jerondu)	Meaning (Ihe ọ pụtata)
O	ri	ri	oriri	*eating/feasting*
ọ	ṅụ	ṅụ	ọṅụṅụ	*drinking*
O	di	de	odide	*writing*
ọ	gụ	gụ	ọgụgụ	*reading*
ọ	mụ	mụ	ọmụmụ	*learning/bearing*

These examples illustrate how nouns can be categorized based on their morphological features, such as the addition of prefix "o/ọ" and two verb roots together to create agent nouns or the transformation of verbs into nouns through by adding prefix "o/ọ", a verb root and infinitive together.

5. Material Criteria:

Material Nouns: Refer to substances or materials from which objects are made. Examples:
"nkụ (*wood*)" (referring to the material obtained from trees and used in construction)
"igwe (*iron/metal*)" (referring to substances like iron, steel, or copper used in manufacturing)
"nnu (*salt*)" (referring to food materials used for cooking and preservation purposes).

These examples of material nouns represent various substances or materials that serve as the building blocks for creating objects, structures, and products (food).

4.3 Common Classes of Noun

1. *Proper Noun (Ahaaka)*: A proper noun is the name given to something to make it more specific. It identifies a particular person, place, or thing (e.g., Nnamdi, Chidi, Awka, Ikwerre, Brian, California). Proper nouns differ from common nouns because common nouns are the words for something in general.

2. *Common Noun (Ahaizugbe)*: refers to people, places, or things in general e.g. abụ (song), ọṅụ (joy), okorobia (boy), nkịta (dog), obodo (city), ụbọchị (day). Common nouns are written with a capital letter only when they start a sentence.

3. *Collective Noun (Ahaigwe)*: refers to a set or group of people, places, animals, or things e.g. Ezinụlọ (family), akwụkwọ (books), igwe (multitude).

4. *Compound Noun (Ahaukwu)*: compound nouns are words for people, animals, places, things or ideas, made up of two or more words, e.g. umu-akwụkwọ (students), umuaka (children), ụlọ-

akwụkwọ (school), ndi-ọrụ (workers), etc.

5. *Abstract Noun (Ahauche/Ahaechereche)*: this refers to ideas, qualities, conditions and things that do not exist physically e.g. ọṅụ (joy), enyi (friendship), ihunanya (love).

6. *Concrete Noun (Aha Ahụrụmnanya):* refers to people and things that exist physically e.g. mmadụ (person), ụwa (planet), osisi (tree), enwe (monkey).

7. *Count Nouns (Aha-agutaraonu)*: countable nouns are nouns that can be counted individually; you can put a number before it as a quantity, e.g. Ụgbọ-ala abụọ (two cars), Nkịta anọ (four dogs), Ụmụnne atọ (three brothers), etc.

8. *Non-count Nouns (Aha-Agutaonu)*: uncountable nouns refer to things that can't be individually counted, and don't take an indefinite article (a or an) in front of them e.g. ego (money), akụ (wealth), mmiri (water), egwu (music), ịhụnanya (love), etc.

Note that money is uncountable but ego-igwe (coin) or ego akwụkwọ (bank notes) are countable. Water is uncountable but glass of water is countable.

9. *Animate Nouns (Aha Adịmụndụ)*: These nouns refer to living beings or things that have the qualities of living beings, such as "mmadụ (human)," "Nkịta *(dog)*," or "osisi *(tree)*."

10. *Inanimate Nouns (Aha Ọdịghịndụ)*: Inanimate nouns refer to non-living objects or things, like "oche *(chair)*," "nkume/okute *(rock)*," or "akwụkwọ *(book)*."

11. *Gender-specific Nouns (Aha ụdịdị okike)*: Gender-specific Nouns refer to nouns that are categorized as masculine, feminine, or neuter based on their gender, For example "nwoke *(man)*", "nwanyị *(woman)*", "di *(husband)*", "nwunye *(wife)*", "ebule *(ram)*", "mkpị *(billy goat)*".

12. *Agent Nouns (Ahaome/Omee)*: These nouns refer to individuals who perform specific actions, often formed by adding prefix and two verb roots together.

Prefix (nganiihu)	Two verb root (Isingwaa abụọ)	Noun Agent (Ahaomee/Omee)	Meaning (Ihe ọ pụtata)
o	de + e	odee	*writer*
o	le + e	olee	*where/how many*
o	me + e	omee	*doer*
ọ	ga + a	ọgaa	*boss*

| ọ | gba + a | ọgbaa | shooter |

13. *Verbal Nouns/Gerunds (Jerọndụ)*: These are nouns formed from verbs by adding prefix and infinitive suffix as shown below.

Prefix (nganiihu)	Verb root (Isingwaa)	Infinitives (Mfinitivu)	Gerund (Jerondu)	Meaning (Ihe ọ pụtata)
o	ri	Ri	oriri	*eating/feasting*
ọ	nyụ	nya	ọnyụnya	*driving*
ọ	ṅụ	ṅụ	ọṅụṅụ	*drinking*
ọ	dị	Da	ọdịda	*falling*

14. *Material Nouns (Aha Mgwọọrụ)*: Material nouns refer to substances or materials from which objects are made, such as "nkụ (*wood*)," "igwe (*iron/metal*)," or "nnu (*salt*)."

These are some of the common classes of nouns in linguistics. It's important to note that different languages may have their own unique categories and rules for classifying nouns. Additionally, some nouns can belong to multiple classes depending on their usage in a sentence.

4.4 Subcategorization, Selection, and Construction of Nouns

The relationships between Igbo nouns and other linguistic elements go far beyond simple categorization. Subcategorization, selection, and construction are essential concepts that shed light on the complex connections between nouns and the words they interact with in sentences.

Subcategorization:

Subcategorization refers to the inherent properties of a verb or other predicate that determine the types of nouns or noun phrases it can combine with in a sentence. For example, the verb "eat" subcategorizes for a direct object, which must be a noun or a noun phrase representing the thing being eaten. You can say, "She eats an apple," where "an apple" is the direct object noun phrase.

Verb Subcategorizing for Direct Object Nouns:

Verb: "Gụọ (Read)"

This verb requires a direct object that is typically a noun or noun phrase representing the material being read.

Example:

Ọ gụrụ akwụkwọ.   *"She read a book."*

Verb Subcategorizing for Indirect Object:

Verb: "Nye (Give)"
This verb requires both a direct object (the thing being given) and an indirect object (the recipient).

Example:

O nyere ya onyinye.   *"He gave her a gift."*

Selection:
Selection is a more general term that encompasses subcategorization and extends to other parts of speech, not just nouns. It refers to the process by which a word, typically a verb or predicate, chooses or "selects" specific types of words or phrases to combine in a sentence.

For instance, the verb "kwu/ekwu *(talk)*" selects for a direct object that is typically a noun phrase representing the topic of conversation. You can say, "Ọ na-ekwu maka ndọrọ ndọrọ ọchịchị *(He talks about politics)*," where "about politics" is the selected noun phrase.

Adjective Selecting Specific Noun Complements:
Adjective: "Obi ụtọ *(Happy)*"
This adjective selects a noun complement that represents the cause of happiness. Example: "Obi dị ya ụtọ maka ezinụlọ ya *(She is happy about her family)*."

Preposition Selecting Noun Object:
Preposition: "n'ime *(in)*"
This preposition selects for a noun object indicating location. Example: "The keys are in the drawer."

4.5 Construction:
Construction refers to the specific way words and phrases are combined in a sentence to convey meaning and grammatical structure. Nouns play a crucial role in constructing sentences by serving as subjects, objects, or other grammatical elements.

For example, in the construction "Nwoke ahụ gburu ọdụm ahụ *(The man killed the lion)*," "Nwoke ahụ *(The man)*" and "Ọdụm ahụ *(the lion)*" are both noun phrases that fulfill the roles of subject and direct object, respectively.

These concepts highlight how nouns, as well as other parts of speech, work together in intricate ways to form meaningful and grammatically correct sentences.

Subject-Verb-Object Construction:
This common sentence structure involves a subject (noun or pronoun), a verb, and a direct object (noun or noun phrase). Example:

"Nwa ahụ kụwara/tiwara efere ahụ."
"Nwa ahụ *(isiahịrị)* kụwara/tiwara *(ngwaa)* efere ahụ *(nnara)*."
"The child *(subject)* broke *(verb)* the ball *(direct object)*."

Prepositional Phrase Construction:
Involves a preposition followed by a noun phrase (the object of the preposition).

Example:

"Ha gara njegharị *n'ebennọkọta ahụ*."
"Ha gara njegharị na ogige nnọkọta ahụ *(Nkebiokwu kembuụzọ)*."
"They went for a walk in the park *(prepositional phrase)*."

These examples showcase how subcategorization, selection, and construction work in various linguistic contexts. Verbs, adjectives, prepositions, and other elements in a sentence often have specific requirements and preferences for the types of nouns or noun phrases they can combine with, resulting in the diverse and structured language we use to communicate.

4.6 Criteria for verbs classification
Verbs in linguistics can be classified into different categories or classes based on various criteria. Some of the criteria used for classifying verbs include the following: Transitivity, Valency, Complementation, and Process-based classifications.

1. Transitivity-based classification:
In the vibrant landscape of linguistic studies, Igbo stands out as a language of remarkable complexity and depth. One aspect that intrigues linguists and language enthusiasts alike is the concept of transitivity within Igbo verbs. It is a subject over which there is continuing disagreement. Before we dive into the specifics, let's establish a foundational understanding of what transitivity means.

Defining Transitivity

Transitivity refers to the grammatical property of verbs that relates to the number of arguments a verb can take. In simpler terms, it deals with whether a verb requires an object to complete its meaning or not.

Nwachukwu's Contribution

The study of transitivity in Igbo gained significant traction thanks to Nwachukwu (1987), whose groundbreaking work recognized the relevance of transitivity and its pivotal role in Igbo syntax. Nwachukwu's work forms the cornerstone of our exploration, as it categorizes Igbo verbs into two main groups: transitive and intransitive.

(a). Transitive Verbs

Transitive verbs in Igbo are those that require an object to make complete sense. In other words, they transfer an action from the subject (the doer) to the object (the receiver). For example, consider the Igbo verb "rie," which means "eat." This verb is transitive because it requires an object to specify what is being eaten, as in "rie ji" (eat yam). Another example is the verb "saa" which means "wash." This verb is a transitive verb because it requires an object to specified what is to be washed as in "saa ahụ gị" (wash your body/take a shower).

(b). Intransitive Verbs

Intransitive verbs, on the other hand, do not require an object to complete their meaning. They stand alone and convey an action or state without involving a direct object. They are verbs whose actions do not directly affect an object, resulting in sentences that lack any object altogether. For instance, consider the sentence "The girl was smiling." In this case, there is no direct object to answer the questions "*what*" or "*whom*." One cannot ask the question, "The girl is smiling *what?* But you can ask the question about what somebody is "playing" which could range from football, basketball, handball, volleyball, cards and so on.

Intransitiveness of Igbo verb is based on pragmatics (social context) and nonverbal cues play a big role. For example, the verb "bịara (came)" is an intransitive verb because when used in a sentence, it does not generate answers to questions like "what" or "whom." For instance, "Ada bịara (Ada came)" or "Ọ bịara (S/he came)." Another example is the verb "rutere (arrived)." "O rutere (S/he arrived). In these sentences, it is not possible to apply the questions "what" or "whom" to identify a direct object. You can only use the "where" question to request information about the location and not object.

Nwachukwu further divides intransitive verbs into two subcategories: unaccusatives and unergatives.

(i). Unaccusative Verbs

Unaccusative verbs describe actions or states that happen to the subject without the subject actively performing the action. it introduces a theme argument in object position. Examples" nọrọ *(remain)*, nọgide *(linger),* bilie *(arise)*, pụọ *(leave/depart)*, hụ *(ensure)*, banye *(enter)*, gbapụ *(escape)*, daa *(fall)*, gaa *(go)*, laghachi *(return)*, bilie *(rise)*,

In linguistics, a theme argument refers to the participant in an action or event that typically undergoes the action, often representing the entity affected by the action. When this theme argument is positioned as the object of a verb in a sentence, it is said to be in "object position."

For instance, the verb "dara" (fall) is unaccusative because it doesn't require a direct object. You can say, "Ọ dara" (It fell) without specifying what was fallen. The "Ọ (It)," coulde be Oroma (Orange fruit), Ube (Pear), and so on.

(ii). Unergative Verbs

Unergative verbs introduce an agent argument in subject position. In linguistics, unergative verbs are a category of verbs that describe actions where the subject of the sentence is actively involved in performing the action. These verbs do not require a direct object to complete their meaning. When an unergative verb is used in a sentence, the agent, or the doer of the action, is positioned in the subject position of the sentence. Examples: kwụsị *(cease)*, gbanwee *(change)*, close *(mechie)*, mgbawa *(crack)*, gbazee *(melt)*, megharia *(move)*, meghe *(open)*, nyefee *(surrender)*, tụgharịa *(turn)*. nkpọnwụ *(wither)*.

These verbs describe actions where the subject is actively involved but still do not require a direct object. An example is "gbasasịa" (to disintegrate), as in "Ọ gbasasịa" (It has disintegrated). There's no need to specify what disintegrated.

Let's illustrate this concept with more examples:
Example 1: Igbo Verb "meghe (open)"
The English verb "meghe (open)" is unergative verb. It describes an action where the subject is actively engaged in opening without the need for a direct object.

Sentence 1: "O meghe (It opened)."
In this sentence, "It" is the subject of the sentence, and "open" is the unergative verb. "It" is the agent, the one performing the action of opening, and it is positioned in the subject position.

Example 2: Verb "kpoọnwụ (wither)"
Another example of an unergative verb in Igbo is "kpoọnwụ (wither)." When something wither,

they are actively participating in the action of withering.

Sentence 2: "Ọ kpọnwụ (It withered)."
In this sentence, "Ọ (It)" is the subject, and "kpọnwụrụ (It withered)" is the unergative verb. "It" is the agent who is actively withering, and he occupies the subject position.

Unergative verbs are those that describe actions where the subject is actively involved in performing the action, and they do not require a direct object. In sentences with unergative verbs, the agent, or the doer of the action, is placed in the subject position.

Nwachukwu's work goes even deeper by acknowledging a subset of intransitive verbs in Igbo that take inherent complements. These are verbs that must co-occur with specific complements that are inherent to them. It's crucial to note that the ability or inability of a verb to take an inherent complement is not a measure of its transitivity.

Conversely, in 2005, Emananjo presented an opposing viewpoint, advocating against the classification of Igbo verbs solely based on transitivity. Instead, Emananjo proposed categorizing these verbs according to the types of complements they use. This perspective underscores the idea that the transitive versus intransitive distinction may not adequately capture the intricate nuances of Igbo verb behavior. Thus, centering the classification on complement types is suggested as a more precise approach.

In his paper titled *"Towards a Classification of Igbo Verbs,"* E. Nolue Emenanjo offers a comprehensive overview of Igbo verb classes. His classification is based on various linguistic aspects, including phonology, morphology, lexicology, syntax, semantics, and pragmatics. Here are the categories of Igbo verbs based to Emenanjo's classification and universal categories that apply to Igbo linguistics:

2. Valency-based classification:
This relies on the concept of valency, which pertains to the number of arguments a verb requires. In this framework, Igbo verbs are categorized into two groups: +valency verbs and -valency verbs. +Valency verbs are finite and capable of full inflection, functioning as predicates. They can also undergo inflection for various grammatical categories, including tense, mood, aspect, negation, and ergativity. On the other hand, -valency verbs are non-finite, dependent, and exhibit deficiencies in verb derivation and extensional morphology.

+valency verbs: +valency" refers to an increase in the valency of a verb, indicating a change in the number of arguments the verb takes. A valency change occurs when a verb acquires more arguments or complements.

For example, a verb may be monovalent (taking only one argument, like an intransitive verb) and then undergo a valency increase to become divalent (taking two arguments, like a transitive verb). This often involves the addition of an object or another argument to the verb.

So, when we talk about "+valency verbs," we are referring to verbs that can increase their valency by taking additional arguments, often resulting in a change from an intransitive to a transitive form, or an increase in the overall number of arguments the verb requires.

The following are examples of +valency verbs in Igbo, where the valency increases by adding an argument:

    Gosi *(Show)*
    Monovalent: Ọ na-egosi *(He/she shows)*.
    Divalent: Ọ na-egosi foto *(He shows a picture)*.

    zụta *(Buy)*
    Monovalent: Ọ na-zụta *(He/she buys)*.
    Divalent: Ọ na-zụta nri *(He/she buys food)*.

    Gụọ *(Read)*
    Monovalent: Ọ na-agụ *(She reads)*.
    Divalent: Ọ na-agụ akụkọ *(She reads a story)*.

Trivalent verbs are those that can take three arguments, typically a subject and two objects. Here are a few examples:

    Nye *(Give)*
    O nyere enyi ya akwụkwọ   *(He/she gave a book to her friend)*.
    Isi ahịrị: "O" (*Nnara*): "akwụkwọ" (*Nnapụta*): "enyi ya".
    (Subject) She *(Direct Object)* a book *(Indirect Object)* to her friend

    Zipu/Ziga *(Send)*
    Ha zigara onye nkụzi ha ozi   *(They sent a message to their teacher)*.
    Isi ahịrị: "Ha" *Nnara*: "Ozi" *Nnapụta*: "onye nkụzi ha".
    (Subject) They *(Direct Object)* a message *(Indirect Object)* their teacher

    Ikuzi (Teach)
    Ọ kụziiri ụmụ akwụkwọ ahụ ihe mmụta   *(He taught a lesson to the students)*.

Isi ahịrị: "O" *Nnara:* "ihe mmụta" *Nnapụta:* "ụmụ akwụkwọ ahụ".
(Subject) He *(Direct Object)* a lesson *(Indirect Object)* to the students

These examples demonstrate trivalent verbs by having a subject and two distinct objects, showcasing the three arguments involved in the action or process described by the verb.

-valency verbs: -Valency verbs are verbs that decrease their valency by removing an argument. For example, the verb "open" is normally divalent (or transitive), meaning it takes two arguments: a subject and an object. However, it can become monovalent (or intransitive) by omitting the object, such as "The door opened."

Examples of valency reduction in Igbo verbs:

Mepee/Meghe (Open)
Divalent: O meghere ụzọ *(He/she opened the door).*
Monovalent: Ọnụ Ụzọ meghere. *(The door opened).*

Mechie (Close)
Divalent: O mechiri akwụkwọ ahụ *(He/she closed the book).*
Monovalent: Akwụkwọ ahụ mechiri *(The book closed).*

Rie (Eat)
Divalent: O riri Garrị. *(He/she ate Garri).*
Monovalent: O riri. *(He/she ate).*

Gụọ (Read)
Divalent: Ọ gụrụ akwụkwọ ahụ. *(He/she read the book).*
Monovalent: Ọ gụrụ. *(He/she read).*

Dee (Write)
Divalent: O dere akwụkwọ ozi. *(He/she wrote a letter).*
Monovalent: O dere. *(He/she wrote).*

Saa (Wash)
Divalent: Ọ sara efere. *(He/she washed the dishes).*
Monovalent: Ọ sara. *(He/she washed).*

These "-valency" verbs typically don't stand alone as complete action words but are used in combination with other words to convey specific meanings or to modify the main action in a sentence.

3. Nhazi Ngwaa nke dabere na mmeju *(Complementation-based classification)*: This classification is based on the type of complement that a verb takes. Emenanjo's (2005) description of the five categories of Igbo verbs is grounded in the morpho-semantic structures of the verbs. Complementation-based classification are as follows:

1. Ngwaa Izugbe Mmeju *(General Complement Verbs)*,
2. Ngwaa Mmeju Nsinachi *(Inherent Complement Verbs)*,
3. Ngwaa Mmeju Ndabe/Ntado *(Bound Complement Verbs)*,
4. Ngwaa Mmeju Nkebiokwu Kembuụzọ *(Prepositional Phrase Complement Verbs)*, and
5. Ngwaa Mmeju Nnabiga *(Ergative Complement Verbs)*.

(A). Ngwaa Izugbe Mmeju *(General Complement Verbs)*:
General complement verbs (GCVs) are verbs that can take any nominal element as their complement, unlike inherent complement verbs (ICVs) that require a specific nominal element to complete their meaning. GCVs are also called non-inherent complement verbs or transitive verbs. In Igbo, GCVs are very common and can be divided into two types: simple GCVs and complex GCVs. Simple GCVs are verbs that take only one complement, while Complex GCVs are verbs that take more than one complement.

In Igbo, GCVs (General Complement Verbs) are common and can be classified into two types: simple GCVs and complex GCVs.

1. Simple GCVs: Simple GCVs are verbs that take only one complement. Here are some examples:

"Kọrọ" *(told):*
Example: Nkechi kọrọ akụkọ. *(Nkechi told a story)*.

"Gbakọ" *(Calculate)*:
Example: Chijioke gbakọrọ ego. *(Chijioke calculated the money)*,

2. Complex GCVs: Complex GCVs are verbs that take more than one complement. Here are examples:

"Nyere" *(Give to)*:
Example: Chima nyere Ngọzị akara. *(Chima gave akara Bean Cake) to Ngọzị)*.

"Kpọrọ" (Call for):

Example: Ifeanyi kpọrọ Chinyere ka ọ lọta ụlọ. *(Ifeanyi called for Chinyere to come home).*

"Zoro" (hide in/under):
Example: Ezoro m n'okpuru oche.   *(I was hiding under the chair).*

"nọdụrụ" (sat on):
Example: Ọ nọdụrụ ala n'elu oche   *(He sat on the chair).*

"tụfuru" (lost/misplaced):
Example: Ọ tụfuru mgbanaka ya n'ụzọ   *(He/she lost her ring on the way).*

In the examples, the simple GCVs take only one complement, while the complex GCVs take more than one complement, often involving both the direct object and an additional prepositional phrase indicating the recipient, destination, or source of the action.

(B). Ngwaa Mmeju Nsinachi *(Inherent Complement Verbs (ICV))*: Inherent complement verbs (ICVs) in Igbo are verbs that require a specific nominal element to complete their meaning. language, Inherent Complement Verbs (ICVs) constitute a subset of stative verbs used to convey adjectival meanings. Examples of Igbo ICVs are: bịá ǹsó, chee echiche, fụ ányà, gba mbọ, kwọ nwá, te ude, etc.

a. Emeka baa-ra   ya   mba   n'ụtụtụ.
   Emeka rebuke-IND   3s (obj)scold   PP.
   Emeka rebuked/scolded him in the morning.

b. Chinedu bịá-ra   ǹsó
   Chinedu come-IND   near.
   Chinedu came nearer.

c. Ada chere   echiche banyere atụmatụ ya.
   Ada think-IND thoughts   PP.
   Ada thought about her plan.

d. Eze fụrụ   yá   ányà
   Eze see-IND 3s (obj) eye.
   Eze saw him/her.

e. Emeka gbara mbọ   ịrụchaa ọrụ ahụ
   Emeka make-effort-IND   INF.

Emeka made an effort to finish the job.

f. O   kpere   ha   ekpere.
    He/she pray-IND 3s (obj)   NP.
    He prayed for them.

e. Nkechi kwọ   nwá   yá.
    Nkechi carry-on-the-back   child   3s.
    Nkechi is carrying her child on the back.

f. Amaka tere   ude   n'ihu nwa ya.
    Amaka apply-IND   cream   PP
    Amaka applied cream to her child's face.

In example "a" above, the phrase "baa mba" comprises the verb root "baa" and the specified noun "mba." These two elements must always appear together in any context describing the action of scolding or reprimanding someone. This is why the Inherent Complement Verb in Igbo is characterized as a 'dual unit morpheme,' emphasizing that these components must consistently co-occur to maintain conceptual integrity.

(C). Ngwaa Mmeju Ndabe *(Bound Complement Verbs (BCV))*: Bound Complement Verbs (BCVs) are a type of verb in which two necessary morphemes combine to generate the verb. The primary morpheme, which expresses the essence of the action, is the verb's basic root. The second morpheme is a structurally derived element that further clarifies or defines the type of action that the verb root expresses. It is shaped by morphological processes. Examples of Bound Complement Verbs in Igbo are: ka nka, kwú ókwú, ñụ ọñụ, pe mpe, ríá ọrịá, sụ̀ nsú

1. Ngọzị dara ada. *(Ngọzị fell down).*
   Ngọzị fall-IND down.

2. Anyị kwùrù ókwú. (We have spoken).
   1ˢᵗpl say-IND talk.

3. O pere mpe. *(It was tiny/little).*
   It is-IND tiny/little.

4. Mgbafọ ríáà ọrịá. *(Mgbafọ was sick).*
   Mgbafọ fall ill-IND sickness.

5. Okeke sụ́rụ ṅsú. *(Okeke stammered).*
   Okeke speak-IND stammer.

In (a), the verb root "da (dara-PST)," which means "fall (fell-PST)," combines with its derivative structure "ada," which means "fell-down". In (b), the verb root "kwú (kwùrù-PST)," which means "speak (spoke-PST)," is paired with its derived form, "ókwú," which means "talk" are complement. The same applies to "c", "d", and "e" in the above examples.

Together, these morphemes provide a rich and harmonic structure that enhances the meaning of the Bound Complement Verb in the Igbo language.

(D). Ngwaa Mmeju Nkebiokwu Kembuụzọ (Prepositional Phrase Complement Verbs (PPCV)): Prepositional Complement Verbs (PPCVs) are formed by verb roots in Igbo that are accompanied by the morpheme "nà" and a noun. In Igbo grammar, the combination of the morpheme "nà" and its accompanying noun is referred to as a prepositional complement. Additionally, this morpheme, "nà," serves various syntactic functions, including being an auxiliary verb, an aspect marker, a conjunction, and a complementizer. Examples include: pụọ n'ụzọ *(get out of the way)*; ka **n**'ọ́nụ́ *(noisy)*; nọ̀ **n**'ọ̀nọ̀dụ̀ *(stay in a situation)*; kwé **nà** chúkwú *(believe in God)*; kwé n'áká *(handshake)*; etc.

   a) Ọ kwụrụ   **n**'ụzọ.   *He/she was in the way.*
      3s stand-IND in the way.

   b) Ọ ka   **n**'ọ́nụ́ .   *Noisy individual.*
      3s better-PRES in mouthing.

   c) Ọ nọ̀ **n**'ọ̀nọ̀dụ̀   ihere.   *He/she is in a shameful situation.*
      3s be in situation   shame.

   d) O kwéré   **nà** omenala.   *He believed in traditional practices.*
      3s agree-IND in tradition.

   e) Ha kwéré   n'áká.   *They exchanged handshakes.*
      3pl agree-IND in hand.

The example in (a) above shows that the verb root "kwụ" which means "stand," and the structure "nà + ụzọ," which serves as a complement to the vthe context of the sentence determines the meaning—which is derived from the clause's context. Similarly, in (b), the predicate structure comprises the verb root "ka" meaning 'better' and the "nà + ọ́nụ́" (in mouthing) structure to express the meaning of the predicate in the clause. Similarly, in example (c), the verb root nọ 'be' and the nà + ọnọdụ (in situation) is structured to derive the meaning of the predicate in the clause. The clause's meaning is clear. in relation to its context.

(E). Ngwaa Mmeju Nnabiga (Ergative Complement Verbs (ECV)): An Ergative Complement Verb (ECV) in Igbo refers to a specific category of verbs that are characterized by the presence of verb roots accompanied by abstract nouns. What sets these verbs apart is their distinctive predicate structure, where the abstract nouns co-occurring with the verbs have the ability to assume the structural position of the subject within an Igbo sentence.

In this particular linguistic construction, the verb roots, which serve as the core elements expressing the action, are intricately connected with abstract nouns. These abstract nouns, rather than traditional concrete objects or subjects, play a crucial role in shaping the predicate structure. Examples of Ergative Complement Verbs are: dà ìbèrìbè *(be stupid)*; kpu ìsì *(be blind)*; kụ ǹgwọrọ *(be lame)*; pụ́ árá *(be mad)*; tụ egwu *(be scared)*; etc.

Unlike many other verb constructions, the abstract nouns in Ergative Complement Verbs hold a unique status. They possess the capacity to function not only as complements but also as subjects, occupying the structural position typically reserved for the doer of the action in a sentence. The following are examples:

1. Uche dà-rà ìbèrìbè *(Uche is stupid)*
   Uche fall-IND stupid.
   Rev: Ìbèrìbè dà-rà Uche *(Uche is stupid)*

2. Chinedu kpụ̀-rụ̀ ìsì *(Chinedu is blind)*
   Chinedu put on-IND blindness.
   Rev: Ìsì kpụ̀-rụ̀ Chinedu *(Chinedu is blind)*

3. Ada kụ̀-rụ̀ ǹgwọ́rọ́ *(Ada is lame)*
   Ada hit-IND lameness.
   Rev: Ǹgwọ́rọ́ kụ̀-rụ̀ Ada. *(Ada is lame)*

4. Nneka pụ̀-rụ̀ árá *(Nneka is mad)*
   Nneka go-out-IND madness.
   Rev: Árá pụ̀-rụ̀ Nneka. *(Nneka is mad)*

5. Obi tụ̀-rụ̀ egwu. *(Obi was scared)*
   Obi throw-IND fear.

Rev: Egwu tụ̀-rụ̀ Obi. *(Obi was scared)*

Since the nouns that co-occur with the verbs might assume the structural role of the subject in a sentence, the predicate structure of these verbs is specific to them. For this reason, Uwalaka (1988) assigned this class of verbs the label "subject-object" switching verbs.

4. Process-based classification:

A process verb or "verb of occurrence" is a verb that expresses an event or a happening that is not directly caused by an agent. Process verbs are also called verbs of occurrence or unaccusative verbs[1]. They differ from transitive verbs, which take an object as their argument, and unergative verbs, which take an agent as their subject.

The main distinguishing factor of "verb of occurrence" is in the manner in which they are questioned. Specifically, questions related to verbs of occurrence are framed differently in the form of:

"NP mere gịnị?" (*"Who/What"* did what?) and
"Gịnị mere NP?" (What happened/is doing to *"Who/What"*?).

However, questions related to verbs of existence are framed in the form of:

"NP dị/dọ/bụ/nọ gịnị?" (*"Who/What"* is what?) and
"Gịnị dị/dọ/bụ/nọ NP?" (What is *"Who/What"*?).

Process verbs or verbs of occurrence refer to a wide range of actions, including process verbs and weather-related verbs. The following are examples of process verb such as: -ba *(burst)*, -bhịa *(crush)*, -cha *(ripe)*, -gbanwe *(change)*, -gbawa *(crack)*, -gbọ *(boil)*, -gbu *(cut short)*, -gha *(sow)*, -kpọ *(dry)*, -kpọ *(hit part of the feet against an object)*. -nwụ *(die)*, -re *(decay)*. -ta *(dry)*, -wa *(break)*, and so on.

The ability of these verbs to convey a change in state or condition in an expression that has a patient is what connects them together. The theme, noun phrase (NP), which is paired with the process verbs in Igbo verb structures, represents the sentence's grammatical subject. This particular characteristic emphasizes the theme's important function in expressing the change or event that these verbs describe.

Process-based classification divides Igbo verbs into six groups: Material Process Verbs, Mental Process Verbs, Verbal Process Verbs, Relational Process Verbs, Existential Process Verbs, and Behavioral Process Verbs[1]

A. Material Process Verbs: Material process verbs are verbs that express physical actions or events that affect the world or other entities. Some examples of material process verbs in English include actions words like tara *(bite)*, tiwa *(break)*, zụta *(buy)*, mebie *(destroy)*, nye *(give)*, ga *(go)*, gbu *(kill)*, mee *(make)*, te *(paint)*, gwuo *(play)*, tinye *(put)*, gba- *(run)*, bụọ *(sing)*, rahụ *(sleep)*, and kwo *(snore)*. For examples:

1. Nkịta tara nwata ahụ.   *(The dog bit the boy).*
2. Emeka tiwara Efere.   *(Emeka broke a plate).*
3. Ngọzị zụtara Oche.   *(Ngọzị bought a chair).*
4. Ụlọ ọrụ ahụ tụlere arịrịọ m.   *(The company considered my request).*
5. Ada mebiri atụmatụ m.   *(Ada destroyed my plans).*

The focus in the material process can take on various roles, such as agent, affected, effected, recipient, beneficiary, range, and instrument. The structures of clauses related to the material process can vary and include intransitive, monotransitive, ditransitive, and complex transitive patterns.

B. Mental Process Verbs: Mental Process Verb are verbs that are characterize by activities associated with thinking, perceiving, or feeling. These verbs depict internal processes taking place within an individual's mind or emotions. We express cognitive processes and affective experiences by using mental action verbs. Mental Process Verb include chee echiche *(think)*, ịghọta *(understand)*, icheta *(remember)*, ikwere *(believe)*, izube *(plan)*, iyochaa *(analyze)*, ịtụ anya *(envision)*, ịmara *(know)*, ịmụta *(learn)*, tụlee *(consider)*, ikwenye (agree), ịrọ nrọ *(dream)*, ịtụgharịa uche *(reflect)*, iyochaa *(evaluate)*, icheta *(recall)*, ichefuo *(forget)*, etc.

a) "Ọ na-arọ nrọ ịgagharị ụwa." (*"He dreams of traveling the world."*)
b) "Ọ na-eche echiche nke ụwa jupụtara ohere." (*"He imagines a world full of possibilities."*)
c) "Ọ na-aghọta echiche ahụ n'ụzọ dị mfe." (*"He understands the concept easily."*)
d) "Ọ na-atụ anya ihe ịma aka na-abịanụ." (*"She anticipates the upcoming challenge."*)
e) "O kwere na ike nke Chineke." (*"She believes in the power of God."*)
f) "Ọ na-enwe obi ụtọ maka ihe ọ rụzuru." (*"She feels happy about her achievement."*)
g) "Ọ na-amụta ihe ọhụrụ kwa ụbọchị." ("She learns new things every day.")
h) "Ọ na-eche echiche nke dị omimi banyere nsogbu ahụ." (*"She thinks deeply about the problem."*)
i) "Ha na-enyocha Njatụle iji chọta ụkpụrụ." (*"They analyze the data to find patterns."*)
j) "Ha na-atụle nhọrọ dị iche iche tupu ha eme mkpebi." (*"They consider different options before making a decision."*)
k) "Ha na-enyocha uru na ọghọm." (*"They evaluate the pros and cons."*)

l) "Ha na-echeta ihe omume ahụ nke ọma." (*"They remember the event vividly."*)

Mental action verbs allow us to convey internal processes, thoughts, and emotions. They help us describe cognitive activities and explore the realm of our minds. By incorporating mental action verbs into our writing and speech, we can express the richness of our thoughts and feelings, creating more engaging and expressive communication.

C. Verbal Process Verbs: Verbal Process Verbs refer to a category of verbs that specifically articulate actions associated with communication and language use. These verbs encompass a diverse range of linguistic activities, reflecting the dynamic nature of verbal processes. In essence, they capture the various ways individuals engage in verbal expression, from straightforward communication to more nuanced forms of language use.

Verbs in this category comprise behaviors like speaking, discussing, narrating, describing, inquiring, and other activities that require active language use. Verbal Process Verbs highlight the variety of interactions that occur when people speak or write ideas, thoughts, feelings, or information through spoken or written means. Examples include: kwu *(say)*, gwa *(tell)*, kwuo *(speak)*, Praise, too *(insult)*, taa ụta *(blame)*, katọọ *(criticize)*, kọọ akụkọ *(report)*, kọwaa *(explain)*, etc.

Here are some sentence examples of verbal process verbs:

a) Ada sị na ọ ga-abịa oriri na ọñụñụ. (*Ada said she'd come to the party.*)
b) Jọn gwara enyi ya aha m. (*John told his friend my name.*)
c) Onye nkuzi na-asụ French nke ọma. (*The teacher speaks French well.*)
d) Onye nkuzi ahụ toro ndị otu ahụ maka imeri ha. (*The coach praised the team that won.*)
e) Ọ kparịrị enyi ya na nzukọ ahụ. (*She insulted his friend at the meeting.*)
f) Ọ tara ndị ọzọ ụta maka mmejọ ahụ. (*He blamed others for the mistake.*)
g) Onye nkuzi ahụ katọrọ ụmụ akwụkwọ ya. (*The professor criticized his students.*)
h) Onye nta akụkọ ahụ kọrọ akụkọ kacha ọhụrụ. (*The journalist reported on the latest news.*)
i) Ị nwere ike ịkọwa ka ekwentị ọhụrụ a si arụ ọrụ? (*Can you explain how the new phone works?*)

These verbs not only signify the act of using language but also emphasize the communicative aspect, elucidating how individuals interact with one another through linguistic expression. Whether it's a straightforward exchange of information or the conveyance of complex narratives, Verbal Process Verbs capture the richness and diversity inherent in human communication and language utilization.

D. Relational Process Verbs: Relational process verbs are a class of verbs that expressly describe a condition or a state of being. These verbs explore the essence of life in language, illuminating the nature of connections, identity, and the fundamental characteristics that distinguish people or things. Relational process verbs draw emphasis to the constant or static features that define an entity's state or condition, in contrast to action verbs, which indicate dynamic activity.

These verbs are used as language tools to express what an entity is or how it existing in a specific state, rather than what it is doing. Thus, relational process verbs are essential for expressing the essential characteristics, relationships, and nature that add to the overall description and comprehension of entities in a particular context. For example: bụ *(to be)*, nwere *(to have)*, yiri *(to resemble)*, ịdị ka (to be like), iweta *(to get)*, iweta *(to obtain)*, ịnata *(to receive)*, ịjụ *(to refuse)*, iketa *(to inherit)*.

Here are some sentence examples of relational process verbs in Igbo language:

a) Nwamba m na-arịa ọrịa. (*My cat is sick.*)
b) Okeke nwere obi ụtọ. (*Okeke is happy.*)
c) O yiri nne ya. (*She resembles her mom.*)
d) Emeka nwetara òkè nke ya. (*Emeka got his own share.*)
e) Enwetara m akwụkwọ ozi ahụ. (*I received the letter.*
f) Eze jụrụ ịnara onyinye ahụ. (*Eze refused to accept the offer.*)
g) ketara nnukwu ego n'aka nne nne ya. (*She inherited a fortune from her grandmother.*)

These verbs are used as language tools to express what an entity is or how it is existing in a specific state, rather than what it is doing. Thus, relational process verbs are essential for expressing the essential characteristics, relationships, and nature that add to the overall description and comprehension of entities in a particular context.

E. Existential Process Verbs: Existential process verbs form a category of verbs designed to articulate the existence or nonexistence of something within a given context. Unlike action verbs that denote activities, existential process verbs delve into the fundamental aspect of existence. Examples include dị, dọ, bụ, nọ.

1. Existential process verbs for status/nature/condition: "dị".
This is used to express the nature of things—that is how they are: texture, quality, taste, and character and so on. In this case, we use "dị" or Bound Complement Verbs (BCVs). Bound Complement Verbs (BCVs) are made up of two morphemes: the root, which expresses the action's fundamental meaning, and a structurally derived element, which provides specifics. Examples of these Bound Complement Verbs are: chara, siri, tere, jọrọ, etc

a) Ije dị anya/ Ije tere anya. *(The journey is far)*.
b) Ikenna dị ike/Ikenna siri ike. *(Ikenna is strong)*.
c) Ọ dị njọ/Ọ jọrọ njọ. *(It is bad)*.
d) Ọ dị ọcha/Ọ chara ọcha. *(It is white)*.
e) Ọ dị ụtọ/Ọ tọrọ ụtọ. *(It is sweet)*.

Following the above examples, the existential process verb for status/nature/condition does not accept other existential process verb like: *"nọ"* or *"bụ"* in place of *"dị"*. Also, in term of colour, texture, and status; *"jiri"* is not interchangeable with *"chara"*. Likewise, *"toro"*, *"tere"*, *jọrọ*, and *"siri"* are not interchangeable with others as well. Therefore, it is wrong to use Existential process verbs for status/nature/condition as follows:

a) *Ọ bụ ogologo /*Ọ nọ ogologo.
b) *Ije nọ anya /*Ije tọrọ anya.
c) *Ikenna nọ ike /*Ikenna tere ike.
d) *Ọ nọ njọ /*Ọ chara njọ.
e) *Ọ nọ ọcha /*Ọ jiri ọcha.
f) *Ọ nọ ụtọ /*Ọ siri ụtọ.

2. Existential process verbs for state of being (adịmadị ihe): "dị".
a) Aja dị n'iyi. *(Sand is in the stream/river)*.
b) Ewu dị n'ọba. *(Goat is in the barn)*.
c) Eze dị n'ọnụ. *(Teeth are in the mouth)*.
d) Mmadụ dị ndụ. *(Human being is alive)*.
e) Okike dị adị. *(The Creator exists)*.

3. Existential process verbs of habitation (ebe obibi): "bi"
a) Ada bi n'ụlọ Ụka. *(Ada lives in the church)*
b) Agbịsị bị n'ọzara. *(Ants lives in the desert)*.
c) Emeka bi na mba mmiri. *(Emeka lives in River state)*.
d) ndị mmụọ ozi bi n'eluigwe. *(Angels live in the heaven)*.
e) Ọdum bi n'oke ọhịa. *(Lion lives in the jungle)*.

4. Existential process verbs for status (abụmabụ ihe): "bụ"
a) Anyị bụ mmadụ. *(We are humans)*.
b) Chukwu bụ onye okike. *(God is the Creator)*.
c) Enwe bụ anụ ọhịa. *(Monkey is an animal)*.
d) Emeka bụ eze Igbo. *(Emeka is an Igbo king)*.

e) Ugo bụ nwata akwụkwọ. *(Ugo is a student).*

5. Existential process verbs for location of things are "nọ" na "dị".
(i). Existential process verbs for location of living things *"nọ."*
   a) Aguiyi nọ n'iyi. *(Crocodile is in the stream/river).*
   b) Chineke nọ n'eluigwe. *(God is in the heaven).*
   c) Ọsa nọ n'elu osisi. *(Squirrel is on the tree).*
   d) Ogechukwu nọ n'ụlọ. *(Ogechukwu is at home).*
   e) Okụkọ nọ n'ọgba. *(Chicken is in the cob).*

(ii). Existential process verbs for location of nonliving things *"dị".*
   a) Ájá dị n'ala. *(Sand is on the ground).*
   b) Akwụkwọ dị n'akpa. *(Book is in the bag).*
   c) Ego dị n'ụlọ akụ. *(Money is in the bank).*
   d) Oche dị na ụlọ oriri na ọṅụṅụ. (Chair is at the dining hall)
   e) Osisi dị n'ọhịa. *(Trees are in the forest).*

Following the above examples, the Existential process verbs for the location of living things is not interchangeable with that of the nonliving. Therefore, it is wrong to use *"dị"* for the animate as well as *"nọ"* for the inanimate.

6. Existential process verbs for liquid substance and solid objects are "dọ" na "dị".
(i). Existential process verbs for liquid substance: *"dọ"*
   a) Mmanụ akwụ dọ n'ite. *(Palm oil is in the pot).*
   b) Mmanya dọ na karama. *(Wine is in the bottle).*
   c) Mmiri dọ n'iko. *(Water is in the cup).*
   d) Ofe Egwusi dọ n'efere. *(Egwusi soup is in the plate).*
   e) Ọgwụ mmiri dọ na karama. *(Syrups is in the bottle).*

(ii). Existential process verbs for liquid objects: *"dị".*
   a) Nri Ji dị n'ikwe. *(There is pounded yam in the mortar).*
   b) Ede dị n'ọba. *(There is cocoyam in the barn).*
   c) Eku dị na tebụl nri. *(There is scoop at the dining table).*
   d) Ite dị n'elu Usekwu. *(The pot is on the stove).*
   e) Ngaji dị na Ngiga. *(There is spoon on the grill).*

Following the above examples, the Existential process verb for liquid substance is not interchangeable with that of the solid objects. Therefore, it is wrong to use *"dị"* for the liquid substance as well as *"do"* for the solid objects.

However, when existential process verb for liquid substance is in a container, the verb to be used is that of the container and Existential process verb for liquid substance. For instance:
   a) Efere mmanụ dị n'elu akwa. *(The bowl of oil is on the bed).*
   b) Iko mmiri dị n'elu okpokoro. *(The cup for drinking is on the table).*
   c) Ite mmanya dị n'okpuru akwa. *(The pot of wine is under the bed).*
   d) Ite ofe dị n'elu Usekwu. *(The pot of soup is on the stove).*
   e) Ngajị ọgwụ dị n'elu oche. *(The spoon for syrups is on the chair).*

F. Behavioral Process Verbs: Behavioral process verbs refer to a category of verbs that describe actions, activities, or behaviors undertaken by individuals or entities. Examples of behavioral process verbs include ịgba ọsọ *(run)*, ịchị ọchị *(laugh)*, ịgba egwu (dance), ịbụ abụ *(sing)*, ịmụ ihe *(study)*, iri nri *(eat)*, iche echiche *(think)*, and ihi ụra *(sleep)*. These verbs help convey activities or behaviors that can be observed, measured, or described in terms of actions.

Here are some sentence examples of behavioral process verbs in Igbo language:

   a) Ụmụaka na-enwe mmasị ịgba ọsọ n'ebennọkọta ahụ. (*Children love to run in the park.*)
   b) Njakịrị ahụ mere ka mmadụ niile chịa ọchị. (*The joke made everyone laugh.*)
   c) Ha kpebiri ịgba egwú abalị dum. (*They decided to dance all night.*)
   d) Ọ na-enwe mmasị ịbụ abụ n'ime mmiri ịsa ahụ. (*She loves to sing in the shower.*)
   e) Ụmụ akwụkwọ kwesịrị ịmụ akwụkwọ maka ule. (*Students need to study for exams.*)
   f) Anyị riri nri abalị n'elekere asaa nke abalị. (*We ate dinner at 7pm.*)
   g) Were obere oge chee echiche tupu i kpebie. (*Take a moment to think before deciding.*)
   h) Mgbe ogologo ụbọchị gasịrị, ana m ehi ụra nke ọma. (*After a long day, I sleep well.*)

These verbs highlight observable and tangible actions, often involving physical or visible manifestations of behavior. Unlike some other verb categories that focus on states of being or existence, behavioral process verbs emphasize actions and conduct.

These criteria are used by Igbo linguists to analyze and categorize verbs, which in turn helps in understanding their syntactic properties within sentences and across different languages.

4.7 Serial Verb Construction

When two or more verbs or verb phrases are strung together in a single clause, it's referred to as verb serialization, also known as verb stacking. Many languages in Africa, Asia, and New Guinea share this characteristic. When expressing several features of a situation as a single cognitive bundle in a single phrase with a single predicate, verb serialization is employed.

Types of verb serialisation
1. The Resultative Serial Verb Construction:
The Resultative Serial Verb Construction (SVC) in Igbo refers to a linguistic structure where two or more verbs are combined to convey a sequence of actions that result in a specific outcome. In this construction, each verb contributes to the overall meaning, and the combination of these verbs forms a cohesive expression.

The first verb typically serves as the main action, and subsequent verbs contribute to describing the result or consequence of the initial action. This sequential arrangement allows speakers of Igbo to convey complex ideas about causation, purpose, or outcome in a concise manner.

In these forms, the result XP is a secondary verb—an open vowel suffix (OVS) that is added to the main verb (V). A participant's condition that develops because of the activity outlined in clause 1 is predicated by the result XP. the inflectional verb class tag: –rV (e.g.-ra)—indicates simple past tense when attached to an active verb, but it takes on a declarative meaning when used with an intransitive verb. The Let's examine five Igbo instances of Resultative SVCs::

Ada soro ya jee. *(Ada went with him.)*
Ada follow -rV (PST) him/her (and) went -OVS.

Here, "soro" (meaning "follow/join") serves as the main verb (V), and "jee" (meaning "went") acts as the result XP.

O were karama kụwaa. *(He took a bottle (and) broke it.)*
He/she take -rV (Past) a bottle (and) break -OVS.

In this construction, "were" (meaning "took") is the main verb (V), and "kụwaa" (meaning "broke") functions as the result XP.

O muyere ọku O ree ya. *(He lit the fire and it burned.)*
He light -rV the fire it burn -OVS it.

Here, "muyere" (meaning "lit") serves as the main verb (V), and "ree" (meaning "burned") is the result XP.

Eze mere Oroma Ọ chaa. *(Eze made the orange ripe.)*
Eze make -rV orange it ripe -OVS.

In this example, "mere" (meaning "made") acts as the main verb (V), and "chaa" (meaning "ripe") serves as the result XP.

> **Ọ gbasara akwa Ọ kọọ.** *(He/she spread clothes and it dried.)*
> *He/she spread rV clothes (and) it dry -OVS.*

Finally, "gbasara" (meaning "spread") is the main verb (V), and "kọọ" (meaning "dry") functions as the result XP.

Igbo Resultative SVC construction enables speakers to communicate not only the actions but also the achieved state or consequence of those actions within a single expression.

2. Sequential Serial Verb Construction:
Sequential Serial Verb Construction (SVC) in Igbo is a linguistic structure where a series of verbs is used to convey a sequence of actions occurring one after the other. Each verb in the sequence contributes to the overall narrative by describing a subsequent action in the chain. This construction allows speakers of Igbo to articulate events or activities in a chronological order, highlighting the step-by-step progression of actions.

Unlike Resultative SVC, where the verbs indicate a sequence leading to a specific outcome, in this construction, each verb shows actions following one after the other in order. They create a depiction of a particular order in which related events, movements, or actions follow each other. This linguistic feature allows speakers of Igbo to express set of scenarios involving successive activities or events in a more efficient and succinct manner. For example:

> **Uche bịara were Ngajị.** *(Uche came to take the spoon.)*
> *Uche come -rV (PST) take -rV (PST) spoon.*

Here, "bịara" (meaning "came") serves as the first verb (V_1), and "were" (meaning "took") is the second verb (V_2), both sits at the same time.

> **Emeka gara tie Obi ihe.** *(Emeka went and beat up Obi.)*
> *Emeka go -rV (PST) hit (-OVS) Obi thing.*

Here, "gara" (meaning "went") serves as the first verb (V_1), and "tịe" (meaning "hit") is the second verb (V_2), both verbs sitting side by side.

> **O jere ree akwụkwọ nri.** *(He/she went and sold vegetables.)*
> *He/she go -rV (PST) sell (-OVS) Vegetable.*

Here, "jere" (meaning "went") serves as the first verb (V₁), and "ree" (meaning "sell") is the second verb (V₂), both verbs sitting side by side.

> **Ada bịara jụọ ese gị.** *(Ada came and asked after you.)*
> *Ada come -rV (PST) ask (-OVS) after you.*

Here, "bịara" (meaning "came") serves as the first verb (V₁), and "jụọ" (meaning "ask") is the second verb (V₂), both verbs sitting beside each other.

> **Mmiri zoro mee ide mmiri.** *(It rained and caused flooding.)*
> *It rain -rV (PST) cause (-OVS) flood.*

Here, "zoro" (meaning "rained") serves as the first verb (V₁), and "mee" (meaning "cause" *INFL*) is the second verb (V₂), both happening at the same time.

In Simultaneous SVC, two or more verbs or verb phrases are strung together within a single clause. It lacks any functional marker (such as conjunctions or affixes) linking the verbs. This construction enhances the language's ability to articulate the concurrency of actions, providing a rich expression.

3. Instrumental Serial Verb Construction (SVC):
Instrumental Serial Verb Construction (SVC) is a linguistic structure where a series of verbs is employed to convey a sequence of actions, with each verb contributing to the expression of using an instrument or tool to perform a certain activity. The verb 'take' characterizes this sort of SVC. It refers to the means or tool used to carry out an action or event. For instance, the event of frightening is achieved by the use of a snake. For example:

a) **O were mma chupu ha.** *(He chased them away with a knife.)*
   3SG take -rV knife chased away 3PL.

b) **Eze were agwo yie ha egwu.** *(Eze frightened them with a snake.)*
   PN take -rV snake frighten -OVS 3PL:OBJ fear.

c) **Nneka ji anụ sie nri.** *(Nneka cooked food with meat.)*
   PN take meat cook food.

d) **Ada jiri nro kpụọ ite.** *(Ada formed a pot from clay.)*
   PN use -rV clay mould -OVS pot.

In this sentence, the Instrumental SVC involves the verbs "used," and "formed," emphasizing the actions related to pottery and the use of a clay as an instrument in the process. The Instrumental SVC allows speakers to express a series of actions involving the use of specific tools or instruments, emphasizing the instrumental role in the performance of each activity within a narrative or description.

4. Locative Serial Verb Construction (SVC):
Locative Serial Verb Construction (SVC) in Igbo is a linguistic structure where a series of verbs is employed to convey a sequence of actions that indicates that the subject NP takes the object along to specific location. This construction emphasizes the spatial aspect of the actions, describing the location or direction in which something is taken to. For examples:

a) **Ha ji akwụkwọ gaa Ụlọ akwụkwọ** *(I went to school with a book.)*
   3PL   take   book   go (-OVS)   school

b) **O ji bọọdụ ụgbọ mmiri ya gaa n'ụsọ osimiri.**
   3SG   took   surfboards   his/her go (-OVS) beach.
   They traveled to the beach with their surfboards.

c) **Ada ji ndepụta izụ ahịa gaa ahịa.** *(He went to the market with a shopping list.)*
   3NP take   shopping list go (-OVS) market.

d) **Anyị ji akpa azụ jiri ụkwụ gaa n'ugwu ahụ.**
   We took backpacks   trekked   on the mountain.
   We hiked to the mountain with our backpacks.

4.8 Individual Verbs, Complements, and Adjuncts

In the lexicon's expansive landscape, verbs emerge as dynamic agents of action and expression. They not only infuse sentences with vitality but also dictate the relationships between different sentence components. Verbs often require complements and adjuncts to convey complete meanings, creating a complex web of dependencies that shape sentence structure.

The concepts of individual verbs, complements, and adjuncts in linguistics:

1. Individual Verbs:
Individual verbs, often referred to simply as "verbs," are a fundamental part of language and play a central role in sentence construction. They are words that typically represent actions, events, or

states. Here are some key points to understand about individual verbs:

a. *Infinitive Verbs (Isingwaa)*: This is a verb form that functions as a noun or is used with auxiliary verbs, and that names the action or state without specifying the subject. In Igbo language, the letter "ị" and "I" plus the root verb comprise the infinitive form of verb.

Examples:

Verb root	English	Verb root	English	Verb root	English
ịbu/ịdị	to be	ịzụta	to buy.	ịta	to chew
isi nri	to cook.	ịgba egwu	to dance	ịṅu	to drink.
ịbanye/ịbata	to enter	isoro	to follow.	ịchọ/chọta	to find/look.
ichefu	to forget.	ighe	to fry	inweta	to get.
inye	to give	inwe	to have/own.	ijide	to hold.
ịchi (chi a)	to laugh.	ịhapụ	to leave	ile (anya)	to look.
ịpụta	to get out	ikpe ekpere	to pray.	icheta	to remember.
inweta	to get.	ịga	to go	ịnụ	to hear.
ịma	to know	ịmụta	to learn.	ige ntị	to listen
ịka (akara)	to mark.	ịgụ	to read	ịgba ọsọ	to run.
ịhụ	to see	ire (ahịa)	to sell.	ịgụ	to sing.
ịbụọ abụ	to sing.	ịpụ	to sit	ịrahụ (ura)	to sleep.
ịsụ	to speak	iguzo/ikuli	to stand.	ịnọ	to stay
ilo	to swallow.	ikuzi	to teach	iche echiche	to think.
ịmetụ	to touch	ịghọta	to understand.	ichere	to wait.
ịga ije	to walk.	ịsa	to wash	iyi	to wear.
ịrụ	to work	ide	to write.		

b. *Linking Verbs (njiko ngwaa)*: This type of verb that connects a noun or a pronoun with a word that identifies or describes it; e.g. is, am, are, etc. Examples:

Igbo	*English*
bụ	*is/am/are.*

c. *Auxiliary Verbs (Enyemaka ngwaa)*: This is a verb that changes or helps another verb, e.g. am, is, are, was, were, be, been, will, has, have, had, do, does, did. In Igbo language, auxiliary verbs often complement verb form to express an action in simple, continuous or future tense. When an auxiliary verb is complementing a simple participle, the auxiliary verb is joined to the complement with a hyphen. This is especially the case when the infinitive accompanying starts with a vowel. The hyphen is used to differentiate/separate the auxillary verb which is a form of prefix of the simple participle from main verb. For example:

Igbo	English
Ben gà-enweta ụgbọ ala.	Ben will catch the bus.
Eze nà-àbia ebe a.	Eze is coming here.
ga-àbịa	Ngọzị will come.
Ọ ga-àbịa	He/She will come.
Eze na-abịa	Eze is coming.
Ọ na-abịa	He/She is coming.

However, when the auxiliary verb takes on the suffix of negation, it is written separately from the complement without a hyphen and as a one word with the suffix. For example:

Igbo	English
Ngọzị agaghị àbịa	Ngọzị will not come.
Ọ gaghị àbịa	He/She will not come.
Eze anaghị abịa	Eze is not coming.
Ọ naghị abịa	He/She is not coming.

2. Complements:

Complements are elements in a sentence that complete the meaning of a verb. They can be nouns, noun phrases, adjectives, or clauses. Complements are essential for understanding the action or state described by the verb. There are two main types of complements:

Direct Object: A direct object is a noun or noun phrase that receives the action of a transitive verb. It answers the question "What?" or "Whom?" For example, in the sentence:

1. Ọ na-agụ akwụkwọ. (*She reads a book*).
   "Akwụkwọ (book)" is the direct object.

2. Ọ na-azụta mkpịsị akwụkwọ. *(He buys a pen).*
   "Mkpịsị akwụkwọ (pen)" is the direct object.

3. Ha hichara ụlọ. *(They cleaned the house).*
   "Ụlọ (house)" is the direct object.

Subject Complement: A subject complement is an element that follows a linking verb and describes the subject of the sentence. This includes: "is," "am," "are," "was," "were," "seem," "become," etc). and provides more information about the subject of the sentence. The subject complement either renames (predicate nominative) or describes (predicate adjective) the subject.

There are two main types of subject complements:

1. *Predicate Nominative*: This is a noun, pronoun, or equivalent that renames or identifies the subject. It follows a linking verb and gives more information about what the subject is. For example:

   1. Ọ bụ ya bụ onyeisi ala, *(He/she is the president)*.

Here, "onyeisi ala (the president)" is a predicate nominative that renames the subject " Ọ (He/she)."

   2. Ọ bụ onye nkuzi. *(Heshe is a teacher)*.

Here, "onye nkuzi (a teacher)" is a predicate nominative that renames the subject " Ọ (He/she)."

2. *Predicate Adjective*: This is an adjective or adjective phrase that describes the subject. It follows a linking verb and provides more information about the qualities or characteristics of the subject. For example:

   1. Okooko osisi mara mma. *(The flowers are beautiful)*.

Here, "mma *(beautiful)*" is a predicate adjective that describes the subject "Okooko osisi *(The flowers)*."

   2. Emeka mara akọ. *(Emeka is clever)*.

Here, "akọ *(clever)*" is a predicate adjective that describes the subject "Emeka *(Emeka -PN)*."

Subject complements are essential for providing additional details about the subject in a sentence and are commonly used in sentences with linking verbs.

3. Adjuncts:
Adjuncts are words, phrases, or clauses that provide additional information in a sentence. Adjuncts are not essential to the sentence's basic structure or meaning, but they enhance and modify the content by offering details, context, or extra information. They are often used to provide answers to questions like " mgbe ole? *(when)*," " ebee? *(where)*," " n'ihi gịnị? *(why)*," " kedu? *(how)*," or " ruo n'ókè ole? *(to what extent)*." The following are types of adjuncts:

1. *Adverbial Adjuncts*: These provide information about the manner, time, place, frequency, or degree of the action in the sentence.

Time Adjunct:	Ọ rutere n'isi ụtụtụ. *(He/she arrived early).*
	Ha mechara na mgbede. *(They finished in the evening).*
Place Adjunct:	Ha zutere n'ebennọkọta ahụ. *(They met at the park).*
	Anyị zutere na cafe ụnyaahụ. *(We met at the Café yesterday,)*
Manner Adjunct:	Ọ bịara ngwa ngwa. *(He came quickly).*
	Ọ na-asụ Igbo nke ọma. *(He speaks Igbo fluently).*
Degree Adjunct:	Ọ rụsiri ọrụ ike. *(She worked very hard).*
	Ọ na-agụ akwụkwọ akụkọ kwa ụbọchị. *(He reads the newspaper daily).*

2. *Adjectival Adjuncts*: These function as adjectives, modifying nouns to provide additional details or descriptions.

   1. Nwata nwanyi nwere okpu uhie bu enyim. (*The girl with the red hat is my friend.*)
      (Adjectival adjunct modifying " Nwata nwanyi (girl)")

   2. Ụlọ nwere ọnụ ụzọ na-acha anụnụ anụnụ bụ nke m. (*The house with the blue door is mine.*)
      (Adjectival adjunct modifying " Ụlọ (house)")

   3. Nwoke ahụ nwere isi awọ bụ papa m. (*The man with the grey hair is my dad.*)
      (Adjectival adjunct modifying "Nwoke (man)").

   4. Ọ bụ nwoke nwere oke amamihe. (*He is a man of great wisdom.*)
      (Adjectival adjunct modifying "Nwoke (man)").

3. *Nominal Adjuncts*: These are noun phrases or clauses that modify other nouns.

   1. Akwụkwọ dị na tebụl na-adọrọ mmasị. (*The book on the table is interesting.*)
      (Nominal adjunct "na tebụl" (on the table) modifying " Akwụkwọ (book)").

   2. Ọ gara ọmụmụ ihe gbasara ise foto. (*She attended a workshop on photography.*)
      (Nominal adjunct "gbasara ise foto" (on photography) modifying "ọmụmụ ihe (workshop)")

3. Anyị tụlere atụmatụ ahụ n'oge nzukọ ahụ. (*We discussed the plan during the meeting.*)
(Nominal adjunct "n'oge nzukọ" (during the meeting)   modifying "tụlere" (discussed)")

4. Enwere m enyi na New York. (*I have a friend in New York.*)
(Nominal adjunct "na New York" (in New York) modifying "enyi" (friend))

Adjuncts add richness and specificity to a sentence but can often be removed without fundamentally altering the sentence's meaning. They are distinguishable from complements, which are more integral to the sentence's structure.

Understanding the roles of individual verbs, complements, and adjuncts is crucial for analyzing sentence structure and meaning in linguistics. These elements work together to form coherent and meaningful sentences in a wide range of languages.

Exercise

1. What is the role of the lexicon in language and communication?
2. How does the lexicon evolve and adapt over time?
3. What are some examples of lexical items besides individual words?
4. In computational linguistics, how is a lexicon used?
5. What are the two main types of vocabulary, and how do they differ?
6. How do teachers facilitate vocabulary expansion in educational settings?
7. What are the semantic layers encompassed within lexical units?
8. How do syntax and lexicon items complement each other in language?
9. Can you explain the process of subcategorization in linguistic terms?
10. How do nouns contribute to sentence construction and grammatical structure?
11. What criteria are used for the classification of Igbo nouns?
12. Could you provide examples of compound nouns in Igbo?
13. What are the distinguishing features of count and non-count nouns?
14. How do animate and inanimate nouns differ in linguistic classification?
15. Can you explain the concept of agent nouns and provide examples from Igbo?
16. What is verb serialization, and which regions or languages commonly employ this linguistic feature?
17. Can you explain the Resultative Serial Verb Construction (SVC) in Igbo, and how does it contribute to expressing complex ideas?
18. In the Igbo language, how does the Resultative SVC differ from the Sequential SVC in terms of conveying actions and outcomes?
19. Provide examples of Resultative SVC instances in Igbo, and analyze how each verb contributes to the overall meaning.
20. What is the Sequential Serial Verb Construction (SVC) in Igbo, and how does it differ from the Resultative SVC?
21. Can you explain how the Instrumental Serial Verb Construction (SVC) functions in Igbo and provide examples to illustrate its usage?
22. Describe the Locative Serial Verb Construction (SVC) in Igbo, and explain how it emphasizes the spatial aspect of actions.
23. Explain the concept of individual verbs in linguistics, and provide examples of infinitive verbs in the Igbo language.
24. What are complements in a sentence, and how do they differ from adjuncts?
25. Provide examples of subject complements in Igbo sentences and explain how they add meaning to the subject.

Chapter 5

Phrasal Categories (*Ọdịdị nke Nkebiokwu Igbo*)

A Phrase (Nkebiokwu) is a group of two or more words that express a single idea but do not form a complete sentence. Phrase usually lacks a finite verb as a result; a phrase can only function as a meaningful unit within a sentence or clause.

The main difference between finite and nonfinite verbs is that finite verbs act as the *main verb*. They indicate person, number, and tense. Nonfinite verbs do not act as a verb in a sentence. They do not indicate person, number, and tense and they do not indicate any inflections. Nonfinite Verbs are *infinitives, gerunds and participles.*

A Phrase cannot stand alone as a sentence because it does not include subject and object that are parts of a sentence without complete sentence cannot be formed.

Examples of Igbo phrase:

Igbo	*English*	*Igbo*	*English*
N'ime Ofe	*inside soup*	N'ime Ụlọ	*in the house*
N'ime anyasị	*at night*	N'anyasị Ụnyahụ	*yesterday's night*
Na mgbede Ụnyahụ	*yesterday's evening*	N'oke ehihe ahụ	*at that noon*
N'ụtụtụ Ụnyahụ	*yesterday's morning*	Nna ya	*his/her father*
Nne ya	*his/her mother*	Nwa Nkịta ya	*his/her puppy*
Nwa ya	*his/her child*	Oba ji nke ha	*their own barn*
Oche ahụ	*that chair*	Onye ahụ	*that person*
Umunne di ya	*his/her husband's in-law*		

PHRASE (NKEBIOKWU)
Igbo Phrase is a term used to describe two or more words that are related and can be used together or as a group but they do not have verb and complete meaning. It can also be defined as a word order that lacks verbs and complete meaning but has an idea with one part of speech.

The main three characteristics of an Igbo phrase are that it lacks verb, does not have complete meaning and it shows one idea. A phrase can function as a noun, an adjective, a preposition or an adverb in a sentence. This is based on the position of the phrase and the construction of the sentence. Based on these two factors, a phrase can fall under the following eight categories:

Translation
Gini bu Nkebiokwu?
Nkebiokwu bụ mkpụrụokwu abụọ ma ọ bụ karịa gakọrọ ọnụ n'ezigbo usoro mana o nweghi ngwaa na nghọta zuru oke. Ọ bụ usoro okwu na-enweghi ngwaa na nghọta zuru oke ma nwee echiche nke isi ya na-egosi otu nkejiasụsụ. Ọ bụ usoro okwu ndi anaghị ezu oke n'ihi na ha enweghi ngwaa. Ejiri mara Nkebiokwu:

a) naghi enwe ngwaa
b) naghi enwe nghota zuru oke
c) na-eziputa naani otu echiche.

Forms and types of Igbo Phrases (Nke n'ụdị Nkebiokwu)
1. Noun Phrase (Nkebiokwu keaha)
2. Adjective Phrases (Nkebiokwu kenkowaaha):
3. Adverbial Phrases (Nkebiokwu kenkwuwa):
4. Prepositional Phrase (Nkebiokwu kembuụzọ)
5. Infinitive Phrase (Nkebiokwu kemfinitiivu)
6. Gerund Phrase (Nkebiokwukejerondu)
7. Demonstrative Phrases (Nkebiokwu kenruaka)
8. Collective Phrases (Nkebiokwu kemkpokọta)
9. Interrogative Phrase (Nkebiokwu kenjụajụjụ)
10. Possessive Phrases (Nkebiokwu kennọchinke)
11. Number Phrases (Nkebiokwu keọnụọgụgụ)

5.1 Noun Phrase (Nkebiokwu keaha)
A noun phrase consists of a noun (a name of a person, animal, place, or thing) and other related words (usually modifiers and Nkwuso *(determiners)*) which modify the noun. A noun phrase acts as a noun in a sentence. Noun phrase (NP) can be a single noun, or a group of words built around a single noun. The headword of a noun phrase is made up of nouns and the modifiers or nkwuso *(determiners)*. Determiners are related words that may come before or after the headword or noun. Both the headword (noun) and the modifiers or determiners (other related words) act as a noun phrase in a sentence.

The basic word order of noun phrase is as follows:
Noun phrase = Noun + Noun (Modifiers or determiners).

Translation
Nkebiokwu keaha = aha + aha. Nkebiokwu keaha nwere ike ị bụ otu aha ma ọ bụ karịa.

Igbo language	*English translation*	*Word Order in Igbo*
Aka ike	*Power (Strong) arm*	Noun + Noun
Akị bekee	*Coconut*	Noun + Noun
Egwu Ọnwụ	*Funeral song*	Noun + Noun
Isi anụ	*Animal's head*	Noun + Noun
Okporouzọ Ọkigwe	*Ọkigwe Road*	Noun + Noun
Onye ahịa ji	*Yam seller*	Noun + Noun
Ụlọ anyị	*Our house*	Noun + Pronoun
Ụlọ nna m	*My father's house*	Noun x 2 + Pronoun
Ụmụ akwụkwọ Aba	*Students of Aba Institutions*	Noun x 3
Ụmụ anụ ọhịa	*offspring of wild animals*	Noun x 3

5.2 Adjective Phrases (Nkebiokwu kenkọwaaha):

An adjective phrase is a phrase the head of which is an adjective. It is a group of words that include an adjective that modifies (changes) a noun or pronoun. Adjective phrases are a great way to describe people, places, objects, and events in an engaging and colorful way.

One of the main functions of adjective phrases is that **they go with nouns and change or add to their meaning**. Shirt: black shirt, brown shirt, white shirt, long-sleeved shirt. An adjective phrase can be a single adjective, or a group of words built around a single adjective, for example:
Emeka has ***clever*** ideas.
It was a **very** *big* meal.
We were **really** *bored* **with the film.**

The basic word order of adjective phrase is as follows:
Adjective phrase = Noun + Adjective (Modifiers or determiners).

Translation: Nkebiokwu kenkowaaha: aha + nkowaaha

Igbo language	*English translation*	*Word Order in Igbo*
Ajọ mmadụ	*Bad person*	Adjective + Noun
Aka mkpụmkpụ	*Shorthand*	Noun + Adjective

Akwa ọcha	*White cloth*	Noun + Adjective
Eze akanwụ	*Grey/silver teeth*	Noun + Adjective
Nwaanyị ọcha	*White woman*	Noun + Adjective
Nwoke ojii	*Black man*	Noun + Adjective
Olu ogologo	*Long neck*	Noun + Adjective
Olu ọma	*Nice voice*	Noun + Adjective
Ọnụ ọjọọ	*Bad mouth*	Noun + Adjective
Ụlọ ọma	*Beautiful house*	Noun + Adjective

5.3 Adverbial Phrases (Nkebiokwu kenkwuwa):

An adverbial phrase is a multi-word that modifies other expressions, including verbs, adjectives, adverbs, adverbials, and sentences. Another common use for adverbial phrases is to describe the frequency of an action. If a phrase is modifying an adjective, verb, or adverb, it is an adverbial phrase. If it is modifying a noun or a pronoun, it is an adjectival phrase. An adverb phrase can be a single adverb or a group of words built around a single adverb, for example:

1. He spoke **very *softly***.
2. I came **here *yesterday***.
3. Jeff was speaking **so *roughly***.
4. John was walking **so *quickly***.
5. Please do it ***now***.
6. Smith was shouting **very *loudly***.
7. They did it **as *fast* as possible**.

The basic word order of adverbial phrase is as follows:
Adverb phrase   =   Noun + Adverb

Translation
Nkebiokwu kenkowaaha: aha + nkowaaha

Igbo language	*English*	*Igbo language*	*English*
ebe a	*here*	ebe ahụ	*there*
echi	*tomorrow*	egwu egwu	*playfully*
kịta kịta	*immediately*	mgbe n'adịghị anya	*soon*
mgbe ụfọdụ	*sometimes*	mma mma	*beautifully*
mma	*well*	n'abalị taa	*tonight*
naanị/sọọsọ	*only*	ngwa ngwa	*hurriedly / quickly / soon*
nwayọọ nwayọọ	*slowly*	nzuzu nzuzu	*foolishly*
ọjọọ	*badly*	ọfụma	*goodly / very well*

ọkụ ọkụ	*hotly*	ọnụ / jikota ọnụ	*together*
ọsịsọ / ọsọ ọsọ	*quickly*	ozugbo ozugbo	*fast / immediately*
rie nne	*very much*	taa / tata	*today*
ugbu a / kịta	*now*	ụjọ ụjọ	*fearfully*
ụnyaahụ	*yesterday*		

5.4 Prepositional Phrase (Nkebiokwu kembuụzọ)

A prepositional phrase is a group of words containing a preposition, a noun or pronoun object of the preposition, and any modifiers of the object. Prepositional phrases are often located at the head of a sentence. It sits in front of (is "pre-positioned" before) its object. Some of the most common prepositions that begin prepositional phrases in English are *to, of, about, at, before, after, by, behind, during, for, from, in, over, under, and with.*

In Igbo, there is only one preposition "na". When preceding a vowel, it drops its vowel sound and letter and takes on the tone of noun that follows it. It is written as n'.

The basic word order Prepositional phrase is as follows:
Prepositional phrase   =   Preposition + Noun

Translation
Nkebiokwu kembuụzọ   =   Mbuụzọ + Aha

	Igbo language	*English translation*
a)	Azu na-ebi **na** mmiri.	*Fishes live in water.*
b)	Emeka bịara **n'**ulo anyi.	*Emeka came to our house.*
c)	Enweghị ihe dị **na** ngwa nju oyi.	*There's nothing in the fridge.*
d)	Ha no **n'**oriri.	*They are in a feast.*
e)	Ha nọ ọdụ **n'**akụkụ osisi ahụ	*They were sitting by the tree.*
f)	Nna ya bi **n'**Aba.	*His father lives in Aba.*
g)	Nwamba ahụ si **n'**oche malie.	*The cat jumped off the chair.*
h)	Ezoro m **n'**okpuru oche.	*I was hiding under the chair.*
i)	Ọ nọdụrụ ala **n'**elu oche	*He sat on the chair.*
j)	Ọ tụfuru mgbanaka ya **n'**ụzọ	*She lost her ring on the way.*

5.5 Infinitive Phrase (Nkebiokwu kemfinitiivu)

An Infinitive Phrase is a group of words consisting of an infinitive and the modifier(s) and/or (pro)noun(s) or noun phrase(s) that function as the actor(s), direct object(s), or complement(s) of the action or state expressed in the infinitive, The *infinitive* is a *grammar* term that refers to a basic verb form that often acts as a noun and is often preceded by the word *to*. An *infinitive* is formed from a verb but doesn't act as a verb. Therefore, one cannot add 's', 'es', 'ed', or 'ing' to the end because it is not a verb. Infinitives can be used as nouns, adjectives, or adverbs.

In Igbo language, infinitive is realized by prefixation using the corresponding i/ị prefix in accordance with vowel harmony to any verb root. That is i/ị + verb root = infinitive. It is important to note that these two prefixes are the possible morphemes used in the realization of infinitive in Igbo language.

Examples with infinitives (Mfinitiivu):

Prefix (nganiihu)	Verb root (Isingwaa)	Infinitives (Mfinitiivu)	Meaning (Ihe ọ pụtata)
ị	Ba	ịbá	to enter
ị	Da	ịda	to fall
ị	Kpa	ịkpa	to discuss
ị	Gba	ịgba	to play/dane
i	De	ide	to write
i	Nyo	Enyo	to peek
i	Ke	ike (wa)	to divide
ị	Ma	ịmá	to know
i	Re	Irè	to sell
i	Zu	Izu	to device/steal

The 'i' and 'ị' of Igbo language are allomorphs because they are different in sound and their spelling is semantically the same. From the example above, you can see that both can be prefixed to the verb root to form infinitives and they are phonological variants of the morpheme. However, they cannot be used interchangeable in the linguistic environment because of Igbo vowel harmony rules.

Furthermore, the infinitive prefixes, 'i' and 'ị' can be used as second person singular pronoun, thus, another form of allomorphs in another grammatical environment. The rule applies here, in all environment where they perform the same grammatical function they cannot be used interchangeably. Some examples of 'i' and 'ị' as pronouns are shown below:

Igbo language   *Meaning*
a) I riri nri.   You ate food.
b) Ị ga-eri nri. You will eat (food).

The basic word order of Infinitive phrase (Nkebiokwu kemfintivu) is as follows:

Infinitive phrase = Infinitive + Noun

Translation
Nkebiokwu kemfintivu = Mfintivu + Aha

Igbo language   *English translation*
a) iri ji ohuu   *to partake in a new yam festival.*
b) Ide akwụkwọ akuko   *to write a story book.*
c) ise onyenyommadu   *to draw someone's shadow.*
d) Izu ohi joro njo.   *Stealing is bad (prohibited).*
e) Anyi akwusila ife arusi.   *We have stopped idolatry.*
f) A maara Aba maka ihe ụkwụ   *Aba is known for shoe making.*

5.6 Gerund Phrase (Nkebiokwukejerondu)

A gerund phrase is a group of words consisting of a gerund and the modifier(s) and/or (pro)noun(s) or noun phrase(s) that function as the direct object(s), indirect object(s), or complement(s) of the action or state expressed in the gerund. The gerund phrase functions as the subject of the sentence. A gerund phrase includes a verbal, a hybrid that functions as a noun (or adjective). Gerund phrases can also function as subjects, such as in the sentence "*Exercising every day keeps you healthy.*" All the words before the verb "keeps" are part of the gerund phrase. More examples include Reading romance novels is relaxing. Swimming with friends helps me unwind.

A *gerund* is like a blend of verbs and nouns. It looks like a verb, but it acts like a noun. In English ending in -ing. For example, the word swimming, asking looking, talking, playing, etc.

In the Igbo language, gerund is a verbal derivation realized by the prefixing of o/ọ to a reduplicated verb root. It is in the form of
     O/ọ + verb root x 2 = Gerund.

Examples with *Gerund* (Jerọndụ):

Prefix (nganiihu)	Verb root (Isingwaa)	Infinitives (Mfinitivu)	Gerund (Jerondu)	Meaning (Ihe ọ pụtata)
O	ri	Ri	Oriri	*eating/feasting*

ọ	nyụ	Nya	ọnyụnya	*Driving*
ọ	ṅụ	ṅụ	ọṅụṅụ	*Drinking*
ọ	dị	Da	ọdịda	*Falling*
O	di	De	Odide	*Writing*
ọ	gụ	gụ	ọgụgụ	*Reading*
O	ri	Re	Orire	*Selling*
ọ	mụ	mụ	ọmụmụ	*learning/bearing*
ọ	hụ	hụ	ahụhụ	*Roasting*
ọ	sụ	sọ	ọsụsọ	*Sweating*
O	bi	Bi	Obibi	*living (home)*
O	ti	Ti	Otiti	*Beating*

The 'o' and 'ọ' of Igbo language are allomorphs because they are different in sound and their spelling is semantically the same. From the example above, you can see that both can be prefixed to the verb root to form infinitives and they are phonological variants of the morpheme. However, they cannot be used interchangeable in the linguistic environment because of Igbo vowel harmony rules.

Furthermore, the infinitive prefixes, 'o' and 'ọ' can be used as third person singular pronoun, thus, another form of allomorphs in another grammatical environment. The rule applies here; in all environments where they perform the same grammatical function they cannot be used interchangeably. Examples of 'o' and 'ọ' as a pronoun is shown below:

Igbo language   *Meaning*
a) *O* dere ihe.   S/he wrote something.
b) *Ọ* gara ahịa.   S/he went to the market.

What are the examples of gerund and gerund phrase?
The fish were swimming in the pond. In this sentence, swimming is a verb because it is the action that the subject (fish) takes. Swimming is my favorite exercise. In this sentence, swimming is a gerund because it is the subject – the thing that the sentence is about.

a) How do you identify a gerund phrase?
b) The phrase will always start with a gerund.
c) The gerund phrase will either have a modifier, an object or both.
d) The entire phrase will function as a noun.
e) The phrase will have singular agreement with a verb.

The basic word order and grouping Gerund phrase (Nkebiokwu kejerọndụ) is as follows:
   Gerund phrase   =   Gerund + Noun

Translation

   Nkebiokwu kejerọndụ   =   Jerọndụ + Aha

Igbo language	*English translation*
a) Ọgụgụ akwụkwọ Igbo	*Reading of Igbo book.*
b) Osisi nri ọha.	*Cooking for the public.*
c) ogbugba egwu	*Dancing to a music.*
d) Oriri na nkwari	*feasting and merriment.*
e) Ọnyụnya ụgbọala dị mma.	*Driving a vehicle is good.*
f) Ọṅụṅụ mmanya dị njọ.	*Drinking (Alcohilism) is bad.*
g) Ọwụwa anyanwụ	*rising of the sun.*
h) Ọdịda anyanwụ	*setting of the sun.*

5.7 Demonstrative Phrases (Nkebiokwu kenruaka)

A demonstrative pronoun is a pronoun that is used to point to something specific within a sentence. These pronouns can indicate items in space or time. Usually a demonstrative pronoun substitutes for a noun phrase that contains the same word being used as a determiner. A *demonstrative pronoun* is a pronoun used to point something out. The demonstrative pronouns are *this, that, these* and *those*.

There are only four demonstrative pronouns, and they are: this, that, these and those. Examples in Igbo language are as follows:

English	*Igbo*	*English*	*Igbo*
This	ihe a	That	ihe ahụ
These	ihe ndị a	Those	ihe ndị ahụ

The basic word order of Demonstrative Phrases (Nkebiokwu kenruaka) is as follows:
Demonstrative phrase = Noun + Demonstrative marker.

Translation

   Nkebiokwu kenruaka   =   aha + Nruaka

Igbo language	*English*	**Word Order in Igbo**
Efere ndị ahụ	*those plates*	Noun + Demonstrative
Ji ndị a	*these yam*	Noun + Demonstrative

Mmanụ nri a	*this (red) oil*	Noun x 2 + Demonstrative
Nkịta nwoke a	*this man's dog*	Noun x 2 + Demonstrative
Nwata akwụkwọ ahụ	*that student*	Noun x 2 + Demonstrative
Oche a	*this chair*	Noun + Demonstrative
Ofe egwusi ahụ	*that melon soup*	Noun x 2 + Demonstrative
Ụlọ a	*this house*	Noun + Demonstrative
Ụmụaka ahụ	*those children*	Noun + Demonstrative

5.8 Collective Phrases (Nkebiokwu kemkpokọta)

A collective noun is a word or phrase that refers to a group of people or things as one entity. In English language, most collective nouns in everyday speech are not specific to one kind of thing. For example, the collective noun "group" can be applied to people or dogs or other things.

Here are some examples of common collective nouns used for things:
A bouquet of flowers, a bunch of flowers, a fleet of ships, a forest of trees, a galaxy of stars, a pack of cards, a pack of lies, a pair of shoes, a heap of rubbish, a hedge of bushes, a library of books, an outfit of clothes, an orchard of fruit trees, a pack of cards, a packet of letters and a pair of shoes.

In Igbo language, Collective Phrases (Nkebiokwu kemkpokọta) refers to a set or group of people, places, animals, or things that are marked with 'dum' (whole/entire) or 'niile' (all).

The basic word order of Collective Phrases (Nkebiokwu kemkpokọta) is as follows:
Collective phrase   =   Noun + Collective marker.

Translation
Nkebiokwu kemkpokọta   =   aha + mkpokọta

	Igbo language	*English translation*	*Word Order in Igbo*
a)	ndị ahịa niile	*All traders*	Noun + Collective
b)	ndị nkuzi dum	*the whole teacher*	Noun + Collective
c)	mmadụ niile	*All human race*	Noun + Collective
d)	ụbụrụ dum	*the whole brain*	Noun + Collective
e)	obodo dum	*the entire community*	Noun + Collective

5.9 Interrogative Phrase (Nkebiokwu kenjụajụjụ)

Most interrogative words in English begin with wh-, content questions in English are often called wh-questions. Although interrogative phrases often consist of single words (interrogative pronouns or interrogative adverbs), they may contain additional words. Content questions are questions that contain an interrogative phrase. For examples:

a. ***Who*** *did you see?*
b. ***Which book*** *do you want to buy?*
c. ***When*** *are you going to leave?*

Interrogative adverbs are used to ask questions. In Igbo, a question can only be initiated by either an interrogative or a personal pronoun. Following interrogatives are commonly used:

Igbo	English	Igbo	English
Kedụ	how, when, where, which?	ebee	where, which place?
olee	how much, how many?	onye	Who?
gịnị/ọ gịnị?	What?	kedụ?	How?
maka gịnị?	Why?	ma ncha	Never
tara akpụ	Rarely	mgbe ụfọdụ	Sometimes
mgbe niīle	Usually	mgbe niīle	Always
nkeọma	Very		

The basic word order of Collective Phrases (Nkebiokwu kenjụajụjụ) is as follows:
Interrogative phrase = Noun + Interrogative (Modifiers or determiners).

Translation: Nkebiokwu kenjụajụjụ = aha + njụajụjụ

Igbo language	**English translation**	**Word Order in Igbo**
Nwa gịnị?	*Which child?*	Noun + Interrogative
Onye ebee?	*Someone from where?*	Noun + Interrogative
Akwụkwọ gini?	*What book?*	Noun + Interrogative
Ego olee?	*How much?*	Noun + Interrogative
Onye gịnị?	*Which person*	Noun + Interrogative

5.10 Possessive Phrases (Nkebiokwu kennọchinke)

Substitution in English grammar is when a word, phrase, or clause in a sentence is replaced by a different word or phrase *(e.g. one, do, this)* in order to avoid repeating the previously used word. A pronoun is defined as a word or phrase that is used as a substitution for a noun or noun phrase, which is known as the pronoun's antecedent. Pronouns are short words and can do everything that nouns can do and are one of the building blocks of a sentence.

Possessive phrase is used in a sentence to show that something belongs to someone; e.g. my, our, your, his, her, its and theirs. There exists an independent form of each of the above possessive pronouns and they are: mine, ours, yours, his, hers, its, and theirs. For example:

English	*Igbo*	*English*	*Igbo*
mine	nke m	Yours	nke gị
His	nke ya	Her	nke ya
Our/ours	nke anyị	Their/theirs	nke ha

The basic word order of Possessive Phrases (Nkebiokwu kennọchinke) is as follows:
Possessive phrase = Noun + Possessive Marker.

Translation
Nkebiokwu kennọchinke = aha + nnọchinke

Igbo language	*English translation*	*Word Order in Igbo*
a) Ụgbọala nke m	*mine (my) car*	Noun + Possessive
b) Ngwá ọrụ nke gị	*yours (your) tools*	Noun + Possessive
c) Nwunye nke ya	*his own wife*	Noun + Possessive
d) Di nke ya	*her own husband*	Noun + Possessive
e) Akwụkwọ nke anyị	*our/ours books*	Noun + Possessive
f) Agbamakwụkwọ nke ha	*their/theirs wedding*	Noun + Possessive

5.11 Number Phrases (Nkebiokwu keọnụọgụgụ)

A number phrase is a phrase that has noun and number marker as a count indicator. A list of English phrases about numbers, include: fifteen minutes, fifth column, four corners, nine days, seven years, six ways, the third degree, the whole nine yards, third time lucky, three sheets, two cents zero tolerance, etc.

The basic word order of Number Phrases (Nkebiokwu keọnụọgụgụ) is as follows:
Number phrase = Noun + Number Marker.

Translation
Nkebiokwu keọnụọgụgụ = aha + ọnụọgụgụ

Igbo language	*English translation*	*Word Order in Igbo*
a) ndị Igbo abụọ	*two Igbo persons*	Noun + Number

b)	nwa akwụkwọ afọ mbụ	*first year student*	Noun + Number
c)	Oche mmadu ise	*five men chair*	Noun + Number
d)	Ọwa asaa	*seventh month*	Noun + Number
e)	Efere anọ	*four plates/bowl*	Noun + Number

Exercise

1. What is a phrase and how does it differ from a complete sentence?
2. Explain the main characteristics of an Igbo phrase.
3. What are the three types of finite verbs, and how do they differ from nonfinite verbs?
4. Provide examples of Igbo phrases and their English translations.
5. How do phrases function within a sentence? Give examples.
6. Define noun phrase and give examples from Igbo language.
7. What are adjective phrases, and how do they modify nouns or pronouns?
8. Explain adverbial phrases and provide examples from Igbo language.
9. Describe prepositional phrases and give examples of their usage.
10. Differentiate between infinitive phrases and gerund phrases.
11. How are infinitive phrases formed in Igbo language? Give examples.
12. What is the structure of gerund phrases, and how do they function in a sentence?
13. Provide examples of demonstrative phrases and explain their usage.
14. What are collective phrases, and how are they formed in Igbo language?
15. Explain interrogative phrases and provide examples of their usage in Igbo.
16. Describe possessive phrases and give examples from Igbo language.
17. What are number phrases, and how are they structured in Igbo?
18. Give examples of each type of phrase discussed in Chapter 5.
19. How do phrases contribute to the overall structure and meaning of a sentence?
20. Discuss the importance of understanding different types of phrases in language comprehension and communication.

Chapter 6

Igbo Phrase Structure Rules (*Iwu Nhazi Nkebiokwu Igbo*)

6.1 Phrase structure rules

Phrase structure rules, also known as syntactic rules or grammar rules, describe the hierarchical structure of sentences in a language. These rules specify how different elements, such as words and phrases, can be combined to form grammatically correct sentences.

Phrase Structure Rules (PSRs) are a foundational concept in linguistics, closely linked to the initial development of transformational grammar by Noam Chomsky in 1957. These rules play a crucial role in elucidating the syntax of a language by deconstructing sentences in that language into their essential components.

In essence, PSRs are a set of guidelines or principles that linguists use to represent the hierarchical structure of sentences in a particular language. They provide a systematic way to analyze and describe the arrangement of words and phrases within sentences. This analysis helps linguists understand how various elements come together to form grammatically correct and meaningful sentences.

Important terms:

Ndebiri (*Abbreviation*)	**Ihe Ọ pụtara** (*Meaning*)	**Ntụghari** (*Translation*)
A	Aha	*Noun*
AO	Ahịrịokwu	*Sentence*
IN	Isingwaa	*Main Verb*
M	Mmeju	*Complement*
MAO	Mmeju Ahịrịokwu	*Complement Sentence*
Mmz	Mmeju Mbuụzọ	*Prepositional Complement*
Mnn	Mmeju Nnara	*Object Complement*

Mnp	Mmeju Nnapụta	*Indirect Object Complement*
Mnt	Mmeju Ntado	*Bound Complement*
Mnw	Mmeju Nkwuwa	*Adverbial Complement*
MO	Mmeju Onwe	*Reflective Complement*
Ngw	Ngwaa	*Verb*
NK	Nkọwaha	*Adjective*
NKA	Nkebiokwu Keaha	*Noun Phrase*
NKm	Nkebiokwu Kembuụzọ	*Prepositional Phrase*
NKN	Nkebiokwu Kengwaa	*Verb Phrase*
NKNk	Nkebiokwu Kenkọwaha	*Adjectival Phrase*
NKnw	Nkebiokwu Kenkwuwa	*Adverbial Phrase*
Nks	Nkwuso	*Determiner*
Nkw	Nkwuwa	Adverb
Nn	Nnọchiaha	*Pronoun*
Nny	Nnyemaka Ngwaa	*Auxiliary Verb*
Ọnọ	Ọnụọgụgụ	*Number*

The application of PSRs involves breaking down sentences into smaller units, such as phrases and clauses, and identifying the relationships and dependencies between these units. By doing so, linguists gain insights into the underlying structure of a language's syntax. This structural analysis is essential for comprehending the rules and patterns that govern how words combine to convey meaning in a coherent and understandable manner.

Rule 1: Ahịrịokwu (AO) (*a sentence (S)*) contains an immediate dominant Nkebiokwu keaha (NKA) (*Noun Phrase (NP)*) and Nkebiokwu kengwaa (NKN) *(a Verb Phrase)* in that order.

  AO → NKA + NKN
(Ahịrịokwu → Nkebiokwu Keaha + Nkebiokwu Kengwaa)

S → NP + VP
(Sentence → Noun Phrase + Verb Phrase)

This rule states that a sentence (S) is composed of a noun phrase (NP) followed by a verb phrase (VP). The noun phrase and verb phrase can then be further analyzed using additional rules, such as:

Ahịrịokwu (AO) *(Sentence (S))*: In linguistic analysis, a Ahịrịokwu (AO) *(sentence (S))* is considered a fundamental unit of expression. According to the specified structure, it is comprised of two main components: a nkebiokwu keaha (NKA) *(noun phrase (NP))* followed by a nkebiokwu kengwaa *(verb phrase (VP))*. This organization helps establish the basic syntactic structure of a sentence.

Example 1: Consider the sentence
"Ọ na-agụ akwụkwọ." ("*She reads a book.*")

The breakdown is represented as:
AO → NKA + NKN, (*S → NP + VP*).

where the nkebiokwu keaha *(noun phrase (NP))* is Ọ ("*She*") and the nkebiokwu kengwaa *(verb phrase (VP))* is na-agụ akwụkwọ ("*reads a book*").

Example 2: Nwamba (NKA) na-ehi ụra (NKN).
The cat (NP) is sleeping (VP).

Rule 2: This rule conveys that a noun phrase, as part of a sentence can contain a determiner that is followed by a noun in that order in English syntax. However, in Igbo language the opposite is the case; Nkebiokwu keaha (NKA) (noun phrase) in Igbo can contain Aha (A) *(a noun)* that is followed by Nkwuso (Nks) *(a determiner)* in that order.

English   Igbo
  NP → Det + N   NKA → A + Nks

Nkebiokwu Keaha (NKA) *(Noun Phrase (NP))*: Nkebiokwu Keaha *(Noun phrases (NP))* are integral elements within a sentence and can take different forms. An NP can consist of an optional Nkwuso *(determiner (Det))*, followed by a Mkpoaha/Aha *(noun (N))*. There is no article in Igbo language This structure is a common way to represent the basic building blocks of a sentence. Please note that there is no article in Igbo language.

Examples:
a) Nwamba ahụ   "*The cat*"
   NKA → Nks A   (*NP → Det N*)

b) Nkịta   "*A dog*"
   Aha (NKA)   (*NP → Det N*)

c) Nwamba ojii.   "*A black cat*"
   NKA + NKNk   (*NP → (Det) + (Adj) + (N)*)

Aha (A) *(Nouns (N))*:

Aha (A) *(Nouns (N))* form the core of noun phrases. A noun can be preceded by an optional nkebiokwu kenkọwaha *(adjective phrase (AP))*, providing additional descriptive information. Additionally, it can be followed by an optional Nkebiokwu Kembuụzọ (NKm) *(prepositional phrase (PP))*, indicating the relationship of the noun to other elements in the sentence.

Examples:

    d) Nnukwu nwamba   "The big cat"
    (A → NKNk + A) *(N → AP + N)*

    e) Nwamba nọ n'elu ụlọ   "The cat on the roof"
    (A → A + NKm)   *(N → N + PP)*

Rule 3: Nkebiokwu kengwaa (NKN) *(verb phrase (VP))* consists of Ngwaa (N) *(verb (V))* followed by Nkebiokwu keaha (NKA) *(a noun phrase (NP))*. This rule generally applies to verbs in a sentence and does not refer to any specific verb, verb phrase or noun phrase.

    NKN → N (NKA)
    VP → V (NP)

A verb phrase is not required to have a noun phrase object to qualify as verb phrase. However, it must have at least one verb (i.e. a verb alone) as shown in the following sentences.

    f) Ịnyịnya ahụ gbapụrụ.   *"The horse galloped."*
       A   Nks   N   *"Det N V"*

    g) Nwoke ahụ (gbara) egwu.   *"The man danced."*
       A   Nks *(verb root)* N   *"Det N V"*

    h) Nwanyị ahụ chiri   ọchị.   *"The woman laughed."*
       A   Nks *(verb root)* N   *"Det N V"*

Verb Phrase (VP): A verb phrase (VP) is a syntactic unit that consists of a verb and its arguments but does not include the subject of an independent or coordinate clause.

    VP → V (NP) (PP)

Example:

    i) Rahụọ jụụ.   *Sleeps peacefully.*
       (VP → V + (NKm)   VP → V + (Adv)

A. Simple Verb Phrases: These are made up of just one primary verb. In a simple verb phrase, the verb denotes the kind of clause as shown below.

Example 1:
Igwefoto gị **na-ese** foto dị egwu. "*Your camera takes fantastic pictures.*"
(Ahịrịmfe, nkebiahịrị nkwupụta) (present simple, declarative clause)

Example 2:
Yiri uwe nke ọma. **Bia** n'oge. "*Dress smartly/well. Arrive on time.*"
(nkebiahịrị okwu dị mkpa) (imperative clauses)

B. *Complex Verb Phrases:* These have the primary verb preceded by one or more auxiliary verbs. The kind and meaning of the auxiliary verbs determine the verbs' placement in a complicated verb phrase.

Example 1:
Ọnụ ahịa ụlọ **nwere ike** *ịda* n'ime ọnwa isii na-abịa.
(ụkpụrụ ngwaa + isingwaa)
"*House prices could fall during the next six months.*"
(modal verb + main verb)

Example 2:
O **nwere ike** *ịbụ* na ị na-egwubu egwuregwu a. "*You may have played this game before.*"
(ụkpụrụ ngwaa + otu nnyemakangwaa) (modal verb + one auxiliary verb)

Rule 4 specifies that a tree can have a NKN (Verb phrase (VP)) that is predominant. This is evident in a sentences preposition phrase and other phrases following verbs.

VP → V (PP)

a) **Nwa nkita na-egwuri egwu n'ebennọkọta ubi.** "*The puppy played in the garden.*"
b) **Ụgbọ mmiri ahụ gbagoro n'osimiri ahụ.** "*The boat sailed up the river.*"
c) **Nkịta atụrụ na-atụgharị n'ime apịtị.** "*The sheepdog rolled in the mud.*"

Rule 5 is a recursive rule. It has structures with multiple prepositional phrases (PPs) and permits the repeats its own category (VP) inside itself. By allowing the grammar structure to generate an infinite set of sentences it creates room for the unboundedness of sentences.

VP → V (PP) (PP) (PP)

Example 1:
Ada   jere [n'okporo ámá] gafee [n'elu ugwu] [site n'ọhịa].
NP   VP   PP   VP   PP   PP
NKA   NKN NKm   NKN NKm   NKm
"Ada walked [down the street] [over the hill] [through the woods]."

Example 2:
Eze [ji egbe] jiri egbe gaa [n'okporo ámá] [n'akụkụ ụlọ akụ].
NP   PP   VP   VP   PP   PP
NKA NKm   NKN NKN   NKm   NKm
"Eze walked [down the street] [with a gun] [toward the bank]."

Rule 6 implies that Prepositional Phrase (PP) must have a Preposition and a Noun Phrase (NP). This rule is used to break down PP into P and NP. Therefore, in a tree, we can use the NP rule twice. After we have applied all the rules that can apply.

PP → P + NP (Det + N)

1. **Akwụkwọ ahụ] dị n'ebe ndebe akwụkwọ ahụ.** (*The book on the shelf.*)
   IS   NKm   m   A   Nks
   Subj   PP (P)   N   Det

2. **Ụgbọ ala ahụ dị n'ebe a na-adọba ụgbọala ahụ.** (*The car is in the garage.*)
   IS   NKm (m +   A   +   Nks)
   Subj   PP (P)   N   Det

3. **Okooko osisi ahụ nọ n'akụkụ ubi/ugbo ahụ.** (*The flowers by the farm.*)
   IS   NKm (m +   A + Nks)
   Subj   PP (P)   N   Det

4. **Ngajị ahụ   dị n'ime akpa ahụ.** (*The spoon in the bag.*)
   IS   NKm (m + A   + Nks)
   Subj   PP   (P) N Det

Rule 7: applies VP which contains complementizer phrase (CP).

Ụmụaka na-atụ anya **na** onye nkụzi ahụ maara **na** onyeisi ụlọ akwụkwọ ahụ kwuru **na** ụlọ akwụkwọ na-emechi n'ụbọchị a.

*The children hope **that** the teacher knows **that** the principal said **that** the school closes for the day.*

    VP → V + CP

In Igbo grammar, **complementizers** are words used to introduce **complement clauses**. These clauses provide additional information and are often introduced by subordinate conjunctions, relative pronouns, or relative adverbs. Let's explore some examples:

1. Ọ ga-amasị m **ma** ọ bụrụ na enwere m ụkwụ ọbọgwụ. (*"I wish **that** I had duck feet."*)
   Nnọ   N   *rel*-Nnọ   Mnn
   Pr   V   *rel*-Pr   CP

2. A-   maghị m **ma** John ọ ga-esonyere anyị. (*"I don't know **if** John will join us."*)
   Nnọ   N   *rel*-Njk   Mnn
   Pr   V   *rel*-Conj   CP

Clausal complement can also start with a adverbial complementizer are regarded which provide additional information. Examples of adverbial words include: mgbe *(when)*; n'ịhị *(because)* etc.

1. **Aga m egwu mmiri *mgbe* anyanwụ pụtara.**
   Nnọ   IN   A   Nkw   Mnw
   Pr   V*root* N   Adv   CP

2. **Ọ nọdụrụ n'ime ụlọ *n'ihi* na mmiri na-ezo.**
   Nnọ   N NKm   Nkw   Mnw
   Pr   V PP   Adv   CP
   *"She stayed indoors **because** it was raining."*

Rule 8 applies to those complementizer phrases (CP) that contain a complementizer (such as *that*) which is followed by an embedded sentence. Other complementizers are *if* and *whether* in sentences.

CP → CS

For example:
1. A-   maghị m *ma* m ga-ekwu maka nke a.
   Nnọ   N   NKm   MAO
   Pr   V   PP   CS
   *"I don't know **whether** I should talk about this."*

2. Eze jụrụ *ma* Ada aghọtara ihe mmụta ahụ.
    A   N   NKm MAO
    Pr   V   PP   CS
*Eze asked **if** Ada understood the lesson.*

6.2 Surface structure:

Surface structure in phrasal structure rules refers to the external or visible form of a sentence, including its words, phrases, and syntax. In generative grammar, the surface structure of a sentence is the representation of the sentence as it appears on the surface, without considering its underlying meaning or structure.

Surface structure is a crucial aspect of syntax in linguistics. In the context of generative grammar, which was developed by Noam Chomsky, syntax is the study of the rules governing the structure of sentences in a language. The structure of a sentence can be analyzed at two levels: deep structure and surface structure.

Deep structure represents the underlying meaning or semantic content of a sentence, while surface structure is the actual arrangement of words and phrases in a sentence. Surface structure is what we observe when we look at a sentence or hear it spoken.

Here are a few reasons why surface structure is considered vital in the study of syntax:

1. Communication and Interpretation: Surface structure is what is visible or audible, and it is what we use to communicate. The arrangement of words and phrases in a sentence influence how the sentence is interpreted by the listener or reader.
For example:

Deep Structure:	**O nyere ya akwụkwọ**.	*"She gave him a book."*
Surface Structure:	**Akwụkwọ o nyere ya**.	*"A book she gave him."*

In this example, the deep structure remains the same, conveying the idea that she gave him a book. However, the word order in the surface structure is changed, showcasing how different surface structures can represent the same underlying meaning.

2. Grammar Rules: The rules of a language that dictate how words and phrases can be combined to form sentences are most directly related to surface structure. These rules include word order, sentence structure, and syntactic categories, among others. An example can be found in Passive Voice Transformation.

Deep Structure: **Nwamba ahụ chụrụ òké ọsọ.**   *"The cat chased the mouse."*
Surface Structure: **Òké ahụ ka Nwamba chụrụ ọsọ.**   *The mouse was chased by the cat.*

Here, the deep structure conveys the action of the cat chasing the mouse. The passive transformation alters the surface structure while retaining the same underlying meaning.

3. Ambiguity Resolution: Surface structure plays a key role in resolving potential ambiguities in language. Different surface structures can sometimes correspond to the same deep structure, and understanding the surface structure helps in disambiguating the meaning of a sentence.
For example:
Deep Structure: **Ahụrụ m nwoke ahụ site na teliskop**   *"I saw the man with the telescope."*
Surface Structures: **Ahụrụ m nwoke ahụ nwe teliskop ahụ.** (*"I saw the man who had the telescope."*)
                    Eji m teliskop hụ nwoke ahụ.   *"I used the telescope to see the man."*

The deep structure is ambiguous, but different surface structures help resolve the ambiguity by offering two possible interpretations.

4. Transformational Processes: Transformational processes, which involve moving or changing elements within a sentence, are applied to deep structure to generate surface structure. These processes are crucial for understanding how different sentences with the same meaning can have different surface structures. Movement and Questions are used to illustrate transformational processes between deep and surface structures.

For example:
Deep Structure: **Jọn ga-eri pizza n'abalị a.**   *"John will eat pizza tonight."*
Surface Structure (Question): **John aga-eri pizza n'abalị a?** (*"Will John eat pizza tonight?"*)

In this case above, the movement of the auxiliary verb "will" transform the deep structure into a question in the surface structure.

These examples highlight how surface structure reflects the observable arrangement of words in a sentence, showcasing transformations, changes in word order, and resolution of ambiguity while retaining the underlying meaning captured in the deep structure.

Surface structure is vital in syntax because it represents the observable form of sentences and is directly related to the rules and principles that govern how sentences are constructed in a language. It provides the basis for communication, the application of grammatical rules, and the resolution of potential ambiguities in language.

6.3 Phrase tree structures

Phrase structure tree (PS trees, for short) also known as a parse tree or syntax tree, is a graphical representation of the syntactic structure of a sentence according to a particular grammar. It shows how the sentence can be divided into phrases, and how those phrases are related to each other. Each node in the tree represents a constituent or a phrase, while the edges represent the hierarchical relationships between these constituents.

PS trees represent three aspects of a speaker's syntactic knowledge:

1. Linearity: This aspect refers to the linear arrangement of words within a sentence. In a phrase structure tree, the linear order of words is depicted from left to right along branches. Each branch corresponds to a constituent (word or phrase), and the overall structure follows the sequential order in which words appear in the sentence.

2. Hierarchy: Hierarchy in phrase structure trees reflects the nested and hierarchical relationships between different syntactic elements. The tree structure illustrates how constituents are hierarchically organized, with larger constituents containing smaller ones. For example, a sentence (S) may consist of a noun phrase (NP) and a verb phrase (VP), each of which can further break down into smaller constituents.

3. Categoriality: Categoriality pertains to the assignment of syntactic categories to different elements in a sentence. Each node in a phrase structure tree represents a specific syntactic category, such as a noun, verb, phrase, or clause. The tree structure visually captures the categorical distinctions and classifications of linguistic elements, highlighting the grammatical roles they play in the overall sentence.

The constituents of sentences, as described by the phrase structure rules, are often visually represented as tree structures or dendrograms. Each word or combination of words is organized hierarchically, with a single node dominating each element. This tree representation helps depict the syntactic relationships within a sentence.

Chomsky's Example:
sentence: "Colorless green ideas sleep furiously"
```
S
 ├── NP (Colorless green ideas)
 └── VP (sleep furiously)
```

Example 1: **Ọ ga-abịa**. *"He will come."*

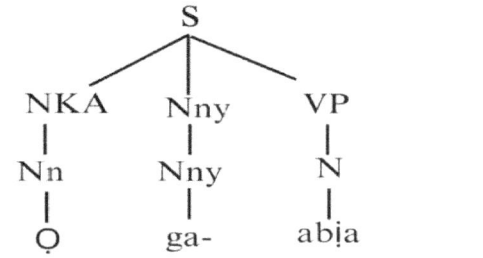
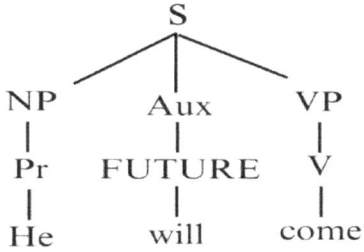

Example 2:

Nnukwu nwoke ahụ pụrụ ngwa ngwa.   *The big man left quickly.*

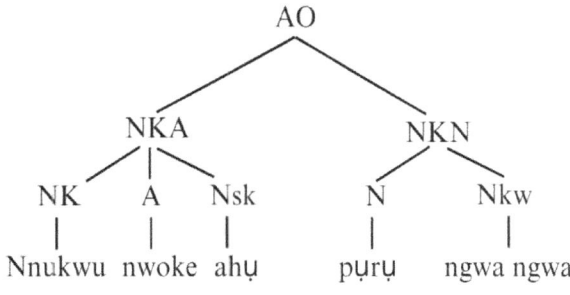
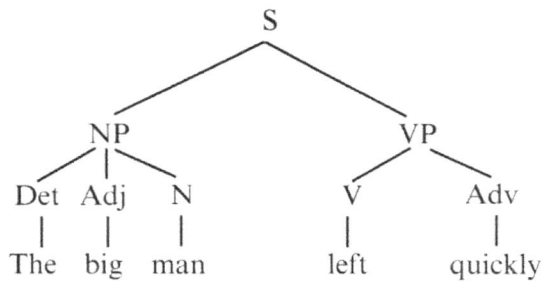

Example 3:

Nwoke ahụ kụrụ bọọlụ ahụ.   *The man hit the ball.*

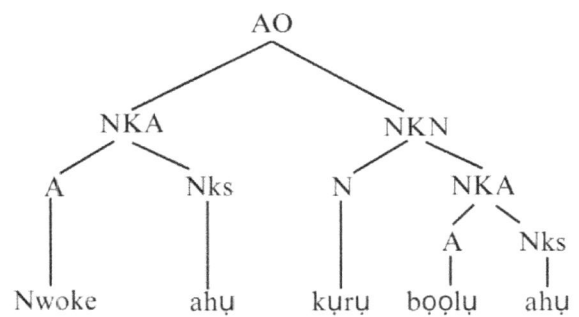
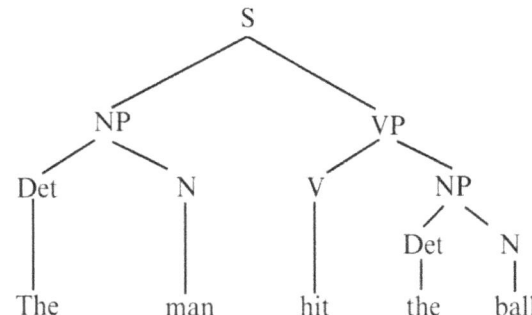

Phrase structure trees serve as a visual tool to represent a speaker's understanding of the linear order (linearity), hierarchical organization (hierarchy), and categorial distinctions (categoriality) within the syntactic structure of a language. These trees provide a comprehensive and structured representation of how words and phrases are combined to form grammatically correct sentences.

Exercise

1. What are phrase structure rules and why are they important in linguistics?
2. How do phrase structure rules help linguists understand the syntax of a language?
3. Can you explain the role of phrase structure rules in breaking down sentences into smaller units?
4. What is the significance of the NP + VP structure in sentence formation according to phrase structure rules?
5. How does Igbo syntax differ from English in terms of the order of elements within a noun phrase?
6. Provide 5 examples of noun phrases (NKA) in Igbo that follow the A + Nks structure?
7. Explain how verb phrases (NKN) are structured in Igbo according to the phrase structure rules.
8. What is the difference between simple and complex verb phrases in Igbo syntax?
9. How does Rule 4 demonstrate the dominance of verb phrases (VP) in certain sentence structures?
10. Give examples of sentences that illustrate the recursive nature of Rule 5 in Igbo phrase structure rules.
11. Explain Rule 6 and its significance in breaking down prepositional phrases (PP) in Igbo.
12. How do complementizer phrases (CP) function in Igbo syntax according to Rule 7?
13. Provide examples of sentences that demonstrate the application of complementizer phrases (CP) in Igbo.
14. What is the purpose of Rule 8 in Igbo phrase structure rules, and how does it relate to embedded sentences?
15. Explain the concept of surface structure in the context of phrase structure rules.
16. How does surface structure differ from deep structure in linguistics?
17. Provide 5 examples of how surface structure influences the interpretation of sentences?
18. Discuss the role of surface structure in resolving ambiguity in language.
19. Explain how transformational processes are applied to derive surface structure from deep structure.
20. What are the three aspects of a speaker's syntactic knowledge represented in phrase structure trees?

Chapter 7
Transformational Grammar (Mgbanwe Ụtọasụsụ)

In transformative grammar, movement rules—also referred to as transformations—are procedures that rearrange or modify syntactic components inside a phrase. They are essential for producing grammatically sound sentences and recognizing the different syntactic patterns present in natural languages.

In order to create distinct structures, transformations control how words and phrases are moved across sentences. They entail moving components around, adding or removing components, or altering the way words relate to one another grammatically.

7.1 Movement Rule in transformative Grammar (Iwu kemgbanwe ọnọdụ)

In transformative grammar, movement rules refer to the processes that involve the displacement or reordering of elements within a sentence. These rules are a crucial part of generative grammar, particularly in the context of transformational-generative grammar developed by Noam Chomsky. Under the umbrella of movement rules, several subtopics can be explored:

Here are a few examples of movement rules commonly used in transformative grammar:

A. *Dative Movement*: Dative movement refers to the transformation or movement of the dative phrase (usually the indirect object) within a sentence. This movement can be observed when the dative phrase undergoes displacement, often for reasons related to emphasis, focus, or stylistic considerations. The dative phrase may move from its original position to a different location within the sentence. This movement is observed in many languages and serves to indicate the recipient or beneficiary of an action. In Igbo language, the direct object (nnara) in the sentence changes its position to the indirect object (nnapụta) position but their function does not change.

Agbaala (Deep structure)	**Agbaelu (Surface structure)**
1. Ha zigara ozi ekele.	Ozi ekele ka Ha zigara.
They sent their greetings.	*Their greetings (was what) they sent.*
2. Ngọzị siri nri.	Nri ka Ngọzị siri.
Ngọzị cooked food.	*Food was (what) Ngọzị cooked.*
3. Osimiri riri nwa nkịta ahụ.	Nwa nkịta ahụ ka osimiri riri.
The river drowned the puppy.	*The puppy drowned in the river.*
4. Ijiji juru ebe niile.	Ebe niile ka Ijiji juru.
Flies were everywhere.	*Everywhere was (full of) flies.*

B. *Wh-Movement*: Wh-movement is the process of moving wh-words, or interrogative words (such as who, what, and where), from one sentence's original position to the one where inquiries are first formed. This movement allows the speaker to ask questions about different parts of a sentence, which is important for building interrogative sentences. It also serves a key purpose in syntax. The wh-phrase include onye *(who)*, Gịnị/kedu *(what)*, Ebee *(where)*, mgbe ole *(when)* and Gịnị (why). Example:

Nsinambu (Original)	**Mgbanwe (Wh-movement)**
1. Ọ ga-eri Garri.	Gịnị ka ọ ga-eri?
She will eat Garri.	*What will she eat?*
2. Jọn siri nri.	"Gịnị ka Jọn siri?"
John cooked food.	*"What did John cook?"*
3. Obi gara ebe oriri na ọṅụṅụ ahụ.	Ebee ka Obi gara?
Obi went to the party.	*Where did Obi went?*
4. Ọ zụtara nwunye ya onyinye	Gịnị ka ọ zụtara nwunye ya?
She bought a gift for his wife.	*What did he buy for his wife?*
5. Ọ hapụrụ ọrụ ịga leta nne ya.	Gịnị mere o ji hapụ ọrụ ya?
He left work to visit her mother.	*Why did he leave his work?*

In examples above, the wh-phrase (what, where, and why) is moved to the beginning of the sentence, marking the transformation from a declarative statement to an interrogative question. This wh-movement allows speakers to seek specific information or clarification.

C. *Topicalization*: Topicalization is the process of moving a constituent to the beginning of a sentence to highlight or emphasize it. This movement allows speakers to bring attention to specific information, setting the stage for what they consider most important or relevant. It adds a layer of expressiveness and flexibility to sentence structure. Topicalization involves moving a constituent (often a noun phrase or adverbial phrase) to the initial position of a sentence to highlight or emphasize it. Here are a few examples of topicalization:

a. Noun Phrase Topicalization:
Original: Agụrụ m akwụkwọ sayensị n'abalị ụnyaahụ.
I read a science book last night.

Topicalization: Akwụkwọ sayensị ahụ, m gụrụ n'abalị ụnyaahụ.
That fascinating book, I read last night.

b. Adverbial Phrase Topicalization:
Original: Ọ gbara egwu nke ọma na nnọkọ ahụ.
She danced gracefully at the ball.

Topicalization: nke ọma, ọ gbara egwú na nnọkọ ahụ.
Gracefully, she danced at the ball.

c. Prepositional Phrase Topicalization:
Original: Anyị hụrụ akụ n'okpuru osisi Iroko.
We found the treasure under Iroko tree.

Topicalization: N'okpuru osisi Iroko, anyị hụrụ akụ ahụ.
Under Iroko tree, we found the treasure.

In each example, the constituent being topicalized is moved to the front of the sentence for emphasis or focus. Topicalization is a syntactic strategy that allows speakers and writers to draw attention to specific information, setting the stage for what they consider important or relevant in a given context.

D. *Passivization*: Passivization is a transformation that involves reordering elements in a sentence to change the focus from the doer of the action to the receiver. It involves transforming an active sentence into a passive one, typically by changing the syntactic structure. The direct object is moved to the sentence-initial position, creating a passive construction. This movement is employed to shift emphasis, obscure the doer of the action, or create a more formal tone.

Example:

Active	**Passive**
1. Nwamba chụrụ òké.	Òké ahụ ka Nwamba chụrụ.
The cat chased the mouse.	*The mouse was chased by the cat.*
2. Onye osi nri siri nri.	Nri ka onye osi nri siri.
The chef cooked a meal.	*A meal was cooked by the chef.*
3. Ada rụchara ọrụ ahụ.	Ọrụ ahụ ka Ada rụchara
Ada completed the job.	*The job was completed by Ada.*
4. Onye ọrụ ubi kụrụ ji.	Ji ka onye ọrụ ubi kụrụ.
The farmer planted yam.	*Yam was planted by the farmer.*
5. Ọ na-ewu ụlọ ọhụrụ.	Ụlọ ọhụrụ ka Ọ na-ewu
He is building a new house.	*A new house is being built by him.*

In each example, the passive voice is formed by rearranging the sentence structure and using the appropriate form of the verb "to be" along with the past participle of the main verb. This results in a construction where the receiver of the action becomes the subject of the sentence, while the doer of the action may be mentioned in a prepositional phrase or omitted.

E. MGBANWE KEESTRAPOZISHỌN (Extraposition)

Extraposition involves moving a constituent (usually a subordinate clause or a phrase) from its original position to the end of a sentence, often for the purpose of improving clarity or stylistic reasons. An extraposition is an interesting linguistic phenomenon in which a clause that functions as a subject gets shifted to the end of a sentence and a dummy "o, ọ, ya (it)" takes its place in the original position. Let's explore some examples:

Original Sentence: O doro anya na e duhiela gị.
    "It is obvious that you have been misled."

Extraposed Version: Na e duhiere gị bụ ihe doro anya.
    "That you have been misled is obvious."

In this case, the subject clause "Na e duhiere gị bụ ihe doro anya." *("that you have been misled")* is extraposed to the end of the sentence.

Original Sentence: Ọ bụ ihe ihere, ihe mere gị na nwanne gị nwanyị.
"It's a shame what happened to you and your sister."

Extraposed Version: Ihe mere gị na nwanne gị nwaanyị bụ ihe ihere.
"What happened to you and your sister is a shame."

Here, the focus shifts to the event "Ihe mere" *(what happened)* by extraposing the subject clause.

In each example, the extraposition involves moving a constituent (such as a subordinate clause or a phrase) from its original position to the end of the sentence. This syntactic transformation is often employed to enhance readability, maintain emphasis, or streamline the structure of complex sentences. Extraposition frequently follows end-weight and end-focus principles, which improves phrase flow and thereby making sentence processing easier.

F. Iwu Nnọgharị Nke Nkebiokwu kengwaa (Verb Phrase hopping):

VP hopping is a phenomenon in transformational grammar that involves the movement of verb phrase from one position to another in a sentence. It is commonly seen in certain languages where the VP moves to a different location to satisfy the specific intention of the speaker.

In Igbo language, verb phrase can jump from their position in the sentence to the to another position in the sentences without altering the sentence structure and meaning. However, the tnoun associated with verb of the sentence will move alongside the verb. Usually, this change of position VP does not exceed two words at a time. It is also the last step in transformative grammar.

For example:
1. Okafọ bụbu Dibịa nwụrụ anwụ.   *The Okafọ was doctor (is) dead.*
   Okafọ nwụrụ anwụ bụbu Dibịa.   *The dead Okafọ was doctor.*

2. Nneka bụbu nwanyị aga mụrụ nwa.   *The Nneka that used to be barren gave birth.*
   Nneka mụrụ nwa bụbu nwanyị aga.   *The Nneka that gave birth used to be barren.*

3. Ngọzị were ahụ bịara ebe a.   *The Ngọzị that took the bag came here.*
   Ngọzị bịara ebe a were akpa ahụ.   *The Ngọzị that came took the bag.*

4. Mgbeke dịbu ime mụrụ nwa.   *Mgbeke that was previously pregnant, gave birth.*
   Mgbeke mụrụ nwa dịbu ime.   *Mgbeke that gave birth was previously pregnant.*

5. Ugochi ahụ dị ọcha dịbu oji. *The fair Ugochi was once black.*
   Ugochi ahụ dịbu oji dị ọcha. *Ugochi that was black is now fair.*

In the hopped sentences above, the verbs "*dị,*" "*dịbu,*" "*bụbụ,*" "*were*" have moved from its original position and hopped over with their individual nouns to a new position and still satisfy the syntactic rules of the Igbo language grammar. Verb Phrase hopping can have implications for sentence structure and meaning.

7.2 Deletion Rule in Transformative Grammar (Iwu nke Mwepu):
This is a deletion of word or group of words in a deep structure sentence so that it does not appear in the surface structure of the sentence. In transformational grammar, there are various deletion rules. They are as follows:

A. Mwepu keaha (Noun Phrase Deletion): NP deletion, or Noun Phrase Deletion, involves the removal or omission of a noun phrase from a sentence while still maintaining clarity and coherence. This is done often under specific conditions. This process is associated with ellipses, where redundant information is omitted because it can be easily inferred from the context.
Here are five examples of NP deletion:

Original: Nnenna zụtara uwe ọhụrụ, Nneka zụtakwara uwe ọhụrụ.
Nnenna bought a new dress, and Nneka bought a new dress too.

NP Deletion: Nnenna zụtara uwe ọhụrụ, *ma* Nneka zụtakwara.
Nnenna bought a new dress, and Nneka too.

Original: Emeka nwere nkịta, Obi nwekwara nkịta.
Emeka has a dog, and Obi has a dog as well.

NP Deletion: Emeka nwere nkịta, *ma* Obi nwekwara.
Emeka has a dog, and Emeka as well.

Original: Ihe nkiri ahụ tọrọ anyị ụtọ, ihe nkiri ahụ tọkwara ha ụtọ.
We enjoyed the movie, and they enjoyed the movie too.

NP Deletion: Ihe nkiri ahụ tọrọ anyị ụtọ, *ma* ha onwe ha kwa
We enjoyed the movie, and they too.

Original: Ọ zụtara ụgbọ ala ọhụrụ, nwanne ya nwoke zụtakwara ụgbọ ala ọhụrụ.
He bought a new car, and his brother bought a new car too.

NP Deletion: Ọ zụtara ụgbọ ala ọhụrụ, *ma* nwanne ya nwoke kwa.
He bought a new car, and his brother too.

In each example, the repeated noun phrase is deleted, and the sentence remains grammatically correct and coherent. NP deletion is a mechanism that helps avoid redundancy in language while conveying the intended meaning.

B. Mwepu keNgwaa (Verb Phrase Deletion): VP Deletion involves the removal or deletion of a verb phrase within a sentence. This often occurs in coordination or conjunction structures where the repeated verb phrase is elliptically omitted to avoid redundancy. VP deletion, or Verb Phrase Deletion, involves removing or omitting part of the verb phrase in a sentence while maintaining its grammatical structure. Here are five examples of VP deletion:

Original: Ha arụchaala ọrụ ahụ, anyị arụchaakwala ọrụ ahụ.
They completed the task, and we have completed the task too.

VP Deletion: Ha arụchaala ọrụ ahụ, ma anyị kwa.
They have completed the task, and we have too.

Original: Anyị nwere ike dozie nsogbu ahụ, ha nwekwara ike dozie nsogbu ahụ.
We can solve the problem, and they can solve the problem as well.

VP Deletion: Anyị nwere ike dozie nsogbu ahụ, ha nwekwara ike.
We can solve the problem, and they can too.

Original: Nwamba ga-ejide òké ahụ, nkịta ga-ejidekwa òké ahụ.
The cat will catch the mouse, and the dog will catch the mouse too.

VP Deletion: Nwamba ga-ejide òké, ma nkịta kwa.
The cat will catch the mouse, and the dog will too.

In each example, part of the verb phrase is deleted to avoid redundancy while still conveying the intended meaning. VP deletion is a grammatical phenomenon that occurs in natural language to streamline expression.

C. Mwepu Kereletiv (Relativization): Relativization is a syntactic process where a relative clause is formed to modify a noun phrase, providing additional information about it. This process involves the use of relative pronouns (e.g., who, which, that) and contributes to sentence complexity.

Examples:

Original: Nwoke ahụ toro ogologo. Nwoke ahụ bụ nwanne m nwoke.
The man is tall. The man is my brother.

Relativization: Nwoke ahụ toro ogologo bụ nwanne m nwoke.
The man who is tall is my brother.

Original: Nwanyị ahụ bụ nwanne m nwanyị.
The woman is my sister.

Relativization: Nwanyị ahụ bụ nwanne m nwaanyị nọ ebe a.
The woman who is my sister is here.

Original: Akwụkwọ ahụ dị n'ebe ndebe akwụkwọ.
The book is on the shelf.

Relativization: Akwụkwọ nke dị n'ebe ndebe akwụkwọ na-adọrọ mmasị
The book that is on the shelf is interesting.

Original: Ụgbọ ala ahụ bụ nke Obi.
The car belongs to Obi.

Relativization: Ụgbọ ala nke Obi na-acha uhie uhie
The car that belongs to Obi is red.

Original: Ụlọ ahụ nwere ọnụ ụzọ na-acha anụnụ anụnụ.
The house has a blue door.

Relativization: Ụlọ nke ọnụ ụzọ ya na-acha anụnụ anụnụ bụ nke m.
The house whose door is blue is mine.

In each example, a relative clause is introduced to provide additional information about the noun phrase, creating a more detailed and specific description. Relativization is a common syntactic process that enhances the richness of sentences in natural language.

D. Mwepu ke ihe n'enweghị njedebe (Deletion based on Indefiniteness): Deletion under the condition of indefiniteness refers to the omission or deletion of information in a sentence when the referent is indefinite or not specified. This deletion often occurs in English to avoid unnecessary repetition.

Example:

Original:	Onye ọ bụla mebiri iwu ga-aga ụlọ nga. *Every law breaker goes to jail.*
Deletion (Indefiniteness):	Onye na-emebi iwu ga-aga ụlọ nga. *Law breaker goes to jail.*
Original:	Ihe ọ bụla bụ omume obiọma nwere ụgwọ ọrụ. *Every act of kindness has a reward.*
Deletion (Indefiniteness):	Omume obiọma nwere ụgwọ ọrụ. *Kindness has a reward.*
Original:	Ihe ọ bụla bụ nri na-edozi ahụ. *All food nourishes the body.*
Deletion (Indefiniteness):	Nri na-edozi ahụ. *Food nourishes the body.*
Original:	Ihe ọ bụla bụ nrubeisi bụ ihe ịrịba ama nke ịhụnanya. *All acts of obedience is a sign of love.*
Deletion (Indefiniteness):	Nrubeisi bụ ihe ịrịba ama nke ịhụnanya. *Obedience is a sign of love.*
Original:	Ihe ọ bụla bụ ọrịa nwere ọgwụgwọ. *Every disease has a cure.*
Deletion (Indefiniteness):	ọrịa nwere ọgwụgwọ. *Disease has a cure.*

In each example, the phrase "Ihe ọ bụla" (every/all) involves deletion under the condition of indefiniteness. The context or the structure of the sentence makes it clear that there is an indefinite item being referred to, allowing for deletion. This linguistic phenomenon helps streamline the expression of information in a sentence.

These syntactic processes contribute to the efficiency and expressiveness of language by allowing speakers and writers to convey information concisely and avoid unnecessary phrase. Understanding these deletion rules is essential in the study of syntax, as they provide insights into the ways in which languages structure and convey information.

7.3 Insertion for Question Formation (Ntinye ke mmebe ajụjụ):

Insertion rules in syntax refer to the addition or insertion of elements into a sentence to fulfill specific syntactic or semantic requirements. One prominent example of insertion rules is in the formation of questions. Let's explore how insertion rules apply to question formation:

A. Ntinye kennọchiaha *(Insertion of Pronoun)*: In Igbo language, questions can be formed by inserting a third person singular pronoun (interrogative pronoun) "o/ọ" or impersonal pronoun "a/e" within a declarative sentence. The insertion of these elements helps transform a statement into an interrogative sentence.

Example:

Declarative: Emeka bịara ụnyahụ
Emeka came yesterday.

Question: Emeka Ọ bịara ụnyahụ?
Did Emeka come yesterday?

Declarative: Ugochukwu gara ụlọ ahịa.
Ugochukwu went to the store.

Question: Ugochukwu Ọ gara ụlọ ahịa?
Did Ugochukwu go to the store?

Declarative: Nkịta ahụ nọ na-agbọ ụja abalị nile.
The dog was barking all night.

Question: Nkịta ahụ ana-agbọ ụja abalị nile?
Was the dog barking all night?

Declarative: Ha nwere ọtụtụ ihe onwunwe.
They have lots of properties.

Question: Ha enwere ọtụtụ ihe onwunwe?
Do they have lots of properties?

B. Ntinye ke "O nwere" *(Insertion of Question maker "is there")*: In Igbo language, questions can be formed by inserting "O nwere" *("is there")* before a sentence. The insertion of this question maker helps transform a statement into an interrogative sentence.

For examples:

1. Amarachi nọ n'ọbá akwụkwọ. (*Amarachi is at the library.*)
2. nwere Amarachi nọ n'ọbá akwụkwọ? (*Is there Amarachi at the library?*)
3. Ụmụaka nọ n'ụlọ akwụkwọ. (*The children are at school.*)
4. nwere ụmụaka nọ n'ụlọ akwụkwọ? (*Are there children at school?*)
5. Akwụkwọ ahụ dị n'elu oche ahụ. (*The book is on the top of the chair.*)
6. nwere Akwụkwọ ahụ dị n'elu oche ahụ? (*Is the book on the top of the chair?*)
7. Nzukọ dị n'ime ụlọ ọgbakọ. (*The meeting is in the conference room.*)
8. nwere Nzukọ dị n'ime ụlọ ọgbakọ? (*Is the meeting in the conference room?*)

These insertion rules in question formation are crucial for understanding how languages convey interrogative meaning through syntactic transformations. They provide a mechanism for speakers to seek information, express curiosity, or engage in conversation effectively.

Exercise

1. What are movement rules in transformative grammar, and why are they important?
2. How does dative movement function in Igbo language sentences?
3. Can you explain the concept of wh-movement and provide examples?
4. What is topicalization, and how does it contribute to sentence structure?
5. Could you elucidate the process of passivization and its significance in syntax?
6. What is extraposition in transformational grammar, and how does it improve sentence clarity?
7. What is verb phrase hopping, and how does it impact sentence structure in Igbo language?
8. What are deletion rules in transformative grammar, and how do they operate?
9. Can you explain NP deletion and provide examples?
10. How does VP deletion streamline sentence expression?
11. What is relativization, and how does it enhance sentence complexity?
12. Could you elucidate deletion based on indefiniteness and provide examples?
13. What are insertion rules in syntax, and how do they contribute to question formation?
14. Can you explain the insertion of pronouns in Igbo language questions?
15. How does the insertion of "O nwere" function in forming interrogative sentences in Igbo?
16. Why is the understanding of transformational grammar important for linguists and language learners?
17. How do movement rules and insertion rules differ in transformative grammar?
18. Can you discuss the implications of dative movement in cross-linguistic syntax?
19. What are the similarities and differences between passivization and extraposition?
20. How do deletion rules contribute to the economy of expression in language?

Chapter 8

Grammatical Functions (Ọrụ Ụtọasụsụ Igbo)

Grammatical function, which is often referred to as syntactic function, describes the function a word or phrase performs inside a particular sentence or clause. It contributes to the general construction and meaning of a phrase and aids in our understanding of how words relate to one another. Sometimes it is simply referred to as function. In Igbo language, grammatical function is primarily determined by a word's position in a sentence as well as by inflection (such as word endings).

There are various grammatical functions, such as subject, object, verb, adverbial, complement, modifier, and more, each serving a specific role in shaping the structure and meaning of sentences. This varied set of grammatical functions work together to produce clear, coherent, and subtle communication in language.

The meaning and overall structure of a sentence are greatly influenced by the placement of words, which is a critical aspect in determining the grammatical functions inside a phrase. In English, word location is frequently prioritized over individual inflections, in contrast to certain other languages where word forms may serve as indicators of roles.

In this language, how words are arranged in a phrase is crucial to communicating grammatical meaning. For example, the verb usually appears in the center, the object near the end, and the subject in the beginning. This positional arrangement aids in establishing a clear and coherent flow of information within the sentence.

A single word can have multiple meanings depending on where it is placed in a phrase, which makes the idea of word position very interesting. When the word "run" is used as the primary action, for instance, it becomes a verb ("She runs every morning"), but when it is used in a different context, it becomes a noun ("He went for a run"). This adaptability makes language use lively and subtle.

8.1 Subject:

The subject is a crucial grammatical function within a sentence, and it generally occupies a prominent position at the beginning. Its primary role is to represent the doer of the action or the entity about which something is being stated. Essentially, the subject is the main focus of the sentence, providing the audience with information about who or what is performing the action described in the sentence.

Example 1 :

a) **Agụ** na-achụ anụ n'abalị.   *"The tigers hunt prey at night."*
b) **Eze** na-agụ akwụkwọ.   *"Eze reads books."*
c) **Okọcha** na-agba bọọlụ   *"Okọcha play soccer."*
d) **Emeka** wuru ụlọ aja.   *"Emeka built a sandcastle."*
e) **Ugonna** riri ofe egwusi.   *"Ugonna ate egwusi soup."*

The subject in (a) above is Agụ (*The tigers*). Here, Agụ (*"The tigers"*) serve as the doers of the action, which is na-achụ anụ n'abalị (*hunting prey at night*). By identifying the subject, we understand that it is the Agụ (*tigers*) who are engaged in the hunting activity.

It's worth noting that the subject is not always a single word; it can also be a noun phrase, pronoun, or even a gerund. Regardless of its form, the subject plays a pivotal role in determining the overall structure and meaning of the sentence.

The following are examples of subjects that are pronouns:

a) **Ị** na-eme nke ọma.   *You are doing great.*
b) **Ọ** sere ọmaricha foto.   *She painted a beautiful picture.*
c) **Ha** lere ihe nkiri.   *They watched a movie.*
d) **O** dere akwụkwọ ozi.   *He wrote a letter.*
e) **Anyị** gara ụlọ ngosi ihe mgbe ochie.   *We visited the museum.*

The following are examples of subjects that are noun phrase:

a) **Ndị ukwe** bụrụ abụ olili ozu.   *The choir sang a funeral song.*
b) **Ndị ọrụ ụzọ** rụziri okporo ụzọ Aba .   *Construction workers repaired Aba Road.*
c) **Onye na-ere ahịa** resiri m ji.   *The market vendor sold yams to me.*
d) **Ụmụ akwụkwọ Aba** gara ọzụzụ ahụ.   *Students of Aba attended the training.*

e) **Ụlọ anụmanụ** dị na mpụga obodo.   *The zoo is located on the outskirts of town.*

The following are examples of subjects that are gerunds:

a) **Oriri** na-ewetara obodo ọṅụ.
   Feasting brings joy to the community.

b) Mmiri **ọṅụṅụ** dị mkpa maka ahụike.
   Drinking water is essential for health.

c) **Odide** ihe na-enyere aka igosipụta echiche na mmetụta uche.
   Writing helps express thoughts and emotions.

d) **Orire** nka ejiri aka mee na-akwado ndị ọrụ nka obodo.
   Selling handmade crafts supports local artisans.

e) **Ọmụmụ** nkà ọhụrụ na-eme ka mmadụ nwekwuo nghọta.
   Learning new skills broadens one's horizons.

f) **Ọsụsọ** bụ nzaghachi ebumpụta ụwa maka mgbatị ahụ.
   Sweating is a natural response to physical exertion.

g) **Obibi** ndụ dị mma na-achọ nhọrọ ndị mara mma.
   Living a healthy lifestyle requires conscious choices.

In the broader context of sentence construction, recognizing the subject is essential for understanding the relationships between different sentence elements. The subject establishes the point of view and sets the stage for the rest of the sentence components, including the verb and object. The subject essentially serves as the focal point around which the other components are centered, which enhances the sentence's coherence and clarity.

The subject in a sentence is the grammatical function that introduces the doer of the action, or the entity being discussed. Identifying the subject is key to grasping the fundamental meaning of a sentence and is an integral aspect of mastering language structure and communication.

8.2 Verb:

The verb holds a central and pivotal role as a grammatical function within a sentence. Its primary function is to represent the action or state expressed in the sentence, serving as the engine that propels the meaning forward. In the context of a sentence, the verb is often the element that conveys what the subject is doing or the condition it is in.

Example:

Agụ **na-achụ** anụ n'abalị. *"The tigers hunt prey at night," the verb is "hunt."*

This verb articulates the action performed by the subject, which, in this case, is the tigers. By identifying the verb, we gain insight into the specific activity taking place—in this instance, the act of hunting.

Verbs can encompass a wide range of actions, including physical activities (like "run," "eat," or "swim"), mental processes (such as "think," "believe," or "imagine"), or states of being (like "is," "am," or "are"). They play a crucial role in shaping the meaning of a sentence and are essential for conveying a dynamic and comprehensive description of events or conditions.

Examples sentences using different physical activity verbs:

a) Ọ **na-agba** ọsọ marathon na ngwụsị izu.
   She runs marathons on weekends.

b) Ọ **na-eri** nri ụtụtụ na-edozi ahụ.
   He eats a nutritious breakfast.

c) Ha **na-egwu** mmiri n'ọdọ mmiri n'oge okpomọkụ.
   They swim in the lake during the summer.

d) Ụmụaka **na-agba** bọọlụ mgbe ụlọ akwụkwọ gasịrị.
   The children play soccer after school.

e) Ana m **ebuli** ibu na ebe mgbatị ahụ maka ọzụzụ ike.
   I lift weights at the gym for strength training.

f) Ọ **na-agba** ígwè ka ọ rụọ ọrụ ka ọ **nọgide** na-arụsi ọrụ ike.
   He bikes to work to stay active.

g) Ha **na-agba egwú** salsa na etiti obodo.
   They dance salsa at the local community center.

Examples of sentences using mental processes verbs:

a) Ọ na-eche nke ọma banyere ajụjụ nkà ihe ọmụma.
She thinks deeply about philosophical questions.

b) O kwere na ike nke echiche ziri ezi.
He believes in the power of positive thinking.

c) Ha na-eche maka ụwa nke jupụtara na imepụta ihe na ihe ọhụrụ.
They imagine a world filled with creativity and innovation.

d) M ga-atụle echiche gị tupu ịme mkpebi.
I will consider your opinion before making a decision.

e) Anyị na-arọ nrọ maka ọdịnihu ka mma maka obodo anyị.
We dream of a better future for our community.

f) Ọ na-atụghari uche n'ihe ndụ pụtara ka ọ na-ele anya na kpakpando.
She contemplates the meaning of life while stargazing.

g) Ọ na-eji anya nke uche hụ ihe ịga nke ọma tupu nzukọ ndị dị mkpa.
He visualizes success before important meetings.

h) Ha na-atụghari uche n'ahụmihe ha ka ha nweta amamihe.
They reflect on their experiences to gain wisdom.

i) Ana m atụghari uche ihe omimi nke eluigwe na ụwa n'oge dị jụụ.
I ponder the mysteries of the universe during quiet moments.

j) Anyị na-atụ anya ihe ịma aka ndị na-abịa site na nchekwube dị mma.
We anticipate the upcoming challenges with optimism.

In these sentences, mental processes verbs are used to convey thoughts, beliefs, imaginations, considerations, and dreams.

Examples of sentences using states of being verbs:

1. Ọ bụ onye na-agụ egwu nwere nkà.   *She is a talented musician.*
2. Ha nwere obi ụtọ maka oriri na-abịanụ.   *They are excited about the upcoming feast.*
3. Ọ bụ nwa akwụkwọ mahadum.   *He is a university student.*

4. Anyị na-anya isi maka ihe anyị mezuru.   *We are proud of our achievements.*
5. Eluigwe chakere mgbe mmiri ozuzo gasịrị.   *The sky is clear after the rain.*
6. Ọ bụ onye ọrụ dị uchu.   *She is a diligent worker.*
7. Ha bụ ụmụnne nwere mmekọrịta siri ike.   *They are siblings with a strong bond.*
8. Enwere m ekele maka nkwado ndị enyi m.   *I am grateful for the support of my friends.*
9. Ha dị njikere maka ihe ịma aka ndị dị n'ihu.   *They are ready for the challenges ahead.*

In these sentences, states of being verbs (is, am, are) are used to describe or identify a state or condition.

Verbs contribute significantly to the overall structure of a sentence. They often dictate the tense, indicating whether the action occurred in the past, is happening in the present, or will occur in the future. Verbs can also alter the mood and tone of a sentence, adding levels of subtlety to the communication.

Understanding the verb is vital for comprehending the temporal and dynamic aspects of a sentence. It not only connects the subject to the rest of the sentence elements but also establishes a foundation for constructing coherent and meaningful language. Whether expressing a swift action or a prolonged state, the verb acts as the linchpin in sentence structure, anchoring the narrative and providing a clear sense of what is happening or being described.

8.3 Object:

The object of a sentence is a grammatical term used to identify a noun, pronoun, or noun phrase that receives the action of the verb or shows the result of the action. The objects in a sentence can help to convey additional information about the subjects and verbs of the sentences. There are two main types of objects, namely: direct and indirect objects.

A. Direct Object:

The direct object is a key component of a sentence that receives the action of the verb. It answers the question "what" or "whom" after an action verb. In the example Obi lụrụ Ada *"Obi married Ada,"* the verb is "married," and "Ada" is the direct object. Here, "Ada" is the entity directly affected by the action of marrying. Identifying the direct object provides additional clarity to the action, specifying the target or recipient.

Examples of direct speech:

Aga m ezute **gị** na ogige nnọkọta echi.   *"I will meet you at the park tomorrow."*
Ọ bụ **ihe ịtụnanya dị egwu**.   *"It is a fantastic surprise!"*
Ị nwere ike inyere **anyị** aka na **oru ngo ahụ**.   *"Can you help us with the project?"*

Ahụrụ m **ihe nkiri** a n'anya.	*"I love this movie."*
Mezue **ihe omume ahụ** ka ọ na-eru Fraịde.	*"Complete the assignment by Friday."*
Gịnị mere **ị** ji noọ ọdụ?	*"Why are you late?"*
Enwere m **ihe nzuzo** ịkọrọ **gị**.	*"I have a secret to share with you."*
Anyị meriri **asọmpi ahụ**!	*"We won the championship!"*

In these examples, the direct speech is enclosed within quotation marks and directly conveys the spoken words of the speaker.

B. Indirect Object:

The indirect object, on the other hand, indicates the recipient or beneficiary of the action and is typically accompanied by a direct object. It answers the questions "to whom" or "for whom" the action is performed. In the example "Sally gave Mary a gift," the verb is "gave," the direct object is "a gift," and the indirect object is "Mary." Here, "Mary" is the one receiving the gift, making her the indirect object. Recognizing the indirect object provides information about the secondary participant involved in the action, often indicating the direction or purpose of the giving.

Here are simple sentences with indirect objects:

a) O nyere **nwanne ya nwanyị** ihe olu mara mma.
   She gave her sister a beautiful necklace.

b) O zigara **enyi** ya akwụkwọ ozi n'ebe ezumike ahụ.
   He sent his friend a postcard from the vacation.

c) Emere m **nwanne** m nwoke sanwichi dị ụtọ.
   I made my brother a delicious sandwich.

d) Onye nkụzi ahụ nyere **ụmụ akwụkwọ** ihe omume.
   The teacher handed the students an assignment.

e) O nyere **onye ọrụ ibe ya** aka.
   He offered his colleague a helping hand.

f) Ọ kụziiri **nwa** ya ihe mmụta bara uru ná ndụ banyere ịkwụwa aka ọtọ.
   She taught her son a valuable life lesson about honesty.

g) Ha gosiri **ndị ọbịa** ha njem nleghari anya n'ebe ndị dị n'akụkọ ihe mere eme.
   They showed their guests a tour of the historical landmarks.

h) Edere m **enyi** m akwụkwọ ozi na-egosi obi ụtọ.
   I wrote my friend a heartfelt letter expressing gratitude.

In these sentences, the indirect objects (sister, friend, parents, brother, students, neighbors, colleague, son, guests, friend) receive the action of the verb.

Understanding the direct and indirect objects contributes significantly to the overall structure and meaning of a sentence. They strengthen and clarify the connections between the subject, verb, and other components. The identification of these objects improves communication by providing a more thorough representation of the dynamics involved in the given event.

While the direct object directly receives the action of the verb, the indirect object indicates the recipient or beneficiary of that action, often working in tandem to provide a comprehensive picture of the relationships within a sentence.

8.4 Complement:
A complement is a grammatical element that furnishes additional information about either the subject or the object within a sentence. These elements serve to further describe, identify, or characterize the subject or object, contributing to a more comprehensive understanding of the sentence.

A. Subject Complement:
A subject complement is a part of a sentence that follows a linking verb (such as bụ *"is/am/are/was/were,"* dị ka *"seem,"* etc.) and provides additional information about the subject. It completes the meaning of the subject by describing or renaming it..

Examples of subject complements:

1. **Ọ bụ onye nka nka.ihe osise.**   *She is a talented artist.*
   Isiahịrị: Ọ   *Subject: "She"*
   Mmeju keisiahịrị: onye nka.ihe osise   *Subject Complement: "a talented artist"*

2. **Ọ dị ka ike gwụrụ ya.**   *He seems exhausted.*
   Isiahịrị: Ọ   *Subject: "He"*
   Mmeju Keisiahịrị: ike gwụrụ ya.   *Subject Complement: "exhausted"*

3. **Achịcha ahụ na-esi ísì ụtọ.**   *The cake smells deliciously sweet.*

Isiahiri: Achicha ahu
Mmeju Kesiahiri: isi uto

Subject: "The cake"
Subject Complement: "deliciously sweet"

4. **Ha bụ ndị meriri n'asọmpi ahụ.**
Isiahiri: Ha
Mmeju Keisiahiri: ndị meriri n'asọmpi ahụ

They were the winners of the competition.
Subject: "They"
SC: "the winners of the competition"

5. **Okooko osisi ahụ na-egbuke na ìhè anyanwụ.**
Isiahiri: Okooko osisi ahụ
Mmeju Keisiahiri: na ìhè anyanwụ

The flowers look vibrant in the sunlight.
Subject: "The flowers"
SC: "vibrant in the sunlight"

6. **Ọ ghọrọ onye ọchụnta ego.**
Isiahiri: Ọ
Mmeju Keisiahiri: onye ọchụnta ego

He became an entrepreneur.
Subject: "He"
Subject Complement: "an entrepreneur"

7. **Akwụkwọ ahụ na-adọrọ mmasị ịgụ.**
Isiahiri: Akwụkwọ ahụ
Mmeju Keisiahiri: mmasị ịgụ

The book seems fascinating to read.
Subject: "The book"
Subject Complement: "fascinating to read"

There are two main types of subject complements: predicate adjectives and predicate nominatives.

A. *Predicate Adjective:* A subject complement that describes or modifies the subject. It typically follows a linking verb and provides information about the subject's characteristics or state. Example: Ọ bụ onye nkuzi *(She is a teacher)*. (Here, onye nkuzi *"a teacher"* is a predicate adjective describing the subject Ọ *"She."*)

B. *Predicate Nominative:* A subject complement that renames or identifies the subject. It follows a linking verb and serves to specify or redefine the subject. Example: Onye meriri bụ Ugochi *(The winner is Ugochi)*. (In this case, "Ugochi" is a predicate nominative, renaming the subject Onye meriri *"The winner."*)

In these sentences, the subject complements provide additional information about the subjects.

B. Object Complement:
An object complement, on the other hand, describes the direct object in a sentence. It provides further information or characteristics about the direct object. In the sentence O weere ihe nkiri ahụ ka ihe gara nke ọma *"(She considered the concert a success)."* the direct object is ihe nkiri ahụ "the concert," and the object complement is ihe gara nke ọma "a success." The object complement enhances our understanding of the direct object ihe nkiri ahụ "the concert" by stating how it went.

Object complements contribute to a more detailed and vivid portrayal of the action carried out on the direct object.

Examples of object complements:

1. **Ha họpụtara ya (dịka) onyeisi oche.**
   - Nnara: ya
   - Mmeju Kennara: onyeisi oche

   They elected her president.
   Direct Object: "her"
   Object Complement: "president."

2. **Anyị na-ahụ ọrụ ahụ dika ihe siri ike**
   - Nnara: ọrụ ahụ
   - Mmeju Kennara: ihe siri ike

   We find the task challenging.
   Direct Object: "the task"
   Object Complement: "challenging."

3. **Ha kpọrọ aha nwa ọhụrụ ahụ Amaka.**
   - Nnara: nwa ọhụrụ ahụ
   - Mmeju Kennara: Amaka

   They named the baby Amaka.
   Direct Object: "the baby"
   Object Complement: "Amaka"

4. **Echere m na atụmatụ a agaghị ekwe omume.**
   - Nnara: atụmatụ a
   - Mmeju Kennara: agaghị ekwe omume

   I deem the plan impractical.
   Direct Object: "the plan"
   Object Complement: "impractical"

5. **O kwuru na ụlọ ahụ enweghị nzerendụ.**
   - Nnara: ụlọ ahụ
   - Mmeju Kennara: enweghị nzerendụ

   He declared the building unsafe.
   Direct Object: "the building"
   Object Complement: "unsafe"

In each example, the object complement provides additional information or characteristics about the direct object in the sentence.

Complements play a vital role in enriching the content and meaning of a sentence. Subject complements expound upon the subject's attributes, while object complements provide additional details about the direct object. Recognizing and effectively using complements enhances the expressiveness of language, allowing for a more nuanced and vivid communication of ideas.

8.5 Adverbial:

An adverbial is a versatile grammatical element that modifies the verb, adjective, or another adverb within a sentence. It serves to provide additional information, specifying aspects such as time, place, manner, or degree, thereby enhancing the overall description of the action or quality.

Let's identify the adverbials in each of the sentences:

a. **Ọ naagba ọsọ ọsọ n'ụtụtụ.** — She runs fast in the morning.
   Adverbial: n'ụtụtụ *("in the morning")*

b. **Anyị naagba bọọlụ na mbara n'azụ ụlọ.** — We play soccer outside in the backyard.
   Adverbial: mbara n'azụ ụlọ *("outside in the backyard")*

c. **Mmiri ahụ zoro nke ukwuu n'elu ụlọ.** — The rain fell heavily on the roof.
   Adverbial: zoro nke ukwuu n'elu ụlọ *("heavily" and "on the roof")*

d. **Emechara m ọrụ ahụ ngwa ngwa.** — I finished the project quickly.
   Adverbial: ngwa ngwa *("quickly")*

e. **Anyanwụ naenwu nke ọma na mbara igwe.** — The sun shines brightly in the sky.
   Adverbial: nke ọma na mbara igwe *("brightly" and "in the sky")*

f. **Ha zutere na mberede n'ụlọ ọñụñụ.** — They met unexpectedly at the cafe.
   Adverbial: mberede n'ụlọ ọñụñụ *("unexpectedly" and "at the cafe")*

g. **Nnụnụ ndị ahụ naeti mkpu ọṅụ na osisi.** — The birds chirped happily in the trees.
   Adverbial: ọṅụ na osisi *("happily" and "in the trees")*.

h. **Ifufe fera nke ukwuu n'oge oké ifufe ahụ.** — The wind blew fiercely during the storm.
   Adverbial: nke ukwuu n'oge oké ifufe ahụ *("fiercely" and "during the storm")*

In each sentence, the adverbials provide additional information about the manner, time, place, or frequency of the actions described in the sentences.

Types of Adverbials:

1. Time Adverbial:
A time adverbial is a grammatical element that provides additional information about when an action takes place within a sentence. It serves to specify the timing or temporal context of the action, offering crucial details that enhance the overall understanding of the sentence.

Varieties of Time Adverbials:

A. Simple Time Adverbials: This is used to indicate specific points in time, such as taa *"today,"* echi *"tomorrow,"* or ụnyahụ *"yesterday."*

- Ha ga-ezute **echi**.	*They will meet **tomorrow**.*
- Anyị gara ụlọ ngosi ihe mgbe ochie **ụnyaahụ**.	*We went to the museum **yesterday**.*

In the sentence Ha ga-ezute **echi** *"They will meet tomorrow,"* the time adverbial is echi *"tomorrow."* Here, echi *"tomorrow"* functions as a time adverbial because it answers the question ole mgbe *"when"* the action of meeting will occur. This adverbial element adds a temporal dimension to the sentence, indicating that the meeting is scheduled for the future, specifically the next day.

B. Duration Adverbials: This is used to specify the length of time an action takes, such as na otu awa *"for an hour"* or kemgbe izu ụka gara aga *"since last week."*

- Ha rụrụ ọrụ ahụ **awa atọ**.	*They worked on the project **for three hours**.*
- A na m amụ Bekee **kemgbe afọ gara aga**.	*I have been studying English **since last year**.*
- Ihe nkiri ahụ mere **n'abalị dum**.	*The concert lasted **throughout the night**.*

C. Frequency Adverbials: This is used to indicate how often an action occurs, like mgbe niile *"always,"* ọtụtụ mgbe *"often,"* or occasionally *"occasionally."*

- Ọ na-aga ụlọ mgbatị ahụ **kwa ụbọchị**.	*He goes to the gym **every day**.*
- Anyị na-ezukọ **ugboro abụọ n'izu**.	*We meet **twice a week**.*
- Ọ na-enyocha ozi-e ya mgbe niile.	*She checks her email **regularly**.*

These examples illustrate how time adverbials provide specific temporal information within sentences. Simple time adverbials pinpoint particular moments, duration adverbials indicate how long an action lasts, and frequency adverbials describe how often an action occurs. Incorporating these adverbials enriches the sentences, offering a more detailed understanding of when an action takes place in relation to time.

Importance of Time Adverbials:
i. *Temporal Precision*: Time adverbials play a key role in conveying temporal precision within a sentence. They assist in specifying whether an action happened in the past, is occurring in the present, or is anticipated in the future.

ii. *Contextual Clarity*: Including time adverbials contributes to the clarity of the sentence by providing a context for the action. This is particularly important for avoiding ambiguity and ensuring that the reader or listener understands the intended timeframe.

iii. *Narrative Flow*: Time adverbials contribute to the smooth flow of a narrative by organizing events chronologically. They help structure information in a way that is coherent and logical, allowing for a more engaging and comprehensible storytelling experience.

Understanding and appropriately using time adverbials contribute to effective communication, allowing speakers and writers to convey not only the action itself but also the temporal context in which it occurs. This helps create a more vivid and precise depiction of events within the broader narrative or discourse.

2. Place Adverbial:
A place adverbial is a grammatical element that provides additional information about the location or spatial context of an action within a sentence. It serves to specify where the action takes place, offering essential details that contribute to a more complete understanding of the sentence.

Example:
O bi nso.   *"He lives nearby."*

In the sentence, O bi nso *"He lives nearby,"* the place adverbial is nso *"nearby."* This adverbial element answers the question ebee *"where"* the action of living occurs. By including nso *"nearby,"* the sentence provides a spatial context, indicating that the person's residence is near the speaker or the point of reference.

Importance of Place Adverbials:
i. *Spatial Precision*: Place adverbials help convey spatial precision within a sentence. They assist in defining the physical location where an action occurs, providing clarity to the reader or listener.

ii. *Contextual Detail*: Including place adverbials adds context to the action, preventing ambiguity and ensuring that the audience can visualize the specific setting of the event.

iii. *Narrative Coherence*: Place adverbials contribute to the overall coherence of a narrative by anchoring actions in specific locations. This helps create a vivid and immersive experience for the audience.

Varieties of Place Adverbials:
A. *Simple Place Adverbials*: Simple place adverbials are grammatical elements that indicate a specific location or place within a sentence. These adverbials provide information about where the action is taking place or where an object is located. They are often simple and straightforward, offering clarity regarding the spatial context of the action or the position of the subject.

Examples of simple place adverbials include words such as ebe a *"here,"* Ebe ahụ *"there,"* and ebe nile *"everywhere."* These adverbials help answer the question ebee *"where"* in a sentence and contribute to a more detailed understanding of the location in which an action occurs, or an object is situated.

For example:

    a) Nwamba na-ehi ụra ebe a.   *The cat is sleeping **here**.*
    b) Ọchị ahụ na-adaba ebe niile n'ime ụlọ ahụ.   *The laughter echoed **everywhere** in the room.*
    c) E liri akụ ahụ ebe a.   *The treasure is buried **here**.*
    d) Ha zutere n' ebennọkọta ahụ.   *They met **at the park**.*
    e) Anyị nwere ike ịhụ udo na jụụ n'ebe ahụ.   *We can find peace and quiet **there**.*
    f) Anyị na-akụ okoko osisi n'ebe ahụ.   *We planted flowers **there**.*

B *Directional Adverbials*: Directional adverbials are grammatical elements that provide information about the direction in which an action is taking place or the movement of someone or something within a sentence. These adverbials specify the orientation or path of the action, offering additional details about the spatial dynamics of the situation.

Examples of directional adverbials include terms such as mgbagoro *"upstairs,"* mgbadata *"downstairs,"* and ngaruu ihu osimiri *"towards the river."* These adverbials help convey the direction in which a person is moving, or an action is happening, contributing to a more vivid and precise description of the scene.

For example:

    a) Ọ gbagoro **mgbago** ụlọ elu ka ọ bute akwụkwọ ya.
    *She went **upstairs** to fetch her book.*

    b) Ha jere ije **ngaru nso** osimiri maka ehihie izu ike.
    *They walked **towards the river** for a relaxing afternoon.*

    c) Ọ rigoro **mgbago** elu ọnụ ụlọ ya.
    *She climbed **upstairs** to her bedroom.*

    d) Osimiri ahụ na-esi n'ugwu **gbada** n'ala.
    *The river flows **downstairs** from the mountains.*

e) Ha jere ije **ngaru nso** osimiri ahụ maka njem udo.
   *They walked **towards the river** for a peaceful stroll.*

In these examples, mgbago *"upstairs,"* mgbada *"downstairs,"* and ngaru nso *"towards the river"* function as directional adverbials, providing essential information about the direction of movement or action within the given context.

C. *Distance Adverbials*: Distance adverbials are grammatical elements that convey information about the physical distance between objects, locations, or individuals within a sentence. These adverbials help specify how far or close something is in relation to a reference point, offering valuable details about the spatial arrangement of the elements mentioned.

Examples of distance adverbials include expressions like tere aka/dị anya *"far away,"* nso nso *"close by,"* or n'ime ntoanya ije *"within walking distance."* These adverbials provide a sense of the proximity or remoteness of the specified locations or objects, enhancing the overall spatial context within the sentence.

For example:

a) Ụlọ ahịa nri kacha nso **dị anya** na mpaghara anyị.
   The nearest grocery store is *far away* from our neighborhood.

b) Ebe a na-eme achịcha **dị nso**, dị n'akụkụ ụsọ.
   The bakery is *close by*, just around the corner.

c) Ụlọ oriri na ọṅụṅụ anyị dị **n'ime ntoanya ije** site n'ọdụ ụgbọ oloko.
   Our hotel is *within walking distance* of the train station.

d) Ebe ọdụ mmanụ ụgbọala kacha nso **dị anya** ebe a.
   The nearest gas station is *far away* from here.

e) Kafe dị **nso**, dị nnọọ n'akụkụ ụsọ.
   The cafe is *close by*, just around the corner.

f) Ụlọ oriri na ọṅụṅụ anyị dị **n'ime ntoanya ije** site n'ụsọ osimiri.
   Our hotel is *within walking distance* of the beach.

g) Ụlọ ahịa ahụ dị **nnọọ n'akụkụ ụsọ**.

The store is ***just around the corner***.

In these examples, tere aka/dị anya *"far away,"* nso nso *"close by,"* or n'ime ntoanya ije *"within walking distance"* function as distance adverbials, offering information about the physical distance between the reference point and the specified locations or objects.

These examples illustrate how simple place adverbials indicate specific locations, directional adverbials specify the direction of an action, and distance adverbials describe the distance from a reference point. Incorporating these adverbials adds valuable spatial context to sentences, making them more descriptive and precise.

Place adverbs provide the physical environment in which activities take place, enabling a more thorough description of those acts when they are included in sentences. This improves the language's richness and distinctiveness, which makes it more interesting and educational.

3. Manner Adverbial:
A manner adverbial is a grammatical element that provides additional information about how an action is carried out within a sentence. It serves to describe the manner or method in which the action occurs, offering crucial details that contribute to a more complete understanding of the sentence.

Example:
- a) O jiri **nlezianya** dozie nsogbu ahụ.   *She solved the problem **carefully**.*
- b) Ọ rụchara ọrụ ahụ **nke ọma**.   *He completed the project **efficiently**.*
- c) Ha na-agba egwu nke **ugwu dị**.   *They danced **gracefully**.*
- d) O **ji obi ike** zaa ajụjụ ahụ.   *She answered the question **with confidence**.*
  (Phrase)

In the sentence O jiri nlezianya dozie nsogbu ahụ *"She solved the problem carefully,"* the manner adverbial is nlezianya *"carefully."* This adverbial element answers the question kedu *"how"* the action of solving the problem is performed. By including nlezianya *"carefully,"* the sentence provides insight into the careful and meticulous approach used to solve the problem.

Importance of Manner Adverbials:
i. *Descriptive Precision*: Manner adverbials add descriptive precision to a sentence by conveying the specific way in which an action is executed.

ii. *Contextual Detail*: Including manner adverbials adds context to the action, providing insights into the attitude, style, or method employed in carrying out the activity.

iii. *Enhanced Communication*: Manner adverbials contribute to effective communication by allowing speakers or writers to convey not only the action itself but also the quality or style with which it is performed.

Incorporating manner adverbials in sentences provides a more nuanced portrayal of actions, allowing for a detailed depiction of the approach, style, or attitude with which the action is carried out. This enhances the expressiveness and clarity of language, making it more engaging and informative.

4. *Degree Adverbial*:
A degree adverbial is a grammatical element that provides additional information about the intensity or degree of an action or quality within a sentence. It serves to specify the extent or intensity to which the action is performed, or the quality is expressed, offering crucial details that contribute to a more complete understanding of the sentence.

Examples:
a) nwere **oke** nkà.
   *He is **extremely** talented.*

b) mere nke oma **n'ụzọ pụrụ iche** n'ule.
   *She performed **exceptionally** well in the exam. (Adverb of Degree)*

c) Ihe nkiri ahụ na-atọ ụtọ **n'ụzọ dị ịrịba ama**.
   *The movie was **remarkably** entertaining. (Intensifier)*

d) Ihu igwe dị **oke** ọkụ maka egwuregwu ahụ.
   *The weather is **too** hot for the game. (Adverb of Degree)*

In the sentence O nwere oke nka *"He is extremely talented,"* the degree adverbial is oke *"extremely."* This adverbial element answers the question ruo n'ókè ole *"to what extent"* or ole *"how much"* the quality of talent is possessed by the person. By including oke *"extremely,"* the sentence emphasizes the high degree or level of talent the person possesses.

Importance of Degree Adverbials:
i. *Intensity Specification*: Degree adverbials help convey the intensity or strength of an action or quality, providing a nuanced understanding of the degree to which it is expressed.

ii. *Contextual Detail*: Including degree adverbials adds context to the sentence, offering insights into the magnitude or scale of the action or quality being described.

iii. *Enhanced Communication*: Degree adverbials contribute to effective communication by allowing speakers or writers to convey not only the action or quality itself but also the level of intensity or degree associated with it.

Incorporating degree adverbials in sentences provides a more nuanced and precise expression of the intensity or degree associated with actions or qualities. This enhances the expressiveness and specificity of language, allowing for a more vivid and detailed communication of ideas.

Adverbials contribute to the richness and precision of language by providing details that go beyond the basic action or description. Understanding the various types of adverbials and their functions enhances one's ability to convey specific nuances in communication, making sentences more vivid and expressive.

8.6 Inflection:
Verbs play a central role in Igbo grammar. They host most of the language's morphology and are considered the most basic category. Many processes in Igbo can derive new words from verbs, but few can derive verbs from words of other classes. In Igbo, verbs undergo inflections to convey various grammatical features, such as tense, aspect, mood, and negation. Different verb forms are used to indicate whether an action has occurred in the past, present, or future, the manner in which the action took place, or whether the action is habitual or completed. For example:

- Infinitive: "iri" (to eat)
- Simple Present: "Ana m eri" (I eat)
- Simple Past: "E riri m" (I ate)
- Future: "Aga m eri" (I will eat)

In this way, inflections on verbs in Igbo not only communicate the temporal aspects of actions but also convey information about how the action unfolds or is perceived.

Examples of how Igbo verbs can undergo inflections to convey different grammatical features:

a) Ọ tetaghị n'isi ụtụtụ. *He did not wake up early.*
b) Ọ naghị eme njem. *He is not traveling.*
c) Ọ ga-akpọ m echi. *He will call me tomorrow.*
d) Ana m agụ akwụkwọ. *I am reading a book.*
e) Ha na-egwu mmiri n'osimiri. *They swim in the river.*
f) Anyị ga-abịa n'isi ụtụtụ. *We will come early.*

g) Anyị ga-ezute echi.   *We will meet tomorrow.*
h) Ị na-ejide aka m.   *You are holding my hand.*
i) Ị na-ehicha ụlọ.   *You clean the house.*
j) Ị na-agba egwu nke ọma.   *You dance well.*
k) Ị kpọtere m n'isi ụtụtụ.   *You woke me up early.*

In these sentences, you can see how Igbo verbs are inflected to express various grammatical features such as tense, aspect, mood, and negation. In Igbo, the inflectional system plays a central role in shaping the grammatical functions of verbs, nouns, and adjectives. The intricacies of these inflections allow for a rich and nuanced expression of ideas, facilitating clear communication within the context of the Igbo language. The relationship between inflections and grammatical functions in Igbo showcases the language's complexity and its capacity to convey precise meanings through morphological modifications.

Exercise

1. What is the primary role of grammatical function in a sentence or clause?
2. How does word arrangement contribute to determining grammatical functions in Igbo language?
3. Explain the significance of identifying the subject in a sentence?
4. Provide examples of subjects in Igbo that are noun phrases.
5. What are the various types of verbs and how do they contribute to sentence meaning?
6. Explain the difference between direct and indirect objects in a sentence.
7. Give 5 examples of sentences with indirect objects.
8. What is a complement, and how does it enhance sentence structure?
9. Describe the role of subject complements in providing additional information about the subject.
10. Provide examples of sentences with subject complements.
11. What is an object complement, and how does it contribute to sentence meaning?
12. Distinguish between predicate adjectives and predicate nominatives in subject complements?
13. Give 5 examples of sentences with object complements.
14. How do complements enrich the content and meaning of a sentence?
15. Why is it important to recognize and understand grammatical functions in language?
16. How do adverbials enhance the overall description of actions or qualities within a sentence?
17. Provide 2 examples of time adverbials and explain how they contribute to specifying temporal context within sentences.
18. What role do place adverbials play in providing spatial context within sentences? Give 5 examples to illustrate.
19. Explain the importance of including manner adverbials in sentences. How do they contribute to communication?
20. Give 5 examples of degree adverbials and discuss how they convey intensity or degree within sentences.
21. In what ways do verbs in Igbo undergo inflections to convey grammatical features such as tense, aspect, mood, and negation?
22. How does the inflectional system in Igbo contribute to the language's ability to convey precise meanings?
23. Provide examples of inflected Igbo verbs and explain the grammatical features they convey.
24. Compare and contrast the functions of adverbials and verb inflections in enhancing sentence structure and meaning.
25. Discuss the significance of understanding adverbials and verb inflections in both Igbo and English grammar for effective communication.

Chapter 9

Heads and Modifiers (*Ọdịdị Ụtọasụsụ* nke *Nkebiahịrị Igbo*)

The relationship between heads and modifiers is crucial for analyzing the structure of sentences and phrases. Different types of phrases, such as noun phrases, verb phrases, and adjective phrases, have a head that defines the main element's syntactic and semantic properties. Modifiers enhance and refine the meaning of the head, contributing to the overall richness and specificity of language expression. This structural understanding is foundational for syntactic analysis and helps linguists describe how words function within sentences and larger linguistic structures.

9.1 Heads, Modifiers, and Meanings
Head-Modifier Construction (Myiri n'ụdị nrụaka/mọdịfaya na isi aha):
The process of "Head-Modifier Construction" is another method of language classification. In the middle of the 20th century, Joseph Greenberg proposed a connection between the Head-modifier pattern and the fundamental functional elements, such as SVO. This suggestion indicates that there are two patterns that can occur in the head-modifier construction: either the head comes first, or the modifier comes first. There are three patterns of considerations when analyzing Head-Modifier construction. They are:

1. Verb/Object construction
2. Noun/Adjective construction
3. Noun/Demonstrative determiner construction
4. Adposition/Noun Phrase construction

(a). Verb/Object construction: In many languages, the verb determines the choice of object and sometimes the case of the objects. As a pattern of arrangement, verbs in relation to object can be considered as the head in Verb/object construction and their objects viewed as their modifiers. For

example: see (hụ), eat (ri),

a) *(to) see the movie [is why he went to the theatre].*
   (ije) hụ ihe nkiri [bụ ihe mere o ji gaa ụlọ ihe nkiri].

b) *(to) eat garri [is why he went to her grandma].*
   (ije) hụ ri garri [bụ ihe mere o ji gaa ụlọ nne nne ya].

(b). Noun/Adjective construction: the relationship between noun and choice of adjective, case of adjective and gender can be used to express Head/Modifier construction of language classification. Nouns in this relationship are often the head and the adjective their modifiers. Examples of adjectives in Igbo are: Big (nnukwu/buru ibu), Small/little (obere), Dark/Black (ojii), White/Clean/bright/light (ọcha), New (ọhụ), Good (ọma), Bad (ọjọọ), Ugly (njọ), old (ochie), Long/tall (ogologo), Dirty (unyi).

English	*Igbo*	*Pattern*
Dirty cloth	ákwà ruru unyi	(N/A)
New book	Akwụkwọ ọhụ	(N/A)
Old chair	Oche ochie	(N/A)
President-elect	Onyeisi oche ahọpụtara	(N/A)
Ugly man	nwoke jọrọ njọ	(N/A)
White cloth	ákwà ọcha	(N/A)

In some occasion the adverb precedes the noun in the relationship to allow meaningful expression. For example:

Tall man	Ogologo nwoke	(A/N)
Long stick	Ogologo osisi	(A/N)

(c). Noun/Demonstrative determiner construction: the relationship between nouns in terms of choice of demonstrative determiners can be used express in the form of Head/Modifier construction of language classification. The noun in this case is the head and the adjective their modifiers. For example:

English Construction		*Igbo Construction*	
That woman	D/N	Nwanyị ahụ	N/D
The sheep	D/N	Atụrụ ahụ	N/D
This man	D/N	Nwoke a	N/D
This book	D/N	Akwụkwọ a	N/D

(d) Preposition/Noun Phrase construction: preposition determines the choice and may be the case of the noun phrase. Therefore, it proceeds the noun phraseas the head as the noun phrase funcrions as the modifier in the construction. Examples of preposition in Igbo language are: at (n'/na), with (soro/wiri/yiri), for (maka), to (n'/na), before (tupu), because of (n'ihi/maka na), during (mgbe), under (n'okpuru), between (n'etiti), in/inside (n'ime), near (nso/n'akuku), beside (n'akuku). above (n'elu), about (ihe dika), and (na).

English	Igbo	Pattern
Under the tree	n'okpuru osisi	P/NP
Inside the room	n'ime ulo	P/NP
Near the bridge	nso akwa mmiri	P/NP
Near the market	n'akuku ahia	P/NP
Because of his wife	n'ihi nwunye ya	P/NP

9.2 Complements and Adjuncts: Enhancing Structure

Complements: Complements are words, phrases, or clauses that complete the meaning of a sentence. They are essential for the sentence to convey its intended message. There are two main types of complements:

Subject Complements: These follow linking verbs (such as bu/di ka, *"be," "become," "seem,"* etc.) and provide additional information about the subject. The most common type of subject complement is the predicate nominative (which renames or identifies the subject) or the predicate adjective (which describes the subject).

Example:
   Ọ bụ dọkịta/dibịa bekee.   *"She is a doctor."*
   (Here, dọkịta *"doctor"* is the predicate nominative.)

Object Complements: These follow certain verbs (such as "mee," "kpọọ," "tule," *"make," "call," "consider,"* etc.) and provide information about the direct object. They often describe or rename the object.
Example:
   Ha họpụtara ya (dị ka) onyeisi oche. *"They elected her president."*
   (Here, onyeisi oche *"president"* is the object complement.)

Adjuncts: Adjuncts are optional elements in a sentence that add extra information but are not necessary for the sentence to be grammatically complete. They can appear in various positions within a sentence (beginning, middle, or end) and serve different purposes:

Adverbial Adjuncts: An adverbial adjunct, in linguistics, is a term used to describe an adverbial that provides additional information in a sentence but is not a required or integral part of the sentence's structure. Adverbial adjuncts often modify the verb and can convey details such as time, place, manner, frequency, degree, or condition. Unlike essential sentence elements, such as the subject, verb, and object, adverbial adjuncts are considered optional and can be omitted without grammatically affecting the core structure of the sentence. They modify verbs, adjectives, or other adverbs. They answer questions like "olee," "mgbe," "ebee," ma ọ bụ " gịnị kpatara ya" (*how, when, where, or why*).

Example:
a) Ọ mere ọsọ ọsọ ka ọ zute bọs *"He ran quickly to catch the bus."*
b) Ọ bụrụ abụ mara mma. *"She sang beautifully."*

In these sentences, ọsọ ọsọ *"quickly,"* mara mma *"beautifully"* is an adverbial adjunct. It provides additional information about how she sang but is not necessary for the basic structure of the sentence.

Adverbial adjuncts can appear in various positions within a sentence and contribute to the overall meaning and context. They play a role in specifying or enhancing the circumstances surrounding the action or state expressed by the verb.

Adjectival Adjuncts: An adjectival adjunct, in linguistics, refers to an adjectival element that provides additional information or description in a sentence. Adjectival adjuncts modify nouns or pronouns, adding details to enhance the specificity or quality of the referred noun. Unlike essential sentence elements such as the subject, verb, or object, adjectival adjuncts are not required for the fundamental grammatical structure and can be omitted without affecting the sentence's core meaning.

Example:
a) Ụgbọ ala **uhie** ahụ gbadara n'okporo ụzọ awara awara ahụ.
   "The red car sped down the highway."

b) Nwanyị ahụ **yi uwe uhie** bụ nwanne m nwanyị.
   "The woman in the red dress is my sister."

In this sentence, yi uwe uhie *"in the red dress"* is an adjectival adjunct modifying the noun "woman." It specifies further information about the woman, describing the color of her dress.

Adjectival adjuncts can take various forms and can appear before or after the noun they modify. They contribute to the overall richness and specificity of language by providing additional details or characteristics associated with the nouns they modify.

Nominal Adjuncts: A nominal adjunct, in linguistics, is an element that functions as an adjective, providing additional information or attributes to a noun within a sentence. Nominal adjuncts, like adjectives, modify and describe nouns, contributing to the specificity or characterization of the referred noun. They are not essential to the core grammatical structure of a sentence and can be omitted without fundamentally altering its meaning.

Example:
   a) Ọbá akwụkwọ ahụ kọleji na-emeghe **ruo etiti abalị**.
      "The college library is open until midnight."

   b) Akwụkwọ **dị na ebendebe akwụkwọ** bụ nke m.
      "The book on the shelf is mine."

In this sentence, dị na ebendebe akwụkwọ *"on the shelf"* is a nominal adjunct modifying the noun "book." It provides additional information about the location of the book.

Nominal adjuncts can take various forms, including prepositional phrases, participial phrases, or relative clauses. They play a crucial role in enriching the language by specifying details related to the noun in question.

In summary, complements are crucial for sentence structure, while adjuncts enhance the meaning by providing extra context.

9.3 Clauses: Building Blocks of Communication

A clause is a group of words that includes a subject and a verb (predicate) and forms a complete thought. Clauses can function independently as a sentence or as part of a larger sentence. They are the building blocks of effective communication, allowing us to convey complex ideas and relationships within sentences. There are two main types of clauses: independent clauses and dependent clauses.

1. Independent Clause:
   An independent clause, also known as a main clause, is a complete thought that can stand alone as a sentence. It contains a subject and a predicate, expressing a complete idea.

Example:
>Ọ gara n'ụlọ ahịa ahụ.   *"She went to the store."*

2. Dependent Clause:

A dependent clause, also known as a subordinate or relative clause, cannot stand alone as a complete sentence because it does not express a complete thought. It relies on an independent clause to form a complete sentence.

Examples:
  a) **N'agbanyeghị na ike gwụrụ ya**, ọ gara nzukọ ahụ.
     "Although she was tired, she attended the meeting."

  b) **N'ihi na mmiri na-ezo**, ọ nọ n'ime ụlọ.
     "Because it was raining, she stayed indoors."

The dependent clause N'ihi na mmiri na-ezo *"Because it was raining"* relies on the main clause to convey a complete thought. (This is a dependent clause because it doesn't provide a complete thought on its own.)

Clauses can be combined to create complex sentences. For instance, a complex sentence may consist of an independent clause and one or more dependent clauses. Understanding clauses is essential for analyzing sentence structure and constructing clear and effective sentences in English.

9.4 Projection from Lexical Heads to Phrases

Projection from lexical heads to phrases is the extension or projection of meaning and structure from central lexical heads. The process involves forming phrases around these central elements, which are often words carrying the primary meaning of the phrase. This projection is essential for imbuing the phrases with both semantic (meaning related) and syntactic (structure related) characteristics.

1. Projection:
Refers to the extension or development of certain features (meaning and structure, in this context) from one element to another.

Example:
Original Sentence: Ikwiikwii maara ihe tiri mkpu n'ime abalị
                       "The wise owl hooted loudly in the night."

In this sentence, we can identify the following elements:

Lexical Head: Ikwiikwii *"owl"* (the central element carrying the primary meaning)
Features: "maara ihe," "tiri mkpu," "n'ime abalị"
"wise," "hooted loudly," "in the night" (modifiers or additional information)

Projection: The features (meaning and structure) extend or project from the central element Ikwiikwii *"owl"* to form the complete phrase Ikwiikwii maara ihe tiri mkpu n'ime abalị *"The wise owl hooted loudly in the night."* The phrase, as a whole, gains meaning and structure by incorporating these projected features.

2. Lexical Heads:
"The central elements in a phrase that carry the primary meaning" refers to the crucial components within a phrase that convey the primary or central idea. These elements are called lexical heads.

Example:
In a noun phrase like nnukwu oroma odo odo ahụ *"the big yellow orange,"* the phrase consists of the following elements:

Determiner: ahụ *"the"*
Adjectives: nnukwu *"big,"* odo odo *"red"*
Noun: oroma *"orange"*

In this example, the lexical head is the noun oroma *"orange."* It is the central element that carries the primary meaning of the phrase. While the adjectives and articles provide additional information, the central focus or primary idea of the noun phrase is conveyed by the lexical head oroma *"orange."*

3. Phrases:
A phrase is a collection of words that operates as a cohesive unit within a sentence. It functions as a single entity and contributes to the overall structure and meaning of the sentence. Phrases are often composed of a central element called the head, which is accompanied by other words that modify or complement it.

For example, consider the sentence:

Nwa akwụkwọ ahụ dị uchu mezuru ọrụ ahụ nke na-ama aka.
"The diligent student completed the challenging assignment."

The words nwa akwụkwọ ahụ dị uchu *"the diligent student"* form a noun phrase, and mezuru ọrụ ahụ na-ama aka *"completed the challenging assignment"* constitutes a verb phrase.

4. Head and Modifiers:
In the noun phrase nwa akwụkwọ ahụ dị uchu *"the diligent student,"* the head is the noun nwa akwụkwọ *"student,"* and the articles ahụ *"the"* and dị uchu *"diligent"* serve as modifiers providing additional information about the student.

In the verb phrase mezuru ọrụ ahụ nke na-ama aka *"completed the challenging assignment,"* the head is the verb mezuru *"completed,"* and the words ọrụ ahụ nke na-ama aka *"the challenging assignment"* function as its object, with ahụ *"the"* and na-ama aka *"challenging"* acting as modifiers.

The phrase's head and its modifiers work together to improve the sentence's distinctiveness and variety of meaning. To grasp sentence structure and successfully express thoughts in language, one must have a thorough understanding of phrases.

5. Pivotal Element:
The process of projection from lexical heads to phrases is highlighted in the examples above as a crucial and essential component of language structure. It emphasizes how important this procedure is as a fundamental and essential part of the larger framework of language formation.

The phrase emphasizes how important the projection process is in creating cohesive and meaningful statements by referring to it as a significant or central element. It implies that the efficient projection of meaning and structure from these key lexical heads is a major factor in the successful formation of phrases. This acknowledgement emphasizes how important the projection process is to the understanding and evaluating language structure.

In summary, the method outlined entails constructing sentences around important lexical heads while making sure that these sentences take on structure and meaning. This is essential for creating coherent and meaningful language sentences.

9.5 Differences between Complements and Modifiers
Modifiers and complements are two separate language components with different purposes in sentences. The following are the main distinctions between modifiers and complements:

1. Function:
Complements: Complements are necessary components that complete the meaning of the main element in a sentence. They often fill essential roles such as the object of a verb or the subject complement, providing crucial information.

Example:
Direct Object: **Ọ na-agụ akwụkwọ**. *"She read a book."*
Subject Complement: **Ọ bụ dọkịta.** *"He is a doctor."*

Modifiers: Modifiers, on the other hand, are optional elements that provide additional information about a word or phrase, enhancing its meaning. Modifiers are not indispensable for the basic structure of a sentence.

Example:
Adjective Modifiers: **Ụlọ elu ahụ** *"The tall building"*
Adverb Modifiers **Ọ na-eje ije ọsọ ọsọ** *"She walks quickly."*

2. Necessity:
Complements: Complements are often required to make a sentence grammatically and semantically complete. Omitting a necessary complement may result in an incomplete or unclear sentence.

Direct Object (Object of the Verb): **Ọ na-agụ akwụkwọ.** *She read a book.*

The direct object akwụkwọ *"a book"* is necessary to complete the meaning of the verb na-agụ *"read."*

Subject Complement (Predicate Nominative): **Ọ bụ dọkịta.** *He is a doctor.*

The subject complement dọkịta *"a doctor"* is necessary to describe and complete the subject Ọ *"He."*

Modifiers: Modifiers are optional and can be added or removed without fundamentally altering the sentence's grammatical structure.

Adjective Modifier (Modifying a Noun): **Ụlọ elu ahụ** *the tall building.*

The adjective modifier elu *"tall/high"* is optional and provides additional information about the noun ụlọ *"building."*

Adverb Modifier (Modifying a Verb): **Ọ na-eje ije ọsọ ọsọ.** *She walks quickly.*
The adverb modifier ọsọ ọsọ *"quickly"* is optional and gives more information about the verb ije

"walks."

Adjective Modifier (Modifying a Pronoun): Ha riri osikapa dị ụtọ. *They ate delicious rice.* The adjective modifier ụtọ *"delicious"* is optional and enhances the pronoun osikapa *"rice."*

Adverb Modifier (Modifying an Adjective):

Ihe nkiri a na-atọ ụtọ nkiri nke ukwuu. *The movie is very entertaining.*

The adverb modifier nke ukwuu *"very"* is optional and modifies the adjective ụtọ nkiri *"entertaining."*

In each example, complements are highlighted as necessary elements to complete the meaning of the main elements in the sentence. Modifiers, on the other hand, are presented as optional elements providing additional information that can be included or excluded without fundamentally changing the sentence's structure.

3. Placement:
Complements: Complements are often positioned immediately after the verb or linked to the subject in a sentence.

For example:
   a) **Ọ na-agụ akwụkwọ.** *She read a book.*
The direct object akwụkwọ "a book" comes after the verb na-agụ *"read."*

   b) **Ọ bụ dọkịta.**   *He is a doctor.*
The subject complement dọkịta *"a doctor"* is linked to the subject Ọ *"He."*

Modifiers: Modifiers can be found in various positions within a sentence, modifying nouns (before or after), verbs, adjectives, or other adverbs.

For example:
   a) **Ụlọ elu ahụ.** *The tall building.*
The adjective modifier elu *"tall/high"* comes before the noun ụlọ *"building."*

   b) **Ọ na-eje ije ọsọ ọsọ.**   *She walks quickly.*
The adverb modifier ọsọ ọsọ *"quickly"* comes after the verb ije *"walks."*

   c) **Ha riri osikapa dị ụtọ.**   *They ate delicious rice.*

The adjective modifier ụtọ "delicious" comes before the noun osikapa *"rice."*

   d) **Ihe nkiri a na-atọ ụtọ nkiri nke ukwuu**.   *The movie is very entertaining.*
The adverb modifier nke ukwuu *"very"* comes before the adjective ụtọ nkiri *"entertaining."*

In these examples, complements are highlighted for their typical placement after the verb or linked to the subject. Modifiers, on the other hand, are shown in various positions, illustrating that they can appear before or after the words they modify.

In summary, complements are essential components that complete the meaning of the main element in a sentence, while modifiers provide optional additional information. Complements are often necessary for sentence completeness, while modifiers enhance and refine meaning without being obligatory.

Exercise

1. What is the significance of understanding the relationship between heads and modifiers in linguistic analysis?
2. Describe Joseph Greenberg's proposal regarding the connection between the Head-modifier pattern and fundamental functional elements.
3. Explain the three patterns of consideration when analyzing Head-Modifier construction.
4. How does the Verb/Object construction contribute to understanding language classification?
5. Provide examples of Noun/Adjective construction in Igbo language and explain their significance.
6. What role do Demonstrative determiners play in Noun/Demonstrative determiner construction?
7. How does Preposition/Noun Phrase construction contribute to the structure of sentences?
8. Define complements and provide examples of both Subject Complements and Object Complements.
9. Distinguish between Subject Complements and Object Complements with examples.
10. What are adjuncts in linguistic analysis, and how do they enhance sentence structure?
11. Provide examples of Adverbial Adjuncts and explain their function within sentences.
12. Differentiate between Adverbial Adjuncts and Adjectival Adjuncts with examples.
13. How do Adjectival Adjuncts contribute to sentence structure and meaning?
14. Explain the role of Nominal Adjuncts in enriching language expression.
15. Define clauses and discuss their importance in communication.
16. Distinguish between Independent Clauses and Dependent Clauses with examples.
17. How are clauses combined to create complex sentences?
18. Describe the process of projection from lexical heads to phrases.
19. What are the key elements involved in the projection from lexical heads to phrases?
20. Differentiate between complements and modifiers, highlighting their functions, necessity, and placement within sentences.

Chapter 10

Constituent Structure (Ndoko Akụrụngwa)

10.1 Definition of Constituent structure:

Constituent structure, in linguistics, refers to the hierarchical arrangement of words and phrases within a sentence. It involves breaking down a sentence into its fundamental components, or constituents, and representing them in a structured and organized manner. The concept of constituent structure is crucial for understanding the syntax, or sentence structure, of a language.

Key points about constituent structure:

10.1.1 *Hierarchical Arrangement:* The concept of hierarchical arrangement in constituent structure underscores the acknowledgment that sentences possess a structured and layered organization. Within this framework, larger units encapsulate or encompass smaller ones, creating a hierarchical relationship among the various components of a sentence.

In linguistic analysis, this hierarchical arrangement reflects the idea that sentences are not merely linear sequences of words but rather intricate structures where elements are nested within one another. The hierarchical nature implies that certain constituents serve as building blocks or foundational units, while others are constructed upon them, forming a tiered structure.

For example,

Nwata nwanyị ahụ gara ahịa ahụ.   *"The girl went to that market."*

In the sentence, Nwata nwanyi ahụ gara ahịa ahụ. *"The girl went to that market,"* the hierarchical arrangement is evident as we can identify larger units like the entire sentence, and within it, smaller units such as noun phrases Nkebiokwu Keaha (NKA) *"Noun Phrase (NP)"* and Nkebiokwu Kengwaa (NKN) *"Verb Phrases (VP)."* This layered organization allows us to comprehend how individual words and phrases contribute to the overall structure of the sentence.

The recognition of hierarchical arrangement in constituent structure is essential for understanding the complexity and systematic organization of language. It provides a framework for linguistic analysis, aiding in the description and representation of how different linguistic elements relate to one another within a sentence.

10.1.2 *Consistency in Grouping:* The principle of consistency in grouping within constituent structure underscores the systematic and reliable nature of how linguistic elements are grouped together based on their syntactic relationships. In this framework, similar constituents, or structural units, can be identified consistently across different sentences or structures, revealing patterns that contribute to a deeper understanding of language organization.

When constituents exhibit syntactic relationships, they share common grammatical roles or functions within a sentence. This shared syntactic nature allows linguists to identify and group similar constituents across various linguistic contexts. For instance, a noun phrase (NP) such as Nwata nwanyị ahụ *"the girl"* consistently represents a grouping of words that function together as a unit, and this NP structure can be identified in different sentences with varied verbs or additional modifiers.

This consistency in grouping becomes particularly evident when considering the recurrence of certain structures or patterns in language. The ability to recognize and apply consistent groupings facilitates linguistic analysis by providing a framework for understanding how elements with similar syntactic properties contribute to the construction of sentences.

By identifying recurring constituent patterns, linguists can uncover the underlying rules and principles that govern the syntactic structure of a language. This systematic approach enhances our understanding of the regularities and variations in language use, contributing to the broader study of syntax and linguistic analysis.

10.1.3 *Phrase Structure Trees:* Phrase Structure Trees serve as a visual and systematic means of representing constituent structure in linguistic analysis. Within this framework, the intricate relationships and hierarchical organization of linguistic elements within a sentence are illustrated through a tree-like structure. In this representation, nodes in the tree correspond to constituents (individual words or groups of words), and branches depict how these constituents are combined to form larger units.

The construction of a Phrase Structure Tree involves breaking down a sentence into its constituent parts and organizing them in a hierarchical fashion. The tree begins with a single node representing the entire sentence, and as we move down the branches, we encounter nodes that represent successively smaller constituents, such as phrases or individual words. This branching structure captures the syntactic relationships and nesting of constituents within the sentence.

For example, consider the sentence "The cat chased the mouse." The corresponding Phrase Structure Tree might look like this:

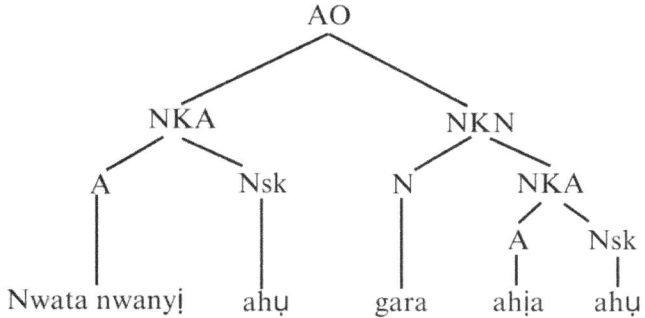

In this tree, the nodes labeled ahịrịokwu [AO] (Sentence), Nkebiokwu Keaha [NKA] (Noun Phrase), Nkebiokwu Kengwaa [NKN] (Verb Phrase), Nkwuso [Nks] (Determiner), Aha [A] (Noun), and Ngwaa [N] (Verb) represent different constituents within the sentence. The branches indicate how these constituents are combined to form larger structures.

Phrase Structure: Trees are invaluable tools for linguists, providing a visual representation that aids in the analysis of sentence structure. They enable a systematic exploration of the hierarchical relationships and syntactic arrangements of constituents, contributing to a deeper understanding of the grammatical structure of a language.

Example Sentence:
Iṇụbiga mmanya ókè nwere ike ịchụpụ ndị ahịa. *"Drunks could put off the customers."*
Here's a simplified diagram of its constituent structure:

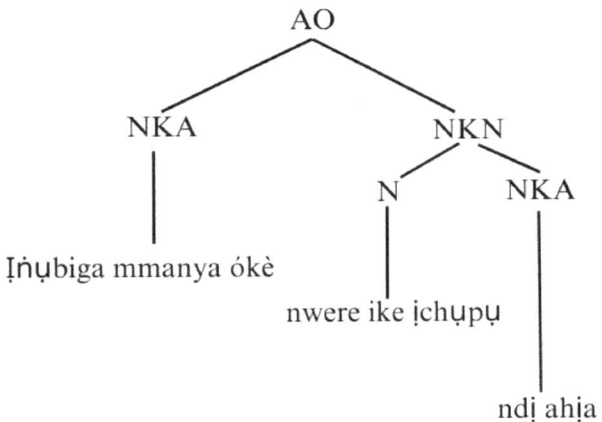

In this example, the constituents include the nkebiokwu keaha *"noun phrases"* (Ịṅụbiga mmanya ókè *"Drunks"* and ndị ahịa *"the customers"*) and the nkebiokwu keaha *"verb phrase"* (nwere ike ịchụpụ *"could put off"*).

Remember, understanding constituents helps us unravel the intricate structure of language.

10.2 Types of Constituents:

Most constituents are phrases. A phrase is a sequence of one or more words (sometimes two or more) built around a head lexical item (such as a noun, verb, or adjective). Phrases function as units within sentences.

Examples of phrases include:
noun phrases: (e.g., nnukwu ose uhie *"the big red pepper"*) and
verb phrases (e.g., Ọ na-aga ije ngwa ngwa "She walks quickly").

Constituent structure in linguistics can be categorized into various types based on the syntactic roles and relationships of the elements within a sentence. Here are some common types of constituent structures:

a. Noun Phrase (NP) *(Nkebiokwu Keaha)*:
A group of words centered around a noun, functioning as a single unit within a sentence. Example: Nnukwu ose uhie.*"The big red pepper."*

b. Verb Phrase (VP) *(Nkebiokwu Kengwaa)*:
A structure centered around a verb, including the verb and its associated elements. Example: Ọ na-agba ọsọ.*"She is running."*

c. Adjective Phrase (AdjP) *(Nkebiokwu kenkọwaaha)*:

A structure containing an adjective and its modifiers, serving as a single unit. Example: Oke ogologo na mma. *"Very tall and elegant."*

d. Adverb Phrase (AdvP) *(Nkebiokwu kenkwuwa)*:
A group of words centered around an adverb, providing information about the manner, place, time, or degree of an action. Example: Ngwa ngwa na nwayọ nwayọ *"Quickly and quietly."*

e. Prepositional Phrase (PP) *(Nkebiokwu kembuụzọ)*:
A structure composed of a preposition and its object, indicating relationships such as location, time, or direction. Example: N'ime ebennọkọta ahụ "In the park."

f. Determiner Phrase (DP) *(Nkebiokwu kenkwuso)*:
A phrase that includes a determiner and its associated elements, often functioning as a specifier for a noun. Example: Nwamba **ahụ** *"The cat."*

g. Clause (CP) *(Nkebiahịrị)*:
A larger syntactic unit containing a subject and a predicate, forming a complete statement, question, command, or exclamation. Example: Ọ na-agụ akwụkwọ *"He is reading a book."*

h. Sentence (S) *(Ahịrịokwu)*:
The highest-level constituent structure, representing a complete grammatical unit that expresses a thought or idea. Example: Ọ na-abụ abụ mara mma *"She sings beautifully."*

These types of constituent structures demonstrate the hierarchical organization of language, where smaller units combine to form larger ones. The identification and analysis of these structures contribute to understanding the syntactic relationships within sentences.

10.3 Tests for Constituents:
Linguists use tests for constituents to identify the constituent structure of sentences. These tests apply to portions of a sentence, providing evidence about its underlying structure. Some commonly used tests include:

Linguists use various tests to identify constituent structures within sentences. These tests help reveal the internal organization of a sentence by examining how words and phrases group together. Here are some common tests used in linguistics:

10.3.1 Substitution Test:
The Substitution Test involves replacing a portion of a sentence with a single word or phrase to observe if the sentence remains grammatical and retains its meaning. Here are examples

demonstrating the Substitution Test:

(a). Sentence: **Mmegbu (mmeso ọjọọ) adịghị mma.**
"Maltreatment is not good."

Substitution Test: Ọ [maltreatment] dịghị [isn't] mma [good].

Result: Ọ *"It"* maintains grammaticality and meaning, suggesting that Mmegbu *"maltreatment"* functions as a constituent.

(b). Sentence: **Ọ na-agụ akwụkwọ akụkọ na-adọrọ mmasị.**
"She is reading a fascinating novel."

Substitution Test: Ọ [She] na-agụ [is reading] ya [it].

Result: Ọ [She] can be substituted with ya [it] without affecting grammaticality, indicating that Ọ [She] is a constituent.

(c). Sentence: **Osisi iroko ochie ahụ guzoro ogologo n'ogige ahụ.**
"The old iroko tree stood tall in the yard."

Substitution Test: Ọ [It] guzoro ogologo n'ogige ahụ [stood tall in the yard].

Result: The substitution is grammatical, indicating that Osisi iroko ochie ahụ [The old oak tree] is a constituent.

These examples illustrate how applying the Substitution Test helps identify constituents within sentences by checking if the substitution maintains grammaticality and meaning.

10.3.2 Movement Test (or Dislocation Test):
The Movement Test, also known as the Dislocation Test, involves shifting a word or phrase to a different position within the sentence to observe if the sentence remains grammatical. Here are examples demonstrating the Movement Test:

(a). Sentence: **Ọ na-agụ akwụkwọ.**
"She read a book."

Movement Test: Akwụkwọ, Ọ na-agụ *"A book, she read."*

Result: The sentence is still grammatical, indicating that Akwụkwọ *"A book"* can be dislocated to the front without affecting the overall structure.

(b). Sentence: **Nwamba ahụ chụrụ òké ọsọ.**
"The cat chased the mouse."

Movement Test: Òké, nwamba ahụ chụrụ ọsọ.
"The mouse, the cat chased."

Result: The sentence remains grammatical, suggesting that òké ahụ *"The mouse"* can be dislocated to the front.

(c). Sentence: **Ha ga-aga na ụlọ ngosi ihe nka ochie echi.**
"They will visit the museum tomorrow."

Movement Test: Echi, ha ga-aga na ngosi ihe nka ochie.
"Tomorrow, they will visit the museum."

Result: The sentence is still grammatical, indicating that Echi *"Tomorrow"* can be dislocated to the front.

(d). Sentence: **Ọ na-agakarị ụlọ mgbatị ahụ**
"He often goes to the gym."

Movement Test: Ụlọ mgbatị ahụ, ọ na-agakarị.
"To the gym, he often goes."

Result: The sentence remains grammatical, showing that Ụlọ mgbatị ahụ *"To the gym"* can be dislocated to the front.

(e). Sentence: **N'ogige ahụ, okooko osisi na-eto eto..**
"In the garden, flowers bloom."

Movement Test: Okooko osisi, n'ogige, na-eto eto.
"Flowers, in the garden, bloom."

Result: The sentence is still grammatical, suggesting that Okooko osisi *"Flowers"* can be dislocated to the front.

These examples illustrate how the Movement Test helps identify constituents within sentences by examining if shifting a word or phrase to a different position maintains grammaticality.

10.3.3 Ellipsis Test:

The Ellipsis Test involves omitting a portion of a sentence to observe if the resulting sentence remains grammatical and retains meaning. Here are examples demonstrating the Ellipsis Test:

(a). Sentence:
Ọ na-amasị ya ịgụ akwụkwọ akụkọ ndị dị omimi, ọ na- enwekwa mmasị ịgụ akwụkwọ akụkọ sayensị. *("She enjoys reading mystery novels, and he enjoys reading science fiction novels.")*

Ellipsis Test: "Ọ na-amasị ya ịgụ akwụkwọ akụkọ ihe omimi, ọ na-enwekwa mmasị na akwụkwọ akụkọ sayensị." *("She enjoys reading mystery novels, and he enjoys science fiction novels.")*

Result: The sentence is still grammatical, suggesting that the ellipsis of ịgụ *"reading"* does not affect overall meaning.

(b). Sentence:
Obi na-ejikarị bọs aga ọrụ, mana Ada na-ejikarị ụgbọ oloko aga ọrụ.
"Obi usually takes the bus to work, but Ada usually takes the train to work."

Ellipsis Test: Obi na-ejikarị bọs aga ọrụ, mana Ada na-ejikarị ụgbọ oloko.
"Obi usually takes the bus to work, but Mary usually takes the train."

Result: The sentence remains grammatical, indicating that the ellipsis of aga ọrụ *"to work"* does not disrupt meaning.

(c). Sentence:
"Ndị otu ahụ mere nke ọma n'oge ọkara nke mbụ, ndị otu ahụ mekwara nke ọma karịa n'oge ọkara nke abụọ. *("The team performed well during the first half, and the team performed even better during the second half.")*

Ellipsis Test:: "Ndị otu ahụ mere nke ọma n'oge ọkara mbụ, ọbụna karịa n'oge ọkara nke abụọ."
"The team performed well during the first half, and even better during the second half."

Result: The sentence is still grammatical, suggesting that the ellipsis of Ndị otu ahụ mere *"the team performed"* is acceptable.

These examples illustrate how applying the Ellipsis Test helps identify constituents within sentences by checking if the omission of certain elements maintains grammaticality and meaning.

10.3.4 Coordination Test:

The Coordination Test involves combining two similar constituents with a coordinating conjunction (e.g., "and", "or") to assess if they form a larger constituent. Here are examples demonstrating the Coordination Test:

(a). Sentence: **"Ọ na-enwe mmasị igwu mmiri, ọ na-enwe mmasị ịgba ọsọ."**
"She likes to swim. She likes to run."

Coordination Test: "Ọ na-enwe mmasị igwu mmiri na ịgba ọsọ."
"She likes to swim and run."

Result: The combined sentence is grammatical, indicating that "igwu mmiri" na "ịgba ọsọ." ["to swim" and "to run"] can be coordinated to form a larger constituent.

(b). Sentence: **Nwamba ahụ dị oji. Nwamba ahụ dị obere.**
"The cat is black. The cat is small."

Coordination Test: Nwamba ahụ dị oji na obere
"The cat is black and small."

Result: The coordinated sentence is grammatical, indicating that oji *"black"* and obere *"small"* can form a larger constituent.

(d). Sentence: **Ha ga-aga Awka. Ha ga-aga na Aba.**
"They will visit Awka. They will visit Aba."

Coordination Test: Ha ga-aga Awka na Aba.
"They will visit Awka and Aba."

Result: The coordinated sentence is grammatical, suggesting that "Awka" and "Aba" can be constituents.

These examples illustrate how the Coordination Test helps identify constituents within sentences by checking if the coordination of similar elements forms a larger grammatical unit.

10.3.5 Clefting Test:

The Clefting Test involves restructuring a sentence into a cleft sentence (e.g., "It is [X] that...") to identify the constituent focused on. Here are examples demonstrating the clefting Test:

(a).   Sentence: **O meriri asọmpi ahụ.**
"She won the championship."

Clefting Test: Ọ bụ asọmpi ahụ ka ọ meriri.
"It was the championship that she won."

Result: The cleft sentence highlights asọmpi ahụ *"the championship"* as the focused constituent.

(b).   Sentence: **Ụmụ akwụkwọ ahụ rụchara arụmarụ ahụ**
"The students completed the project."

Clefting Test: Ọ bụ arụmarụ ahụ ka ụmụ akwụkwọ ahụ rụchara.
"It was the project that the students completed."

Result: The cleft sentence emphasizes arụmarụ ahụ *"the project"* as the focused constituent.

(c).   Sentence: **Ọ doziri nsogbu ahụ tara akpụ.**
"He solved the difficult problem."

Clefting Test: Ọ bụ nsogbu ahụ tara akpụ ka o doziri.
"It was the difficult problem that he solved."

Result: The cleft sentence brings attention to nsogbu ahụ tara akpụ *"the difficult problem"* as the focused constituent.

(d).   Sentence: **O dere uri mara mma.**
"She wrote a beautiful poem."

Clefting Test: Ọ bụ ọmarịcha uri o dere
"It was a beautiful poem that she wrote."

Result: The cleft sentence points to ọmarịcha uri *"a beautiful poem"* as the focused constituent.

These examples illustrate how the Clefting Test helps identify constituents within sentences by reorganizing the sentence to emphasize a particular element, revealing the focused constituent.

10.3.6 Pronominalization Test:

The Pronominalization Test involves replacing a constituent with a pronoun to determine if the sentence maintains grammaticality and meaning. Here are examples demonstrating the Pronominalization Test:

(a).   Sentence: **Eze zụtara ụgbọala ọhụrụ. Eze nwere obi ụtọ maka ụgbọala ahụ.**
"Eze bought a new car. Eze is excited about the car."

Pronominalization Test: Eze zụtara ụgbọala ọhụrụ. Ọ nwere obi ụtọ maka ya.
"Eze bought a new car. She is excited about it."

Result: The pronoun ọ *"it"* maintains grammaticality, indicating that ụgbọala ahụ *"the car"* can be pronominalized.

(b).   Sentence: **Ugo na Ada na-abia oriri ahụ. Ugo na Ada ga-ebute nri.**
"Ugo and Ada are coming to the party. Ugo and Ada are bringing food."

Pronominalization Test: Ugo na Ada na-abia oriri ahụ. Ha na-ebute nri
"Ugo and Ada are coming to the party. They are bringing food."

Result: The pronoun Ha *"They"* preserves grammaticality, suggesting that "Ugo and Ada" can be pronominalized.

(c).   Sentence: **Nwamba ahụ jidere òké. Nwamba ahụ ji òké ahụ egwuri egwu.**
"The cat caught a mouse. The cat played with the mouse."

Pronominalization Test: Nwamba ahụ jidere òké. O ji ya egwuri egwu.
"The cat caught a mouse. It played with it."

Result: The pronoun O *"It"* is grammatical, indicating that òké ahụ *"the mouse"* can be pronominalized.

(d).   Sentence: Ndị otu ahụ meriri asọmpi ahụ. Ndị otu ahụ mere ememe mmeri ahụ.
"The team won the championship. The team celebrated the victory."

Pronominalization Test: Ndị otu ahụ meriri asọmpi ahụ. Ha mere ememe mmeri ahụ
"The team won the championship. They celebrated the victory."

Result: The pronoun Ha *"They"* maintains grammaticality, suggesting that Ndị otu ahụ "the team" can be pronominalized.

(e). Sentence: **Ngọzi na-agụ akwụkwọ. Alice nwere mmasị n'akwụkwọ ahụ.**
"Ngọzị is reading a book. Ngọzị found the book interesting."

Pronominalization Test: Ngọzi na-agụ akwụkwọ. O nwere mmasị na ya
"Ngọzị is reading a book. She found it interesting."

Result: The pronoun O *"She"* is grammatical, indicating that akwụkwọ ahụ *"the book"* can be pronominalized.

These examples illustrate how applying the Pronominalization Test helps identify constituents within sentences by checking if replacing a portion with a pronoun maintains grammaticality and meaning.

10.3.7 Question Formation Test:
The Question Formation Test involves transforming a declarative sentence into a question to analyze the resulting structure and identify constituents. Here are examples demonstrating the Question Formation Test:

(a). Sentence: **Ọ na-aga ụlọ ahịa.** *"She is going to the store."*
Question Formation Test: Ọ na-aga ụlọ ahịa? *"Is she going to the store?"*

Result: The question maintains grammaticality, indicating that Ọ *"She"* and na-aga ụlọ ahịa *"going to the store"* are constituents.

(b). Sentence: **Ha arụchaala arụmarụ ahụ.** *("They have completed the project.")*
Question Formation Test: Ha arụchaala arụmarụ ahụ? *("Have they completed the project?")*

Result: The question is grammatical, suggesting that Ha *"They"* and arụchaala arụmarụ ahụ "completed the project" are constituents.

(c). Sentence: **Ọ ga-aga nzukọ ahụ.** *"He will attend the meeting."*
Question Formation Test: Ò ga-aga nzukọ ahụ? *"Will he attend the meeting?"*

Result: The question is grammatical, suggesting that Ọ *"He"* and aga nzukọ ahụ *"attend the meeting"* are constituents.

(d). Sentence: **Ụmụaka na-egwuri egwu n'ebennọkọta ahụ.**
"The children played in the park."

Question Formation Test: Ụmụntakịrị ahụ ana-egwuri egwu n' ebennọkọta ahụ?
"Did the children play in the park?"

Result: The question maintains grammaticality, indicating that Ụmụntakịrị ahụ *"The children"* and egwuri egwu n' ebennọkọta ahụ *"played in the park"* are constituents.

These examples illustrate how the Question Formation Test helps identify constituents within sentences by transforming them into questions and examining the resulting structure.

10.3.8 Topicalization Test:
The Topicalization Test involves moving a constituent to the front of a sentence to determine if it retains grammaticality and meaning. Here are examples demonstrating the Topicalization Test:

(a). Sentence: **Ọ gbochiri nsogbu ahụ ngwa ngwa.** (*"She solved the problem quickly."*)
Topicalization Test: (Na) Ngwa ngwa, O doziri nsogbu ahụ. (*"Quickly, she solved the problem."*)

Result: The sentence is still grammatical, indicating that Ngwa ngwa *"Quickly"* can be topicalized.

(b). Sentence: **Ụmụ akwụkwọ ahụ rụchara ihe omume ha n'oge.**
"The students completed their assignments on time."

Topicalization Test: N'oge, (ka) ụmụ akwụkwọ ahụ rụchara ihe omume ahụ.
"On time, the students completed their assignments."

Result: The sentence remains grammatical, suggesting that N'oge *"On time"* can be topicalized.

(c). Sentence: **Ha ga-aga n'ụlọ ngosi ihe mgbe ochie ama ama echi.**
"They will visit the famous museum tomorrow."

Topicalization Test: Echi, ha ga-aga n'ụlọ ngosi ihe mgbe ochie ama ama.
"Tomorrow, they will visit the famous museum."

Result: The sentence maintains grammaticality, suggesting that echi *"Tomorrow"* can be topicalized.

(d). Sentence: **Nwamba ahụ jidere òké n'abalị ụnyaahụ.**
"The cat caught a mouse last night."

Topicalization Test: N'abalị ụnyaahụ, nwamba ahụ jidere òké.
"Last night, the cat caught a mouse."

Result: The sentence remains grammatical, indicating that N'abalị ụnyaahụ *"Last night"* can be topicalized.

These examples illustrate how applying the Topicalization Test helps identify constituents within sentences by assessing if moving an element to the front preserves grammaticality and meaning.

10.3.9 Fragment Test:
The Fragment Test involves examining whether a sentence fragment, which is an incomplete sentence, can be considered a grammatical unit while retaining meaning. Here are examples demonstrating the Fragment Test:

(a). Sentence: **Mgbe mmiri ozuzo kwụsịrị.** *"After the rain stopped."*
Fragment Test: Mmiri ozuzo kwụsịrị. *"the rain stopped."*

Result: The fragment is grammatical but still lacks a main clause.

(b). Sentence: **gbaaọsọ n'ime ọhịa.** *"Running through the forest."*
Fragment Test: N'ime n'oké ọhịa *"Through the forest."*

Result: The fragment is not a complete sentence and lacks a main clause.

(c). Sentence: **N'egbughị oge ma ọ bụ ịtụ egwu.** *("Without hesitation or fear.")*
Fragment Test: igbu oge ma ọ bụ ịtụ egwu. *("hesitation or fear.")*

Result: The fragment is not a complete sentence and lacks a main clause.

These examples illustrate that sentence fragments, while grammatical, often lack the necessary components to function as complete sentences, specifically a main clause. The Fragment Test helps identify whether a group of words constitutes a grammatical unit or if it requires additional elements for completeness.

10.3.10 Intonation Test:

The Intonation Test involves using the rising or falling pitch of the voice to turn a statement into a question or vice versa. Here are examples demonstrating the Intonation Test:

(a). Statement: **Ị na-abịa oriri na ọṅụṅụ ahụ.** *"You're coming to the party."*
Intonation Test (Question): Ị na-abịa oriri na ọṅụṅụ ahụ? *"You're coming to the party?"*

Result: By raising the pitch at the verb, it transforms the statement into a question.

(b). Question: **Ị rụchara ọrụ omume ụlọ gị?** (*"Did you finish your homework?"*)
Intonation Test (Statement): Ị rụchara ọrụ omume ụlọ gị. (*"Did you finish your homework."*)

Result: By lowering the pitch at the verb, it turns the question into a statement.

(c). Statement: Ọ bụ ọmarịcha ụbọchị. *"It's a beautiful day."*
Intonation Test (Question): Ọ bụ ọmarịcha ụbọchị? *"It's a beautiful day?"*

Result: Raising the pitch at the verb turns the statement into a question.

These examples demonstrate how altering the pitch through intonation can influence whether a sentence is perceived as a statement or a question.

These tests, when applied systematically, help linguists uncover the constituent structure of sentences, contributing to a more comprehensive understanding of syntax and sentence organization in a given language.

Constituent structure is a fundamental concept in syntax, helping linguists analyze and describe the underlying organization of sentences in a language. It provides a systematic way to represent the relationships between different parts of a sentence and contributes to our understanding of how sentences are formed and interpreted.

Exercise

1. What is constituent structure in linguistics, and why is it important for understanding sentence syntax?
2. How does hierarchical arrangement contribute to the concept of constituent structure in sentences?
3. Can you explain the principle of consistency in grouping within constituent structure?
4. What are Phrase Structure Trees, and how do they help represent constituent structure visually?
5. Give an example of a sentence and its corresponding Phrase Structure Tree to illustrate constituent structure.
6. What are the different types of constituents in linguistics, and how do they function within sentences?
7. Explain the concept of a Noun Phrase (NP) and provide an example.
8. What is a Verb Phrase (VP), and how is it structured within a sentence?
9. Describe an Adjective Phrase (AdjP) and provide an example.
10. What role does an Adverb Phrase (AdvP) play in sentence structure? Give an example.
11. Define a Prepositional Phrase (PP) and provide a sentence example.
12. What is a Determiner Phrase (DP), and how does it function in sentence structure? Give an example.
13. Explain the concept of a Clause (CP) and its role in forming sentences.
14. Define a Sentence (S) in terms of constituent structure and provide an example.
15. How do linguists use tests for constituents to analyze sentence structure?
16. Describe the Substitution Test and how it helps identify constituents within sentences.
17. Explain the Movement Test (or Dislocation Test) and its significance in identifying constituents.
18. What is the Ellipsis Test, and how does it aid in identifying constituents within sentences?
19. Describe the Coordination Test and its role in identifying constituents.
20. Explain the Clefting Test and its significance in identifying constituents within sentences.

Chapter 11
Igbo Clauses (Ọdịdị Nkebiahịrị Igbo)

11.1 The Grammatical Nature of Igbo Clauses:

In syntax, A Clause (Nkebiahịrị) is a is a grammatical unit that consists of a subject and a predicate. It functions as a building block of a sentence and can express a complete thought. A clause can be independent, meaning it can stand alone as a complete sentence, or dependent, meaning it cannot stand alone as a complete sentence and functions as a part of a larger sentence. Dependent clauses in Igbo often function as adjectives or adverbials, modifying nouns or verbs in the main clause.

Igbo clauses can also be classified based on the type of verb they contain. There are two types of verbs in Igbo: transitive and intransitive. Transitive verbs take a direct object, while intransitive verbs do not. Igbo clauses can also be finite or non-finite. Finite clauses contain a finite verb form, which indicates tense and aspect, while non-finite clauses contain non-finite verb forms, such as infinitives or participles.

For examples:
- a) Ọ tụtụtara okooko osisi n'ogige ahụ — *She picked flowers in the garden.*
- b) Nne m mere Achịcha awaị maka nri ụtụtụ. — *My mother made a sandwich for breakfast.*
- c) Ewi ahụ manyere n'ahịhịa ahụ. — *The bunny hopped in the grass.*
- d) Papa m kọrọ akụkọ banyere anụ ọhịa bea. — *Daddy told a story about a bear.*
- e) Anyanwụ pụtara mgbe mmiri ozuzo gasịrị. — *The sun appeared after the rain.*
- f) Ụgbọala ahụ gbagharịrị gburugburu ime ụlọ. — *The little car zoomed around the room.*
- g) Nkịta ahụ fere ọdụ ya n'obi ụtọ. — *The puppy wagged its tail with excitement.*
- h) Anyị gụrụ kpakpando ọnụ tupu oge ụra. — *We counted stars before bedtime.*
- i) Enyí ahụ were ogwe ya fesa mmiri. — *The elephant sprayed water with its trunk.*
- j) Akụkọ oge ụra nwere foto ụmụ anụmanụ. — *The bedtime story had pictures of animals.*
- k) Anyị na-agba egwú n'ọnụ ụlọ. — *We danced to music in the living room.*
- l) Urukurubụba ji ọmarịcha nku na-efeghari. — *The butterfly fluttered by with pretty wings.*
- m) Anyị bụkọrọ abụ mmeri ahụ ọnụ. — *We sang the victory song together.*
- n) Anyị na-akụ mkpụrụosisi n'ubi ahụ. — *We planted tiny seeds in the garden.*
- o) Ụmụ ọkụkọ yoro anya n'ụlọ ọzụzụ ọkụkụ. — *The baby chicks peeped in the barn.*

There is a structure for main and subordinate clauses in the world of clauses. Subordinate clauses depend on major clauses for meaning, but main clauses stand alone. This structure makes it possible to construct complex sentences that explain complex relationships between ideas.

11.2 Main/Independent Clause

An independent clause is a group of words that forms a complete and meaningful sentence on its own. It contains both a subject and a predicate, allowing it to express a complete thought independently. The components of independent clause are:

(i). *Subject*: The subject is the part of the sentence that indicates who or what the sentence is about. It typically consists of a noun or pronoun. Example: Ọ *"She"*

In the sentence Ọ gara ụlọ ahịa. *"She went to the store,"* "She" is the subject of the independent clause.

(ii). *Predicate*: The predicate is the part of the sentence that provides information about the subject, usually containing a verb and sometimes additional elements. Example: gara ụlọ ahịa; *"went to the store."*

In the same sentence, gara ụlọ ahịa *"went to the store"* is the predicate of the independent clause, describing the action performed by the subject Ọ *"She."*

Examples of independent clause:

1. Mama m siri kuki na-esi ísì ụtọ. (*Mommy baked cookies that smelled delicious.*)
2. Osisi ahụ na-enye ndò n'ụbọchị anwụ na-acha. (*The tree provided shade on a sunny day.*)
3. Ụgbọala mgbanyụ ọkụ ahụ nwere nnukwu siren. (*The fire truck had a loud siren.*)
4. Mama m mere koko na-ekpo ọkụ n'ụbọchị oyi. (*Mommy made warm cocoa on a cold day.*)
5. Obere ọbọgwụ ahụ gwuru mmiri n'ọdọ mmiri ahụ. (*The little duck swam in the pond.*)
6. Akụkọ ịlakpu ụra ahụ nwere njedebe n'emeobi ụtọ. (*The bedtime story had a happy ending.*)
7. Papa m mere ihu ọchị iji mee ka anyị chịa ọchị. (*Daddy made funny faces to make us laugh.*)
8. Katuun kacha amasị m nwere ndị na-akpa ọchị. (*My favorite cartoon had funny characters.*)
9. Ihu igwe tụgharịrị dị ka agba mara mma n'oge ụra. (*The sky turned pretty colors at bedtime.*)

Combining the subject and predicate, we have the complete independent clause: "She went to the store." This clause forms a standalone sentence because it conveys a full and coherent idea. Independent clauses are the building blocks of sentences and serve as the foundation for constructing more complex structures in written and spoken language.

Independent clauses, in addition to being stand-alone sentences, can be further classified based on their structure and function. Here are some common types of independent clauses:

11.2.1 Declarative clauses:
Declarative clauses, also known as statements, are a type of independent clause that serves the purpose of making straightforward statements or declarations. These clauses convey information, express facts, or communicate opinions in a direct and assertive manner. Here's an expansion of the example provided:

Example: Ọ gara ụlọ ahịa.   *"She went to the store."*

In this declarative clause, the subject Ọ *"She"* is the one performing the action, and the predicate "went to the store" indicates the specific action taken. This type of clause is commonly used to share information, describe events, or state facts without posing a question, giving a command, or expressing strong emotion.

More examples of Declarative clause:

a) Ọnwa pụtara na mbara igwe n'ime abalị.   *The moon appeared in the night sky.*
b) Ọ bụrụ abụ gbasara mbe.   *He sang a song about tortoises.*
c) Nne m mere anyị kuki dị ụtọ.   *My mom made yummy cookies for us.*
d) Ada chiri ọchị maka okwu njakịrị ahụ.   *Ada giggled at the joke.*
e) Anyị hụrụ nkume ka anyị na-aga ije.   *We found rocks on our walk.*

Declarative clauses are fundamental in everyday communication, allowing individuals to convey information in a clear and concise manner. They are commonly used in both written and spoken language to share details, narrate events, or present arguments.

11.2.2 Interrogative clauses:
Interrogative clauses, also known as questions, are a type of independent clause designed to elicit information or prompt a response. These clauses are characterized by their inquiry into a particular subject and often begin with question words. Here's an expansion of the example provided:

Example: Ọ gara ụlọ ahịa?   *"Did she go to the store?"*

Here are more seven examples of interrogative clauses:

a) Ebee ka ụlọ ahịa nri kacha nso dị?　*Where is the nearest grocery store?*
b) Onye na-abịa oriri na ọṅụṅụ?　*Who is coming to the party?*
c) Kedu oge ihe nkiri ahụ na-amalite?　*What time does the movie start?*
d) Gịnị mere nwamba ahụ ji rịgoro osisi?　*Why did the cat climb the tree?*
e) Kedu akwụkwọ ị na-agụ?　*Which book are you reading?*
f) Mmiri ọ ga-ezo echi?　*Is it going to rain tomorrow?*
g) Kedu ka ị siri mụta ịnya igwe?　*How did you learn to ride a bike?*

Interrogative clauses play a crucial role in communication by facilitating conversation, seeking clarification, or prompting discussion. The variety of question words, such as onye, gịnị, mgbe, ebe, na kedu, (who, what, when, where, why, and how), enables the formation of diverse interrogative clauses that can range from seeking factual information to exploring opinions or motivations.

11.2.3 Imperative clauses:

Imperative clauses, also known as commands or instructions, are a type of independent clause designed to convey a direct request, command, or guidance. These clauses play a decisive role in communication by expressing a desire for someone to perform a specific action. Here's an expansion of the example provided:

Example: Gaa n'ụlọ ahịa.   *"Go to the store."*

In this imperative clause, the verb Gaa (*"Go"*) serves as the command, and the subject is typically implicit, referring to the person being addressed. Imperative clauses are characterized by their brevity and assertiveness, as they cut straight to the point, instructing the listener or reader on what action to take.

Here are more examples of imperative clauses:

a) Mechie ụzọ ahụ n'azụ gị.　*Close the door behind you.*
b) Biko nyefee m nnu ahụ.　*Please pass me the salt.*
c) Echefula ịbịa echi.　*Don't forget to come tomorrow.*
d) Jiri nlezianya gụọ ntuziaka ahụ.　*Read the instructions carefully.*
e) Dozie ime ụlọ gị tupu ị lakpuo ụra.　*Clean up your room before bedtime.*
f) Gee onye nkuzi ntị n'oge nkuzi.　*Listen to the teacher during the lesson.*

Imperative clauses are ubiquitous in everyday communication, ranging from simple requests to authoritative commands. They are commonly employed in various contexts, including giving directions, issuing orders, or making polite requests.

11.2.4 Exclamative clauses:
Exclamative clauses, also known as exclamations, are a type of independent clause designed to convey intense emotions, enthusiasm, or strong reactions. Exclamative clauses are powerful linguistic tools that allow speakers or writers to convey heightened feelings, excitement, surprise, or awe.

Here are examples exclamatory sentences:

a) Chei, lee ọdịda anyanwụ mara mma! — *Wow, what a beautiful sunset!*
b) Ee e, echefuru m nri ehihie m n'ụlọ! — *Oh no, I forgot my lunch at home!*
c) Ngwa ngwa, anyị meriri asọmpi! — *Hurray, we won the championship!*
d) Ee, akwafuru m ihe ọṅụṅụ m n'ala! — *Oops, I spilled my drink on the floor!*
e) Ah, isi nke okooko osisi ọhụrụ n'ogige! — *Ah, the aroma of fresh flowers in the garden!*
f) Aaaa, ị rụrụ nnukwu ọrụ n'arụmarụ a! — *Bravo, you did a great job on the project!*
g) Ewoo, ụbọchị a na-atụ anya ya abịala! — *Alas, the long-awaited day has finally come!*

These clauses are characterized by their expressive nature. Exclamative clauses add a vibrant and passionate dimension to language, providing a way to articulate emotions with emphasis. They are commonly used to express positive or negative sentiments, depending on the context, and contribute to the overall tone and mood of the communication. The distinctive feature of exclamative clauses lies in their ability to capture and convey the intensity of the speaker's emotions, making them a valuable element in both written and spoken language for expressing enthusiasm, admiration, or even astonishment.

11.3 Subordinate/Dependent Clause

A dependent clause, also known as a subordinate clause, is a group of words that contains a subject and a verb but cannot stand alone as a complete sentence. It relies on an independent clause (main clause) to give it meaning and context. The subject in a dependent clause typically performs an action or is described by the verb within that clause.

(i). *Subject*: Similar to an independent clause, a dependent clause has a subject, which is the part of the sentence that indicates who or what the sentence is about.

For example:

Independent Clause: "Ọ gara n'ụlọ ahịa."   *"She went to the store."*
Dependent Clause: "N'ihi na ọ chọrọ ngwa nri." *"Because she needed groceries."*

In this example, "N'ihi na ọ chọrọ ngwa nri." "Because she needed groceries" is a dependent clause with the subject "Ọ" *"she."* It cannot function independently and relies on the main clause for its meaning.

(ii). *Predicate*: The predicate is the part of the sentence that provides information about the subject, usually containing a verb and sometimes additional elements.

Example: "chọrọ ngwa nri."   *"needed groceries."*

In the above dependent clause, "chọrọ ngwa nri." *"needed groceries."* is the predicate, describing the action or state of the subject.

Now, if we look at the dependent clause "N'ihi na ọ chọrọ ngwa nri." *"Because she needed groceries."* by itself, it doesn't form a complete idea or a standalone sentence. It leaves the reader or listener expecting more information. To make it complete, it needs to be combined with an independent clause. For example:

Independent Clause: "Ọ gara n'ụlọ ahịa."   *"She went to the store."*
Dependent Clause: "N'ihi na ọ chọrọ ngwa nri." *"Because she needed groceries."*

Combined Sentence: "Ọ gara n'ụlọ ahịa n'ihi na ọ chọrọ ngwa nri."
        "She went to the store because she needed groceries."

In this combined sentence, the dependent clause "N'ihi na ọ chọrọ ngwa nri." (*"Because she needed groceries"*). is now joined with the independent clause "Ọ gara n'ụlọ ahịa." (*"She went to the store"),* creating a complete thought and a grammatically correct sentence. Dependent clauses often serve to add additional information, provide context, or express conditions in conjunction with independent clauses.

Dependent Clauses can also be further categorized based on their structure and function. Some common types include noun clauses, verb clauses, adjective clauses, adverb clauses, The grammatical structure and function of clauses can affect how a sentence is understood and can be used to express complex ideas and relationships between different elements within a sentence.

11.3.1 Noun clauses:

Noun clauses function as nouns within sentences and can be used in place of nouns to refer to people, places, things, or ideas.

Here are examples noun clauses:

a) **Ihe o kwuru** tụrụ ndị niile nọ n'ime ụlọ ahụ n'anya.
   What she said surprised everyone in the room. (Noun clause: *What she said*)

b) doghị anya **ma ọ ga-abịa oriri na ọṅụṅụ**
   Whether he will come to the party remains uncertain. (Noun clause: *Whether he will come to the party*)

c) **Ọ bụrụ na mmiri zoo echi**, anyị nwere ike ịkagbu picnic.
   If it rains tomorrow, we might have to cancel the picnic. (Noun clause: *If it rains tomorrow*)

d) A ga-ekwupụta **onye ga-emeri** n'abalị a.
   Who the winner is will be announced later tonight. (Noun clause: *Who the winner is*)

e) **Ihe mere o ji mee mkpebi ahụ** ka bụ ihe omimi nye anyị.
   Why he made that decision remains a mystery to us. (Noun clause: *Why he made that decision*)

f) **Ma ọ masịrị gị ma ọ bụ masịghị gị** agbanweghị ọnọdụ ahụ.
   Whether you like it or not doesn't change the situation. (Noun clause: *Whether you like it or not*)

g) **Ihe o mere** nwere mmetụta dị ukwuu na ihe si na ya pụta.
   What she did had a significant impact on the outcome. (Noun clause: *What she did*)

h) **Ma ha nwere ike isonyere anyị** dabere n'usoro ihe omume ha.
   Whether they can join us depends on their schedule. (Noun clause: *Whether they can join us*)

Noun clauses serve as the subjects or objects of verbs and can act as the subjects or objects of other noun clauses.

11.3.2 Adjective clauses:
Adjective clauses, also known as relative clauses, modify a noun or pronoun in a sentence. They

provide additional information about the noun or pronoun they modify. For example, "The book, which I read last night, was fascinating." Here, the adjective clause "which I read last night" modifies the noun "book."

For examples:

a) Akwụkwọ **nke ọ tụrụ aro ya** magburu onwe ya na mma
   The book that she recommended is excellent. (Adjectival clause: that she recommended)

b) Ụgbọ ala ahụ, **nke a dọwara n'akụkụ okporo ụzọ**, nwere taya dara ada.
   The car, which was parked by the curb, had a flat tire. (Adjectival clause: which was parked by the curb)

c) Ahụrụ m **onye ma nwanne gị nwanyị**.
   I met a person who knows your sister. (Adjectival clause: who knows your sister)

d) Ụlọ **ebe ha ebibu** bụzi ugbu a ihe agbahapụrụ.
   The house where they used to live is now abandoned. (Adjectival clause: where they used to live)

e) Ihe nkiri ahụ **nke anyị lere n'abalị ụnyaahụ** tọrọ ụtọ.
   The movie that we watched last night was thrilling. (Adjectival clause: that we watched last night)

f) Uwe elu ahụ, **nke a na-ere ere**, bụ agba kacha amasị m.
   *The shirt, which is on sale, is my favorite color. (Adjectival clause: **which is on sale**)*

g) Enwere m enyi **onye nwere ike ịsụ asụsụ ise**.
   I have a friend who can speak five languages. (Adjectival clause: who can speak five languages)

h) Ugwu ahụ **nke guzoro n'ebe dị anya** bụ Ugwu Everest.
   The mountain that stands tall in the distance is Mount Everest. (Adjectival clause: that stands tall in the distance)

i) Achịcha ahụ, **nke uzommeputa ya bụ ihe nzuzo ezinụlọ**, na-atọ ụtọ.
   The cake, whose recipe is a family secret, is delicious. (Adjectival clause: whose recipe is a family secret)

Adjective clauses, also known as relative clauses, modify nouns and provide additional information about them.

11.3.3 Adverb clauses:

Adverb clauses provide additional information about the verb in a sentence, such as when, where, why, or under what circumstances something occurs. They usually begin with a subordinating conjunction (such as "when," "where," "why," "because" etc). and provide information about the time, place, reason, or manner of the action described by the verb. For example, "I will visit you after I finish work." In this sentence, the adverb clause "after I finish work" provides information about the time when the speaker will visit the other person.

For examples:

a) Ọ gbasiri mbọ ike **ka o nwee ike imezu ebumnuche ya**.
   She worked hard so that she could achieve her goals. (Adverbial clause: *so that she could achieve her goals*)

b) **Mgbe mmiri ozuzo kwụsịrị**, ha gawara n'èzí ka ha gwurie egwu.
   After the rain stopped, they went outside to play. (Adverbial clause: *After the rain stopped*)

c) Aga m akpọ gị **ma m rụchaa ọrụ m**.
   I'll call you when I finish my work. (Adverbial clause: *when I finish my work*)

d) **Ebe ọ bụ na mmiri na-ezo**, a kagburu picnic.
   Since it was raining, the picnic was cancelled. (Adverbial clause: *Since it was raining*)

e) **N'agbanyeghị na ọ gụrụ akwụkwọ nke ọma**, ọ gafeghị ule ahụ.
   Although he studied hard, he didn't pass the exam. (Adverbial clause: *Although he studied hard*)

f) **Tupu anyị apụ,** ka anyị hụ na ụzọ niile juru mechiri.
   Before we leave, let's make sure every door is closed. (Adverbial clause: *Before we leave*)

g) Ọ na-abụ abụ mara mma **mgbe obi dị ya ụtọ**.
   She sings beautifully when she is happy. (Adverbial clause: *when she is happy*)

h) Nwamba ahụ zoro n'okpuru akwa **n'ihi na égbè eluigwe gbara**.
   The cat hid under the bed because there was a thunderstorm. (Adverbial clause: *because there was a thunderstorm*)

i) Ndị otu ahụ meriri **n'agbanyeghị ọnọdụ ịma aka (ha zutere)**.
   The team won despite the challenging conditions. (Adverbial clause: *despite the challenging conditions*)

Adverb clauses modify verbs, adjectives, and other adverbs and provide information about time, place, and manner.

11.3.4 Non-finite clauses:
Non-finite clauses are usually not marked for tense and do not have a subject, making them different from finite clauses, which are complete sentences with a subject and a finite verb marked for tense and are limited to a particular number and person.

For example, in the sentence Ọ na-masị m ịkpọ ụbọ akwara. *"I like to play the guitar,"* ịkpọ ụbọ akwara; *"to play the guitar"* is an infinitive clause serving as an object of the verb mmasị "like." In the sentence Ọkpụkpọ nke ụbọ akwara na-atọ ụtọ; *"Playing the guitar is fun,"* in the sentence, Ọkpụkpọ (nke) ụbọ akwara; "Playing the guitar" is a gerund clause serving as the subject of the sentence.

Non-finite clauses typically serve as verbal nouns, verbal adjectives, or verbal adverbs, and they cannot stand alone as complete sentences. There are three types of non-finite clauses: infinitive clauses, participle clauses, and gerund clauses.

(a). *Infinitive clauses*: Infinitive clauses begin with the word "to" and serve as verbal nouns, which can function as subjects, direct objects, indirect objects, or objects of prepositions.

For examples:

a) Ọ chọrọ **ịmụta ka e si akpọ piano**.
   She wants to learn how to play the piano. (Infinitive clause: *to learn how to play the piano*)

b) Enwere m olileanya **ịga Paris n'oge okpomọkụ na-abịa**.
   I hope to visit Paris next summer. (Infinitive clause: to visit *Paris next summer)*

c) kpebiri **ịmalite azụmahịa ọhụrụ**.
   He decided to start a new business. (Infinitive clause: *to start a new business*)

d) Ọ dị mkpa **iri nri kwesịrị ekwesị**.
   It's important to eat a balanced diet. (Infinitive clause*: to eat a balanced diet)*

e) Ebumnobi m bụ **ịghọ onye ode akwụkwọ ihe na-agara nke ọma**.
My goal is to become a successful writer. (Infinitive clause: *to become a successful writer*)

f) Ha na-eme atụmatụ **ịrụgharị ụlọ ha n'afọ ọzọ**.
They plan to renovate their house next year. (Infinitive clause: *to renovate their house next year*)

g) Ọ ga-amasị m **ịgaghari gburugburu ụwa otu ụbọchị**.
I would like to travel around the world someday. (Infinitive clause: *to travel around the world someday*)

h) Nzọukwụ mbụ bụ **ịghọta nsogbu ahụ**.
The first step is to understand the problem. (Infinitive clause: *to understand the problem*)

i) kpebiri na ya **agaghị ewere ọrụ ahụ**.
He decided not to take the job offer. (Infinitive clause: *not to take the job offer*)

(b). *Gerund clauses*: Gerund clauses begin with a gerund and serve as verbal nouns, which can function as subjects, direct objects, indirect objects, or objects of prepositions.

For examples:

a) **Oriri nri na-atọ ụtọ** bụ ihe a na-eme n'ememe ezumike.
Feasting on delicious food is a highlight of holiday celebrations. (Gerund clause: *Feasting on delicious food*)

b) **Ọnyụnya ụgbọ ala nke nlezi anya na ajọ ọnọdụ ihu igwe** dị mkpa maka nchekwa.
Driving carefully in adverse weather conditions is important for safety. (Gerund clause: *Driving carefully in adverse weather conditions*)

c) **Odide uri** na-enye ohere nke igosipụta echiche na mmetụta.
Writing poetry allows for creative expression of thoughts and emotions. (Gerund clause: *Writing poetry*)

d) **Ọgụgụ akwụkwọ** na-amụba uche ma na-amụba ihe ọmụma.
Reading books broadens the mind and enhances knowledge. (Gerund clause: *Reading books*)

e) **Orire ihe ejiri aka mee n'ahịa obodo** bụ ihe na-akpatara ya ego.
Selling handmade crafts at the local market is a source of income for her. (Gerund clause: *Selling handmade crafts at the local market*)

f) **Ọmụmụ asụsụ ọhụrụ** na-emepe ụzọ maka ọdịbendị na echiche dị iche iche.
Learning new languages opens doors to different cultures and perspectives. (Gerund clause: *Learning new languages*)

g) **Odidi ihe isi ike na nọgidesie ike** na-ewulite ike nke agwa.
Bearing hardships with resilience builds strength of character. (Gerund clause: *Bearing hardships with resilience*)

h) **Ọsụsọ mgbe mgbatị ahụ gasịrị** na-egosi ogo nke ọrụ mgbati ahụ.
Sweating after a workout indicates level of exertion. (Gerund clause: *Sweating after a workout*)

Non-finite clauses are often used in various combinations with finite clauses to form complex sentences. They provide additional information and add variety to sentence structures, making them an important aspect of grammar in many languages, including Igbo.

The grammatical structure and function of clauses play a crucial role in how sentences are understood. Different types of clauses allow speakers and writers to convey a variety of meanings and intentions. The choice of declarative, interrogative, imperative, or exclamative clauses can shape the overall tone and purpose of a sentence.

Moreover, the arrangement and combination of independent and dependent clauses within a sentence contribute to expressing complex ideas and illustrating relationships between different elements. By manipulating clauses, writers can create sentences that convey a range of information, from simple statements to intricate and nuanced meanings. Understanding these variations in clause types and their functions enhances one's ability to communicate effectively in written and spoken language.

Exercise

1. What are the two main types of clauses in Igbo grammar, and how do they differ?
2. How are transitive and intransitive verbs related to the classification of Igbo clauses?
3. Provide 5 examples of finite and non-finite clauses in Igbo?
4. What is the function of a dependent clause in Igbo syntax?
5. How do dependent clauses contribute to the construction of complex sentences in Igbo?
6. What are the components of an independent clause in Igbo, and how do they work together?
7. Can you explain the difference between declarative and interrogative clauses in Igbo?
8. How do imperative clauses function in Igbo communication?
9. What role do exclamative clauses play in Igbo language expression?
10. Give 5 examples of noun clauses in Igbo sentences?
11. How do adjective clauses modify nouns in Igbo sentences?
12. What types of information do adverb clauses provide in Igbo grammar?
13. How do infinitive clauses function as verbal nouns in Igbo?
14. Can you explain the purpose of gerund clauses in Igbo sentences?
15. What distinguishes non-finite clauses from finite clauses in Igbo syntax?
16. How do writers in Igbo use clause combinations to convey complex ideas?
17. In what ways does understanding clause structure enhance language proficiency in Igbo?
18. How do Igbo clauses contribute to the richness and variety of sentence structures?
19. Provide 5 examples of complex sentences in Igbo that demonstrate the use of different types of clauses?
20. How does the choice of clause type affect the tone and meaning of a sentence in Igbo communication?

Chapter 12

Cleft Sentence in Igbo Grammar (Nkewaa *Ahịrịokwu dị n'asụsụ Igbo*)

12.1 The syntax of clefts clauses

Cleft sentences typically involve two clauses. The cleft sentence in Igbo often begins with a pronoun, which serves as the subject of the sentence. This pronoun is followed by a copula, a verb-like element that links the subject to the rest of the sentence. In Igbo, the copula often takes the form of a specific verb that indicates a state of being.

In syntax, clefts and relative clauses are two distinct structures that play different roles in organizing and expressing information within a sentence. The structure of Igbo cleft sentences involves a combination of a pronoun, a copula, an informationally prominent phrase, and an embedded clause.

Cleft sentences are constructions that highlight a particular element in a sentence by dividing it into two clauses – the main clause and the cleft (subordinate) clause. Clefts often employ the subordinating conjunctions "it" or "what" to introduce the subordinate clause.

Example:
Original Sentence: O meriri asọmpi ahụ.   *"She won the championship."*
Cleft Sentence: Ọ bụ asọmpi ahụ ọ meriri.   *"It was the championship that she won."*

Syntax:
Main Clause: Ọ bụ   *"It was"*
Cleft Clause: asọmpi ọ meriri   *"the championship that she won"*

Clefts serve to emphasize a specific part of a sentence, drawing attention to the focal element.

They are commonly used to bring focus to the subject, object, or any other constituent in a sentence.

A cleft sentence (also known as a cleft construction or cleft clause) is a type of complex sentence that divides its content into two distinct parts: An emphasized part and A de-emphasized part.

Emphasized Part (Contrasting Topic): The emphasized part in a cleft sentence is the element that we want to highlight or draw attention to. It often contrasts with other possibilities or expectations.

Examples:
(a). Ọ bụ Obi ka Ada hụrụ. *"It was Obi that Ada saw."*
(Emphasizing Obi as the specific person Ada saw.)

(b). Ihe Ada zụtara bụ mbipụta mbụ. *"What Ada bought was a first edition."*
(Emphasizing the specific thing Ada purchased.)

De-emphasized Part: The de-emphasized part provides context or background information. It typically follows the emphasized part.

Examples:

(a). Ọ bụ Obi ka Ada hụrụ na asọmpi ahụ. *"It was Obi that Ada saw at the competition."*
(Background context: Ada saw someone at the competition.)

(b). Ihe Ada zụtara bụ mbipụta mbụ nke akwụkwọ ahụ.
"What Ada bought was a first edition of the book."
(Background context: Ada made a purchase of a book.)

By structuring sentences this way, we achieve several effects: We direct attention to the emphasized part. The cleft construction clarifies the intended meaning. We contrast the emphasized part with other possibilities.

12.2 Cleft Construction:

Cleft constructions in Igbo involve the use of specific sentence structures to emphasize or highlight constituents. These constructions often serve to provide focus on a specific element, and their syntax plays a pivotal role in shaping the discourse. Similarly, relative clauses in Igbo are employed to add descriptive or identifying information about a noun phrase within a sentence, contributing to the specificity and clarity of expression.

The core of the cleft construction lies in the informationally prominent phrase. This phrase is the focus of the sentence, the element that is being emphasized or highlighted. It could be a noun, a pronoun, or another kind of phrase that carries significance in the context. After the copula and the informationally prominent phrase, there is typically an embedded clause. This subordinate clause provides additional information about the focused element, adding detail or context to the main statement. It contributes to the overall complexity and depth of meaning in the cleft sentence.

Cleft constructions are fascinating sentence structures that play a crucial role in emphasizing specific elements within a sentence. Cleft constructions allow us to emphasize specific information while providing necessary context. They are powerful tools for precision and rhetorical impact in English sentences.

Types of Cleft Constructions:
1. It-Cleft Sentence:
An it-cleft is a specific sentence structure where a single clause is split into two parts, each with its own verb. The purpose of an it-cleft is to emphasize a particular element within the sentence.

Basic Structure of an It-Cleft Sentence:

Form: "It was [X] that [Y]."

Example:

a). Ọ bụ Obi ka Ada hụrụ.   *"It was Obi that Ada saw."*
It + be verb + subject/object + that/who relative clause.

The "it" in the beginning is nonreferential and serves as the "cleft pronoun."

b). Ọ bụ nne ya na-emepụta ihe ngọpụ mgbe niile.
"It was her mother that always came up with excuses."
(Emphasizing her mother as the one who put forward the excuses.)

It-clefts allow precise focus on specific information. They clarify meaning and create coherence in discourse. Often used in spoken English to connect understood information with new information.

2. Wh-Cleft/Pseudo-Cleft Sentence:
Wh-cleft sentences (also known as pseudo-cleft sentences) share similarities with cleft sentences

but are formed using the pronoun "what." These structures allow us to emphasize specific information within a sentence:

Structure of Wh-Cleft/Pseudo-Cleft Sentences:

A wh-cleft sentence consists of two main parts:

i)The what-clause: Begins with "what" and contains information that is already understood or known.
ii). *The phrase after the what-clause + be*: This is the emphasized part, providing new information.

Form: "[Wh-word] [Y] was [X]."

Examples of Wh-Cleft/Pseudo-Cleft Sentences:

a) Ihe Amaka zụtara bụ mbipụta nke mbụ.   *"What Amaka bought was a first edition."*

b) Ihe dị mkpa bụ ka I we ezigbo ụra.   *"What you need is a good sleep."*
(Emphasizing the necessity for rest.)

c) Ihe na-amasịghị m bụ njedebe nke ihe nkiri ahụ.
"What I didn't like was the end of the movie." (Highlighting the disliked part.)

d) Ihe gbanwere obi ya bụ akwụkwọ ahụ ọ gụrụ.
"What changed his mind was a book he'd read." (Focusing on the influencing factor.)

e) Ndị m zutere bụ ndị nnọchiteanya.
"The people who/that I met were members of the delegation."
(Referring to specific individuals.)

f) Ihe ị ga-eme bụ degara onyeisi ọrụ ahụ akwụkwọ ozi.
"What you should do is write a letter to the manager."
(Emphasizing the recommended action.)

(a). Verb Forms in Wh-Clefts: The verb after "be" usually corresponds to the form used in the what-clause. For example:

i). Ihe m chọrọ bụ ihi ụra.

"What I want is to sleep."

ii). Ihe ọ enweghị ike inabata bụ ibili n'isi ụtụtụ.
"What he can't stand is getting up early."

(b). Past Simple and Present Perfect Patterns: In these tenses, we can use the following structures:

i). Ihe m mere n'ikpeazụ bụ laa n'ụlọ
"What I did in the end was (to) go home."

ii). Ihe m mere bụ idegara onye nchịkọta akụkọ akwụkwọ ahụ ozi
"What I have done is (to) write a letter to the editor."

3. Reversed Wh-Cleft/Inverted Pseudo-Cleft Sentence: Like pseudo-clefts but with inverted word order. A reversed wh-cleft (also known as an inverted pseudo-cleft) is a type of cleft sentence where the nominal relative clause appears at the end of the sentence. Unlike standard cleft sentences, where the focus element comes after the verb "be," in a reversed wh-cleft, the focus element is brought to the front of the sentence.

Examples of Reversed Wh-Cleft/Inverted Pseudo-Cleft Sentences:

Ezechi na-agwa Amarachi okwu.	*"Ezechi was talking to Amarachi."*
Amarachi bụ onye Ezechi na-agwa okwu.	*"Amarachi was who Ezechi was talking to."*
Achọrọ m udo na jụụ	*"I want some peace and quiet."*
Ụfọdụ udo na jụụ bụ ihe m chọrọ	*"Some peace and quiet is what I want."*
Achọrọ m ịga ebe dị anya na ebe a.	*"I want to go to a place so far away from here."*
Ebe dị anya na ebe a bụ ebe m chọrọ ịga.	*"A place so far away from here is where I want to go."*

Reversed wh-clefts allow us to emphasize specific information by placing it at the beginning of the sentence. They create a clear focus on the desired element while maintaining coherence in discourse. Reversed wh-clefts provide an alternative way to structure sentences, emphasizing the focus element right from the start.

12.3 The cleft pronoun in Igbo:
In Igbo, the cleft pronoun cannot be used interchangeably with demonstratives. Igbo's cleft pronoun is non-referential, which makes sense when considering cleft structures from an expletive perspective. The cleft pronoun in Igbo involves focus-fronting, and it is clearly expletive. the only

exception is where is the cleft clause is a relative clause and the cleft pronoun is to be regarded as referential. Igbo has two kinds of cleft constructions: *focus fronting* and *relativization*.

Cleft Pronoun as Expletive:

In cleft constructions, a pronoun is often used to introduce the structure. This pronoun is typically a placeholder or an expletive, meaning it doesn't carry significant meaning on its own. Instead, its role is often syntactic, fulfilling a grammatical requirement in the sentence.

Example 1: Cleft Pronoun
Original Sentence: Ọ bụ nwamba ahụ kụpụrụ ite ahụ
"It was the cat that knocked over the vase."

Demonstrative form: Nke a bụ nwamba ahụ kụpụrụ ite ahụ
"This was the cat that knocked over the vase."

Example 2: Cleft Pronoun
Original Sentence: Ọ bụ akwụkwọ akụkọ ahụ na-atọ m ụtọ ịgụ.
"It is the novel that I enjoyed reading."

Demonstrative form: Nke ahụ bụ akwụkwọ akụkọ ahụ na-atọ m ụtọ ịgụ
"That is the novel that I enjoyed reading."

Example 3: Cleft Pronoun
Original Sentence: Ọ bụ ihe nkiri ahụ anyị lere n'abalị ụnyahụ .
"It is the movie that we watched last night."

Demonstrative form: Nke a bụ ihe nkiri anyị lere n'abalị ụnyaahụ
"This is the movie that we watched last night."

In these examples, the cleft pronoun "it" serves a referential role, pointing to a specific element in the sentence. The alternation involves replacing the cleft pronoun with a demonstrative ("this" or "that"), maintaining the overall meaning and referential function.

Nancy Hedberg, a linguist, has extensively studied the fascinating world of cleft sentences. Her insights into Cleft Sentences uncovered that a cleft sentence is a specific type of sentence structure where a single clause is divided into two parts and these two parts serve distinct purposes:

The clefted constituent (often introduced by the pronoun "it") expresses an exhaustive focus.
The cleft clause conveys a pragmatic presupposition.

Hedberg's Contributions:
Nancy Hedberg's research sheds light on the nature of cleft sentences, particularly the role of the cleft pronoun (often "it"). She argues that the cleft pronoun is not merely an expletive or grammatical filler. Instead, it has semantic content. In her view, the cleft pronoun functions pragmatically as a definite article in a discontinuous definite description.

This description involves equating the clefted constituent (the emphasized part) with the referent via the copula. In other words, the cleft pronoun plays a crucial role in creating the focus and presupposition in cleft sentences.

Consider the following examples:
a) Ọ bụ Okoro meriri.   *"It was Okoro who won."* (Emphasizing Okoro as the focus)
b) Onye meriri bụ Okoro. *"The one who won was Okoro."* (Same emphasis)

These sentences demonstrate how the cleft pronoun "it" introduces the focus (Obama) and sets up the presupposition. Nancy Hedberg's work enriches our understanding of cleft sentences, emphasizing the significance of the cleft pronoun and its role in creating nuanced meaning.

Hedberg's suggests that the cleft pronoun can be seamlessly interchanged with demonstratives, showcasing the flexibility of these constructions in English and other European languages. Hedberg's argument highlights the referential nature of cleft pronouns and their ability to be alternated with demonstratives. However, he also notes that this alternation is not observed in other instances of the pronoun "it," specifically in raising structures and weather predicates. Let's elaborate on this distinction with examples:

12.4 kinds of cleft constructions in Igbo:
12.4.1 Focus Fronting:
Focus fronting is a syntactic construction where emphasis is placed on a particular element within a sentence by bringing that element to the front of the sentence. This construction highlights the focused element, drawing attention to it and often conveying a sense of emphasis or importance. Focus fronting is often employed in contexts where the speaker wants to highlight or stress a particular piece of information. It can be applied to various sentence structures, providing flexibility in emphasizing different elements.

A focus marker is a linguistic element that signals the presence of focus or emphasis on a particular part of a sentence. It is often used to highlight new or contrastive information, indicating what the speaker considers the most important element in the utterance. "Ka" is focus marker in Igbo cleft sentence.

The typical structure of an English it-cleft consists of a pronoun, copular verb, the focused phrase (XP), and the cleft clause. When the object is moved to the beginning of the cleft clause, there is morphological extraction marking. Following this object, a focus marker is present. The focus marker "ka" cannot be used with subject clefts. This distinction in ka-marking reflects a broader pattern of dissimilarity between subjects and non-subjects in out-of-place focus constructions in the language. Subject and non-subject clefts differ fundamentally because the complementizer "ka" is required for clefted non-subjects but not suited with subjects clefted within the clause. There is no focus marking with local subjects since the subject does not move to Spec-FocP.

Cleft Pronoun: Expletive

Example
Original Cleft Pronoun: Ọ bụ Nneka gara ahịa.
                                "It was Nneka that went to the market."

Demonstrative 1:   *Nke a bụ Nneka gara ahịa.
                                "This was Nneka that went the market."

Demonstrative 2:   *Nke ahụ bụ Nneka gara ahịa.
                                "That was Nneka that went the market."

In the above cleft constructions, the pronoun "it" serves an expletive function and cannot be smoothly replaced by a demonstrative without loss of meaning. While most English it-cleft are referential and can be smoothly replaced by demonstratives, in raising structures and weather predicates, "it" functions differently; it doesn't refer to a specific entity but serves as a syntactic placeholder. Attempting to substitute "it" with a demonstrative in these contexts disrupts the grammatical structure. For example:

2. Raising Structures: Example
Original Raising Structure: O dị ka obi adị ya ụtọ.
                                "It seems that she is happy."

Attempted Demonstrative Alternation:
                                *Nke a dị ka obi dị ya ụtọ. *
                                "This seems that she is happy."

In raising structures, where "it" serves as a placeholder subject, attempting to replace "it" with a demonstrative disrupts the grammatical structure, and the sentence becomes ungrammatical.

3. Weather Predicates:
Original Weather Predicate Example: Mmiri na-ezo.   *"It is raining."*
Attempted Demonstrative Alternation: *"Nke a na-ezo."*   *"This is raining."*

In weather predicates, such as "It is raining" or "It is snowing," replacing "it" with a demonstrative result in an ungrammatical construction. The pronoun "it" in weather expressions doesn't refer to a specific entity but serves as a syntactic placeholder.

Expletive analysis is a better way of describing clefts involving focus fronting in Igbo. This is because attempts to alternate Igbo cleft pronoun with a demonstrative has been found to result to ungrammatical structure of language expression. Therefore, Igbo cleft pronoun is expletive. This means that in Igbo, the cleft pronoun and the cleft clause form a continuous definite description as proposed by the specificational approach.

Understanding focus fronting allows for effective communication by strategically placing emphasis on key elements within sentences. A focus marker and a copula serve distinct functions in a sentence, and their co-occurrence depends on the language and its syntactic structures.

12.4.2 Relativization:

Relativization in the syntax of clefts involves the process of forming relative clauses within the structure of cleft sentences. In English, cleft constructions often include a relative clause that provides additional information about the clefted element. Here's how it works:

The basic structure of a cleft sentence includes a clefted element, a copular verb, and a cleft clause. For example, in the sentence "It was the book that I read," "the book" is the clefted element, "was" is the copular verb, and "that I read" is the cleft clause.

Igbo exhibits distinctive cleft construction, particularly one that incorporates relativization. Within these constructions, the cleft pronoun takes on a non-expletive role. Notably, when it comes to cleft sentences involving relativization, the initial pronoun assumes a non-expletive and referential nature, setting it apart from the pronoun deployed in cleft constructions emphasizing focus. The potential variations in the initial cleft pronoun, as outlined above, serve as evidence that this pronoun carries a referential function, especially within clefts featuring relative clauses.

Example:

a) Ọ bụ akwụkwọ ahụ Sera gụrụ.   Nke a bụ akwụkwọ ahụ Sera gụrụ.
   3sg cop akwụkwọ ahụ Sera gụụ-sfx   *DEM* cop akwụkwọ ahụ Sera gụụ-sfx

It is the book that Sarah read.   *This is the book that Sarah read.*

b) Ọ bụ ihe nkiri ahụ anyị lere.   Nke a bụ ihe nkiri ahụ anyị lere.
3sg cop ihe nkiri ahụ anyị lee-sfx   *DEM* cop ihe nkiri ahụ anyị lee-sfx
It is the movie that we watched.   *This is the movie that we watched.*

c) Ọ bụ abụ ahụ o dere.   Nke ahụ bụ abụ ahụ o dere.
3sg cop abụ ahụ o dee-sfx   *DEM* cop abụ ahụ o dee-sfx
It is the song that he composed.   *That is the song that he composed.*

d) Ọ bụ obodo ahụ ọ gara.   Nke ahụ bụ obodo ahụ ọ gara.
3sg cop obodo ahụ ọ gaa-sfx   *DEM* cop obodo ahụ ọ gaa-sfx
It is the city that she visited.   *That is the city that she visited.*

Relativization allows for the inclusion of descriptive or restrictive information within the cleft construction, giving more context to the focused element. It helps to clarify or specify which book, person, or thing is being emphasized in the cleft sentence.

a) Ọ bụ ugwu ahụ ka ha rigoro.   *It is the mountain that they climbed.*
3sg cop ugwu ahụ FOC ha rigo-sfx

b) Nke ahụ bụ ugwu ahụ ha rigoro.   *It is the mountain that they climbed.*
3sg cop ugwu ahụ ha rigo-sfx

In the first example mentioned, the clefted element offers a 'value' for a 'variable,' allowing the cleft sentence to function as a response to a question like "*What did we climb?*" where the clefted constituent corresponds to the wh-phrase. In this context, the cleft structure in example 1 aligns with the characteristics of a specificational sentence. Conversely, in the second example, the clefted element following the copula does not assign a value to a variable; rather, it predicates information about the subject. Consequently, the cleft sentence in example 2 cannot serve as an answer to the question "*What did we climb?*" This distinction in interpretation indicates that the copula used in these two cleft sentences is not identical. Specifically, the copula employed in cleft constructions involving relativization is a predicational copula.

12.5 Igbo copular clauses

Igbo copular clauses involve a verb copula "bụ/dị", which connects the subject of the clause with a subject complement, expressing a relationship or providing additional information about the subject. Here's an elaboration on the provided examples:

In Igbo, distinct copulas are employed in specificational and predicational sentences, as illustrated in the examples provided below (1-4). In the predicational copular sentence (b), the "dị" copula is utilized, whereas the "bu." copula is present in the cleft construction in (10-a).

a) Ọ bụ ihe nkiri ọhụrụ ka m lere na ụlọ ihe nkiri.
3sg cop ihe nkiri ọhụrụ FOC 1sg watch-PST na ụlọ ihe nkiri.
It was a new movie that I watched in the theater.

b) Ihe nkiri ahụ m lere n'ụlọ ihe nkiri *dị/*bụ* ọhụrụ.
Ihe nkiri ahụ 1sg watch-PST n'ụlọ ihe nkiri cop new.
The movie that I watched in the theater was new.

a) Ọ bụ nri ọhụrụ ka m riri na ụlọ oriri na ọṅụṅụ.
It was a new meal that I enjoyed at the restaurant.

b) Nri m riri n'ụlọ oriri na ọṅụṅụ *dị/*bụ* ọhụrụ.
The meal that I enjoyed at the restaurant was new.

a) Ọ bụ egwuregwu na-akpali akpali ka m gwuru n'ebennọkọ ahụ.
It was a thrilling game that I played at the park.

b) Egwuregwu m gwuru na ogige nnọkọta ahụ dị/*bụ ọhụrụ.
The game that I played at the park was new.

a) Ọ bụ akwụkwọ na-adọrọ mmasị ka m gụrụ na mbara ihu ụlọ.
It was a fascinating book that I read on the balcony.

b) Akwụkwọ m gụrụ na mbara ihu ụlọ dị/*bụ ọhụrụ.
The book that I read on the balcony was new.

The specificational and predicational copula "bụ."
The copula "bu." in Igbo serves dual roles as both a copula of specificational and a predicational copula. This means that "bu." can function in both specificational and predicational capacities. Given its role as a copula of specification, "bu." is employed in cleft constructions involving focus movement, particularly in cases where sets are involved.

For Example:

Predicational copular clause:

a.   Ada bụ nwa akwụkwọ.   "*Ada is a student*." (Predicational)

This is an example of a predicational copular clause where the copula "bụ" links the subject "Ada" to the predicative adjective " nwa akwụkwọ." In this structure, the copula asserts a condition/state about the subject.

Specificational copular clause:

b.   Onye isi oche otu Igbo bụ Ojukwu Okeke.
       "*The Chairman of Igbo Union is Ojukwu Okeke.*" (Specificational)

In this specificational copular clause, the copula "bụ," connects the subject " Onye isi oche otu Igbo" to the subject complement " Ojukwu Okeke." The focus here is on identifying or specifying the subject rather than describing a quality.

Identificational copular clause:

c.   Nwanyị ahụ bụ Nneka.
       "*That (woman) is Nneka.*" (Identificational)

This sentence represents an identificational copular clause. The copula "bụ," links the subject " Nwanyị ahụ" to the subject complement "Nneka." The primary purpose is to establish the identity of the subject, indicating that " Nwanyị ahụ" is indeed Nneka.

Equative copular clause

d.   Pete Edochie bụ Ogadagidi.   "*Pete Edochie is Ogadagidi*." (Equative)

In an equative copular clause, such as this example, the copula "bụ" asserts an equivalence or identity between the subject "Pete Edochie" and the subject complement "Ogadagidi." This structure is often used to equate two different names or expressions referring to the same entity.

B. The predicational copula nature of "dị."
One fundamental distinction between predicational copular clauses with "bụ." and those with "dị" lies in the fact that the "dị" copula is associated with descriptive nouns. Descriptive nouns are often equivalent to English adjectives. For instance, in the predicational "bụ." clause in (1a) below, the copula "bụ." cannot be substituted with the "dị" copula in (1b). Similarly, in a sentence (2-4), where the predicate complement are the descriptive noun, only "dị" is acceptable. The

predicational "bụ" is not permissible, as demonstrated by the incorrect example in (*).

a. Ada bụ nwa akwụkwọ.   "*Ada is a student.*" (Predicational)
b. *Ada dị nwa akwụkwọ.   "*Ada is a student.*" (incompatible Predicational)

	Copular sentence	**Not permissiable**	**English translation**
a)	Laptọọpụ dị ọhụrụ	*Laptọọpụ bụ ọhụrụ.	"*The laptop is new.*"
b)	Kọfị dị ọkụ,	*Kọfị bụ ọkụ.	"*The coffee is hot.*"
c)	Ofe Egwusi dị ụtọ.	*Ofe Egwusi bụ ụtọ.	"*Egwusi soup is delicious.*"
d)	Ọ dị n'ime ụlọ.	*Ọ bụ n'ime ụlọ.	"*It is inside the house.*"

The "dị" copula is also used with locational XPs, as demonstrated in the examples provided earlier. In sentence (1b) above, the extraction of the post-copular locative prepositional phrase is illustrated. Furthermore, sentences (2-5) indicate that the pre-copular and post-copular elements in the "dị" copula cannot be inverted. These characteristics align with the expectations for a predicational copula. Additional evidence supporting the idea that "dị" functions exclusively as a copula of predication is found in the fact that some clauses with the "dị" copula can be expressed using non-copular predicative verbs, as demonstrated in the sentences in (4).

Exercise

1. What are the typical components of a cleft sentence in Igbo grammar?
2. How do cleft sentences in Igbo differ from relative clauses?
3. What role does the copula play in Igbo cleft sentences?
4. Can you explain the syntax of cleft constructions in Igbo?
5. What is the purpose of cleft constructions in Igbo?
6. How do cleft sentences emphasize specific elements in a sentence?
7. What distinguishes a cleft sentence from a relative clause in Igbo?
8. Provide 5 examples of cleft sentences in Igbo?
9. What are the two types of cleft constructions discussed in Igbo grammar?
10. How does focus fronting contribute to cleft sentences in Igbo?
11. What is the role of the cleft pronoun in Igbo grammar?
12. Can the cleft pronoun be replaced with demonstratives in Igbo cleft constructions?
13. How does Nancy Hedberg's research contribute to our understanding of cleft sentences?
14. Explain the distinction between focus fronting and relativization in Igbo cleft sentences.
15. What is the function of the copula in Igbo copular clauses?
16. How does Igbo utilize the copula "bụ" in specificational and predicational copular clauses?
17. Give 5 examples of specificational copular clauses in Igbo?
18. What distinguishes the copula "dị" from "bụ" in Igbo predicational copular clauses?
19. How does relativization contribute to the complexity of cleft sentences in Igbo?
20. Can you explain the equative copular clause in Igbo grammar?

Chapter 13

The Structure and Formation of Igbo Sentence (*Nhazi na Mmebe* Ahịrịokwu Igbo)

13.1 A sentence—grammatical unit:
A sentence is a grammatical unit consisting of one or more words that express a complete thought or idea and typically have a subject and a predicate. It is a coherent group of words that express a complete thought or idea. It usually consists of a subject, which is the person, place, thing, or idea being discussed, and a predicate, which provides information about the subject.

A sentence typically begins with a capital letter and ends with punctuation, such as a period, exclamation point, or question mark. Sentences can express a wide range of thoughts, such as statements, questions, commands, and exclamations. In written language, sentences are used to convey information and to express ideas, thoughts, and emotions. In spoken language, sentences are used to make conversation and to convey information in a clear and organized manner.

13.2 Types of Sentences based on SUBJ-PRED construction.
The structure of SUBJECT-PREDICATE is a linguistic pattern observed in many languages. It comprises a subject (SUBJ) and a predicate (PRED) within a sentence, serving as a basic framework for communicating details about an action, state, or connection. This construction is essential for conveying information effectively and capturing the attention of audiences in diverse linguistic contexts. There are two sentences based on SUBJ-PRED construction, namely: Major and Minor Sentence.

13.2.1 MINOR SENTENCE:
A minor sentence is a sentence fragment that still conveys meaning despite lacking all the required components to be a complete sentence. They are sentences that do not always have to be complete. Minor sentences also referred to as, Sentence fragments, are partial sentences that lack a subject or main verb. These fragments can be utilized for various purposes, including:

1. Adding a conversational tone
2. Emphasizing a point
3. Building drama
4. Conveying surprise.

Linguistic technique of substitution and transformation do not apply to minor sentence. Minor sentences do not have SUBJ-PRED as in the case of major sentences. For examples:

a)	Aruo n'aja, Erie na ndo.	*Labour in the sun, enjoy in shade.*
b)	Ezi ekeresimesi	*Merry Christmas*
c)	Ekwe kuo. Ama Agba	*When the gong goes out, messages are given.*
d)	Ma ahuhu adighi. uru agaghi adi.	"No pain, no gain.'
e)	Gaa!	*"Go!" (Imperatives)*
f)	Ka o di / Ka emesia	*"Good-bye."*
g)	Kedu maka ndi a ebe a?"	*"How about these?" (At the market)*
h)	Di ka nna, di ka nwa.'	*"Like father, like son." (Aphoristic Expressions)*
i)	Amaka ebe a.	*"Amaka, here." (Self-Identification)*
j)	Daalu .	*"Thanks."*
k)	Chai!	*"Wow!" (Exclamations and Interjections)*
l)	Gi n'ebe a!	*"You over there!" (Vocatives)*

13.2.2 MAJOR SENTENCE

Major sentences are identified syntactically by the following factors:

1. Subject-Predicate
2. Substitution
3. Transformation

Substitution: Substitution is a linguistic technique in which one word or phrase is replaced with another word or phrase to change the meaning or structure of a sentence. For example, in the sentence Nwamba ahu noduru na ute; *"The cat sat on the mat"*, the word Nwamba *"cat"* can be substituted with nkita *"dog"* to change the sentence to Nkita ahu noduru na ute *"The dog sat on the mat"*. Substitution is often used in linguistic analysis to test the grammaticality of a sentence or to understand its underlying structure.

Transformation: Transformation is a process in which the structure of a sentence is changed without altering its meaning. Transformations can include operations such as subject-verb inversion, passive voice construction, and questions formation. For example, the sentence

Nwamba ahụ nọdụrụ na ute *"The cat sat on the mat"* can be transformed into a question by inverting the subject and verb to form Nwamba ahụ ọ nọdụrụ na ute? *"Did the cat sit on the mat?"*

Subject-Predicate Structure: The subject-predicate structure refers to the basic organization of a sentence, in which the subject and predicate are the two main components. The subject is the noun or noun phrase that the sentence is about, and the predicate is the verb phrase that provides information about the subject. For example, in the sentence Nwamba ahụ nọdụrụ na ute. *"The cat sat on the mat"*, Nwamba ahụ *"The cat"* is the subject, and nọdụrụ na ute *"sat on the mat"* is the predicate.

The subject-predicate structure is a fundamental aspect of linguistic structure and is present in all major sentence types, including declarative, interrogative, imperative, exclamatory and optative sentences.

13.2 Types of Sentences based on Functions.

Types of sentences based on function refer to the different purposes or intentions behind the sentences in communication. Each type serves a distinct function in conveying information, expressing emotions, asking questions, or issuing commands. These functions are categorized into various types such as declarative, interrogative, imperative, exclamatory, and optative sentences. Understanding these types helps individuals comprehend the intent behind the sentences they encounter and enables them to use language more effectively in different contexts.

13.2.1 Declarative Sentences:

Declarative sentences, which are the most prevalent type in language, serve the primary function of making statements or assertions. They are the standard mode of communication for conveying information, expressing opinions, or presenting facts. In essence, declarative sentences aim to communicate what the speaker believes to be true or factual about a particular subject. By structuring a declarative sentence, individuals articulate their thoughts, share knowledge, or express their viewpoints in a clear and straightforward manner.

For instance, the sentence Ọnwa na-acha n'abalị *"The moon shines at night,"* exemplifies a declarative statement. Here, the speaker asserts a universally recognized fact about the natural phenomenon of the moon. Through this declarative sentence, the speaker communicates a piece of information about the moon's operation, contributing to the listener's understanding of astronomical principles.

More examples:

    a) Nwamba na-arahụ ụra na oche.   *The cat is sleeping on the chair.*

b) Obi na Ada gara ihe nkiri n'abalị ụnyahụ.   *Obi and Ada went to the movies last night.*
c) Ụwa na-agba gburugburu anyanwụ.   *The Earth orbits around the sun.*
d) Mbara igwe na-acha anụnụ anụnụ.   *The sky is blue.*
e) Akwụkwọ ahụ dị na tebụl.   *The book is on the table.*
f) Ọnwa na-acha n'abalị.   *The moon shines at night.*
g) Nwanne m nwanyị na-egwuri egwu n'èzí.   *My sister is playing outside.*

Declarative sentences play a pivotal role in various contexts, including formal discourse, informal conversations, academic writing, and everyday interactions. They serve as the foundation for conveying information accurately and effectively, facilitating comprehension and clarity in communication. Whether presenting findings in a scientific report, expressing personal beliefs in a discussion, or sharing observations in casual conversation, declarative sentences form the backbone of effective communication in language.

13.2.2 Interrogative Sentences:
Interrogative sentences serve a crucial function in communication by prompting inquiries and seeking clarification on various topics. These sentences are designed to elicit information, opinions, or explanations from the listener or reader. They are characterized by their use of question words, such as who, what, where, when, why, or how, which initiate the interrogation process and guide the focus of the inquiry.

For example, consider the interrogative sentence Ebee ka ọbá akwụkwọ kacha nso dị? *"Where is the nearest library?"* Here, the speaker seeks specific information regarding the location of the nearest library. By employing the question word "where," the speaker directs attention to the spatial aspect of the inquiry, prompting the listener to provide details about the precise whereabouts of the library.

More examples:

a) Kedu ihe na-akụ?   *What time is it?*
b) Ebee ka ị na-aga?   *Where are you going?*
c) Kedu onye bụ ezigbo enyi gị?   *Who is your best friend?*
d) Gịnị mere i ji bịa ebe a?   *Why did you come here?*
e) Kedu ka Ị mere taa?   *How are you feeling today?*
f) Kedu oge bụ ụbọchị ọmụmụ gị?   *When is your birthday?*
g) Ị nwere ike ịsụ Igbo?   *Can you speak Igbo?*
h) Ihe nkiri ahụ ọ masịrị gị?   *Did you enjoy the movie?*
i) Ị na-abịa oriri na ọṅụṅụ ahụ?   *Are you coming to the party?*
j) Kedu agba ka amasị gị?   *Which colour do you prefer?*

    k)   Ị chọrọ ka m na gị gwukọrịta egwu?   *Do you want to play with me?*

Interrogative sentences facilitate active engagement in conversations, interviews, investigations, and various forms of discourse where seeking information or clarification is essential. They enable individuals to gather knowledge, clarify uncertainties, or solicit opinions, thereby enhancing understanding and fostering meaningful interactions.

In everyday communication, interrogative sentences play a vital role in facilitating dialogue, encouraging participation, and promoting exchange of ideas. Whether in formal settings such as interviews, surveys, or academic discussions, or in informal conversations among friends or colleagues, interrogative sentences serve as powerful tools for generating discourse, exploring perspectives, and deepening comprehension of the world around us.

13.2.3 Imperative Sentences:
Imperative sentences fulfill a distinct function in language by conveying commands, requests, or instructions to the listener or reader. These sentences are characterized by their direct and authoritative tone, as they aim to prompt action or compliance from the recipient. Imperative sentences can vary in their intensity, ranging from forceful commands to polite requests, depending on the context and interpersonal dynamics involved.

For instance, the imperative sentence Mechie ụzọ *"Close the door"* exhibits a straightforward and authoritative command, instructing the listener to perform a specific action without room for negotiation or delay. In this context, the speaker asserts control over the situation and expects immediate compliance from the listener.

More examples:

    a)   Biko nyefee nnu.   *Please pass the salt.*
    b)   Gbanyụọ ọkụ.   *Turn off the lights.*
    c)   Emetụla ya aka!   *Don't touch that!*
    d)   Nọrọ jụụ n'oge ihe nkiri.   *Be quiet during the movie.*
    e)   Wepụ ihe mkpofu ahụ.   *Take out the trash.*
    f)   Chichaa ezé gị tupu ị lakpuo ụra.   *Brush your teeth before bed.*
    g)   Gee ndị mụrụ gị ntị.   *Listen to your parents.*
    h)   Richaa akwụkwọ nri gị.   *Finish your vegetables.*
    i)   Nọdụ ala ma zuru ike.   *Sit down and relax.*
    j)   Kpọọ m mgbe ị rutere ebe ahụ.   *Call me when you get there.*

Conversely, imperative sentences can also adopt a softer and more polite tone, particularly when making requests or issuing instructions in a courteous manner. For example, the sentence Biko, nyefee nnu *"Please pass the salt"* combines the imperative form with the use of the polite word "please," conveying a respectful and considerate request rather than a demanding command. In this case, the speaker acknowledges the listener's autonomy and extends a polite invitation for assistance.

Imperative sentences play a vital role in various contexts, including everyday interactions, instructional settings, and emergency situations. Whether directing individuals in emergency procedures, providing guidance in instructional manuals, or requesting assistance in social settings, imperative sentences facilitate clear and efficient communication of directives and expectations.

13.2.4 Exclamatory Sentences

Exclamatory sentences serve as potent vehicles for conveying intense emotions or reactions, infusing language with heightened expressiveness and fervour. Distinguished by their distinctive punctuation, the exclamation mark, these sentences resonate with fervent excitement, profound surprise, visceral anger, or other powerful sentiments, capturing the essence of the speaker's emotional state.

For example, let's look at the exclamation, "Oh wow, that's delicious!" The phrase "Oh wow" expresses surprise or amazement, while the word "delicious" emphasizes the speaker's appreciation for the taste of the food. With this exclamation, the speaker not only expresses admiration for the food's flavour but also their strong appetite for enjoyment.

More examples:

a) Chei, nke ahụ dị ịtụnanya! — *Wow, that was amazing!*
b) Ohoo, lee nwa nkịta mara mma! — *Oh, what a cute puppy!*
c) Ihe ịtụnanya, anyị meriri egwuregwu ahụ! — *Amazing, we won the game!*
d) Chei, nke ahụ na-atọ ụtọ! — *Oh wow, that's delicious!*
e) Lee ka okooko osisi si maa mma! — *How lovely the flowers look!*
f) Oo chimoo,, nke ahụ atọgbuo m! — *Oh, my goodness, that's hilarious!*

Exclamatory sentences encompass a broad spectrum of emotions, ranging from jubilation and delight to indignation and outrage. They serve as powerful vehicles for expressing enthusiasm, awe, joy, frustration, or any other intense feeling that resonates deeply with the speaker's innermost sentiments.

In everyday communication, exclamatory sentences add vibrancy and emphasis to language, imbuing expressions with passion, energy, and urgency. Whether exclaiming in delight at a surprising revelation, expressing dismay at an unfortunate turn of events, or conveying gratitude for a kind gesture, exclamatory sentences amplify the emotional impact of the speaker's words, fostering connection and resonance with the listener.

13.2.5 Optative Sentences

Optative sentences serve as vessels for expressing wishes, desires, or blessings, embodying aspirations and heartfelt sentiments for oneself or others. These sentences convey a sense of hope, goodwill, or benevolence, encapsulating the speaker's sincere wishes for a positive outcome or experience.

For example, consider the optative sentence, Gaa nke oma/Ije ọma *"May you have a wonderful journey."* Here, the speaker extends a heartfelt wish for the listener's journey to be filled with joy, adventure, and fulfilment. The use of "may" imbues the sentence with a sense of possibility or potential, as the speaker invokes blessings and positive energy to accompany the listener on their travels.

More examples:

a)	Ka ị nwee ọmaricha ụbọchị!	*May you have a wonderful day!*
b)	Ka nrọ gị mezuo.	*May your dreams come true.*
c)	Ka ị nweta obi ụtọ na afọ ojuju.	*May you find happiness and fulfilment.*
d)	Ka udo diri unu mgbe nile.	*May peace be with you always.*
e)	Ka njem gị bụrụ nke dị mma ma dị ụtọ.	*May your journey be safe and pleasant.*
f)	Ka ọganihu soro gị ebe ọ bụla ị na-aga.	*May success follow you wherever you go.*
g)	Ka ọchịchọ gị bịa na mmezu.	*May your wishes be granted.*
h)	Ka Chineke nọnyere gị na ezinụlọ gị.	*May God be with you and your household.*
i)	Ka ị nweta ume n'oge mkpagbu.	*May you find strength in times of adversity.*
j)	Ka Chukwu meere gi ebere.	*May God have mercy on you.*

Optative sentences encompass a diverse range of expressions, from well-wishes for personal endeavours to blessings bestowed upon others. They reflect the universal impulse to convey goodwill and positive intentions, fostering connections and nurturing relationships through acts of kindness and empathy.

In everyday communication, optative sentences serve as gestures of support, encouragement, and affection, uplifting spirits and inspiring optimism in both the speaker and the recipient. Whether offering words of encouragement before a significant event, expressing gratitude for blessings received, or sending heartfelt wishes for a brighter future, optative sentences foster a sense of warmth, camaraderie, and shared humanity.

13.3 Types of Sentences based on Structures.

Understanding the structural complexity of sentences goes beyond merely recognizing their functions. It involves delving into the intricate arrangements of words and phrases within sentences to convey meaning effectively. By comprehending different sentence structures, individuals can wield language more skillfully, crafting nuanced expressions and communicating with precision.

13.3.1 Simple Sentences (Ahịrịokwu mfe)

Simple sentences, the most basic form of sentence structure, are composed of just one independent clause. This clause typically contains a subject and a predicate, with the subject being the doer of the action and the predicate expressing what the subject does or is. Simple sentences are concise and clear, expressing a complete thought in a straightforward manner. They stand alone as coherent units of communication, making them essential building blocks of written and spoken language. In Igbo language, simple sentences do not have more than one verb.

For instance, take the simple sentence Ọ na-abụ abụ nke oma. *"She sings beautifully."* Here, "she" is the subject, and "sings beautifully" is the predicate. The subject Ọ *"she"* performs the action of singing, while the predicate na-abụ abụ nke oma *"sings beautifully"* describes how she sings, conveying the idea that she sings with beauty or skill. This single independent clause forms a complete thought on its own, requiring no additional information to convey its meaning effectively.

More examples:

a) Elekere na-akụ nwayọ. *The clock ticks quietly.*
b) Nneka na-abụ abụ. *Nneka sings a song.*
c) Nkịta na-agbọ ndị ọbịa ụja. *The dog barks at strangers.*
d) Osisi na-ama jijiji na ifufe. *The tree sways in the wind.*
e) Nnụnụ na-efe ufe na mbara igwe. *Birds fly in the sky.*
f) Osimiri ahụ na-asọ nwayọọ nwayọọ. *The river flows gently.*
g) Obi na-aracha oroma. *Obi eats an orange.*
h) Anyanwụ na-ada na mgbede. *The sun sets in the evening.*
i) Amaka na-agba egwu nke ọma. *Amaka dances gracefully.*
j) Mmiri na-ezo nwayọọ nwayọọ. *The rain falls softly.*

Simple sentences are versatile and widely used in everyday communication, from casual conversations to formal writing. They are particularly useful for conveying straightforward ideas, making statements, or providing essential information without unnecessary complexity. By mastering the construction and usage of simple sentences, individuals can communicate clearly and efficiently, ensuring their messages are understood with ease.

13.3.2 Compound Sentences (Ahịrịokwu nha)

Sentences that are compound—a step above simple sentences in complexity—have a dynamic structure that combines several independent clauses. These independent clauses, each with a subject and a predicate, are connected by coordinating conjunctions to function as separate units inside the sentence. These conjunctions, such as "ma," "ma ọ bụ," "ma ọ bụghị," "maka," "mana," na "ya mere," ("but," "or," "nor," "for," "yet," and "so,") facilitate the seamless integration of related ideas or actions, creating a cohesive narrative flow. In Igbo language, compound sentences are sentences that have two verbs and two different meanings.

For examples:

a) Achọrọ m ịga oriri na ọṅụṅụ, ma enwere m ọtụtụ ihe omume ụlọ.
   I wanted to go to the party, yet I had too much homework.

b) Ha gara n'ikpere mmiri, mana mmiri malitere izo.
   They went to the beach, but it started to rain.

c) Achọrọ m osikapa maka nri abalị, mana nwanne m nwoke chọrọ akpụ.
   I wanted rice for dinner, but my brother wanted cassava.

d) Ọ na-enwe mmasị ịgụ akwụkwọ, ma ọ naghị enwe ohere maka ya.
   He likes to read books, yet he rarely has time for it.

e) Achọrọ m ịga igwu mmiri, ya mere, etinyere m uwe mwụda mmiri.
   I wanted to go swimming, so I put on my swimsuit.

f) chefuru nri ehihie ya, ya mere ọ ga-azụrịrị ya n'ụlọ akwụkwọ.
   He forgot his lunch, so he had to buy it at school.

Compound sentences offer a versatile framework for expressing complex relationships between ideas or events. They enable writers and speakers to juxtapose contrasting concepts, present alternatives, or illustrate cause-and-effect relationships with clarity and precision. By harnessing the power of coordinating conjunctions, individuals can craft engaging narratives, persuasive arguments, or compelling descriptions that captivate audiences and convey meaning effectively.

13.3.3 Complex Sentences (Ahịrịokwu ukwu)

Complex sentences have a precise structure that combines independent and dependent clauses. These sentences are crucial to complex communication. These elaborate and detailed sentences have one or more dependent clauses and at least one independent clause that can stand alone as a complete sentence. The independent clause must supply context and meaning for these dependent clauses, which are essential parts of the sentence.

Whereas independent clauses can stand alone as complete sentences, dependent clauses cannot. Sometimes, they start with subordinating conjunctions, like n'agbanyeghị *"although,"* n'ihi na *"because,"* ma ọ bụrụ *"if,"* mgbe *"when,"* or kemgbe *"since,"* which create a logical connection with the independent sentence.

For instance, consider the complex sentence: N'agbanyeghị na mmiri na-ezo, ha kpebiri ijegharị. *"Although it was raining, they decided to go for a walk."* In this example, the independent clause ha kpebiri ijegharị *"they decided to go for a walk"* forms a complete thought, expressing an action taken by the subjects. However, the dependent clause N'agbanyeghị na mmiri na-ezo, *"Although it was raining"* provides context and introduces a condition under which the action occurs. Together, these clauses construct a narrative that conveys the resilience or determination of the subjects despite adverse weather conditions.

More examples:

a) N'agbanyeghị na mmiri na-ezo, ha kpebiri ijeagharị..
   Although it was raining, they decided to go for a walk.

b) Mgbe ihe nkiri ahụ mechara, ha gara rie nri abalị.
   After the movie ended, they went out for dinner.

c) Ebe ọ bụ na chi ejiela, ha kpebiri ịpụ oriri ahụ.
   Since it was getting late, they decided to leave the party.

d) Mgbe mgbịrịgba ahụ kụrụ, ụmụ akwụkwọ ahụ ji ọsọ pụọ na klaasị ahụ.
   When the bell rang, the students rushed out of the classroom.

e) N'ihi na O nwetaghị bọs ahụ, ọ jiri ụkwụ gaa ụlọ akwụkwọ.
   Because he missed the bus, he had to walk to school.

f) Mgbe ha richara nri abalị, ha gawara ịgagharị na ogige nnọkọta.
   After they finished dinner, they went for a stroll in the park.

g) N'ihi na ọ bụ ụbọchị ọmụmụ ya, ha mere ya oriri oriri ịtụnanya..
   Because it was his birthday, they threw him a surprise party.

h) Mgbe ọ ruchara ọrụ ya, e kwere ka ya na ndị enyi ya pụọ.
   After she finished her chores, she was allowed to go out with her friends.

i) Ebe ọ bụ na o chefuru nche anwụ ya, mmiri wee matọọ ya.
   Since he forgot his umbrella, he got soaked in the rain.

Complex sentences offer a versatile framework for weaving together multiple ideas, establishing causal relationships, or expressing conditional statements with precision and clarity.

13.3.4 Compound-Complex Sentences (Ahịrịokwu nhaukwu)

Compound-complex sentences, the pinnacle of sentence complexity, seamlessly integrate the characteristics of both compound and complex structures. Within these sentences, multiple independent clauses coexist alongside at least one dependent clause, resulting in a sophisticated framework for conveying intricate relationships between ideas.

In essence, compound-complex sentences offer a wealth of detail and flexibility, allowing writers and speakers to interweave various elements of information, causality, and contingency. This elevated level of complexity enables the expression of nuanced thoughts, elaborate narratives, or multifaceted arguments with precision and coherence.

For example, consider the compound-complex sentence:

"Ọ gara ụlọ ahịa, ma ọ chefuru ịzụrụ mmiri ara ehi, nke pụtara na ọ ga-alaghachi azụ ma emechaa."
"She went to the store, but she forgot to buy milk, which meant she had to go back later."

Here's is the breakdown:
Ọ gara ụlọ ahịa; *"She went to the store* (independent clause), ma ọ chefuru ịzụrụ mmiri ara ehi *but she forgot to buy milk* (independent clause), nke pụtara na ọ ga-alaghachi azụ ma emechaa *which meant she had to go back later* (dependent clause)."

In this sentence, each independent clause — Ọ gara ụlọ ahịa *"She went to the store"* and ọ chefuru ịzụrụ mmiri ara ehi "she forgot to buy milk" — functions as a standalone unit, articulating distinct actions performed by the subject. Meanwhile, the dependent clause nke pụtara na ọ ga-alaghachi azụ ma emechaa *"which meant she had to go back later"* introduces a causal relationship, explaining the consequence of forgetting to buy milk.

More examples:

j) Ọ bụ ezie na ọ mụsiri ihe ike maka ule ahụ, ọ nweghị akara mmụta dị mma, ma ọ maara na ọ pụrụ inwe oganihu ma ọ nọgide na-ịrụsi ọrụ ike.
Although she studied hard for the test, she still didn't get a good grade, but she knows she can improve if she keeps working hard.

k) Mgbe ha rutere na mmemme ahụ, onye ọ bụla na-agba egwu, n'ihi ya, ha sonyere ha, mana ha pụrụ n'oge n'ihi na ha nwere ihe ọzọ ime n'isi ụtụtụ echi.
When they arrived at the event, everyone was already dancing, so they joined in, but they had to leave early because they had an early morning the next day.

l) Mgbe ọ nụrụ akụkọ ahụ, ọ wụrụ ya akpata oyi, ya mere, ọ kpọrọ enyi ya ka ọ gwa ya okwu maka ya, ma enyi ya azaghị ya, nke mere ka ọ na-echegbukwu onwe ya.
When he heard the news, he was shocked, so he called his friend to talk about it, but his friend didn't answer, which made him feel even more anxious.

m) Mgbe ha rutere n'ụsọ osimiri, ha doziri nche anwụ na akwa nhicha ha, mana ifufe siri ike nke ukwuu, n'ihi ya, ha gara ebe ọzọ, ebe ọ dị jụụ.
When they arrived at the beach, they set up their umbrella and towels, but the wind was too strong, so they had to move to a different spot, where it was calmer.

n) Ebe ọ bụ na ọ kpakọbara ego zuru ezu, o kpebiri ịzụ ụgbọ ala ọhụrụ, ma ọ pụghị ikpebi agba ọ chọrọ, nke a mere oge mkpebi ya ji dị anya.
Since he had saved up enough money, he decided to buy a new car, but he couldn't decide on the color, which delayed his decision.

Compound-complex sentences enable authors and speakers to communicate complicated narratives, in-depth analyses, or thorough explanations by skillfully combining independent and dependent clauses. This complex arrangement improves communication's depth and coherence, enabling the nuanced expression of concepts and encouraging audience participation and understanding.

Exercise

1. What are the essential components of a sentence?
2. Explain the difference between a major and a minor sentence.
3. How do minor sentences differ from major sentences in terms of linguistic analysis techniques?
4. Provide examples of minor sentences and explain their usage.
5. What are the characteristics of declarative sentences?
6. Give examples of declarative sentences and explain their function in communication.
7. How do interrogative sentences facilitate communication, and what are their defining features?
8. Provide examples of interrogative sentences and discuss their role in seeking information.
9. What distinguishes imperative sentences from other types of sentences, and how are they used?
10. Give 5 examples of imperative sentences and explain their function in communication?
11. What purpose do exclamatory sentences serve, and how do they differ from other sentence types?
12. Provide examples of exclamatory sentences and discuss their role in expressing emotions.
13. What defines optative sentences, and how are they used to convey wishes or blessings?
14. Give examples of optative sentences and explain how they contribute to communication.
15. What are simple sentences, and how do they differ from other sentence structures?
16. Provide examples of simple sentences and discuss their significance in communication.
17. How are compound sentences structured, and what role do coordinating conjunctions play in their formation?
18. Give examples of compound sentences and explain how they enhance communication.
19. What characterizes complex sentences, and how do they contribute to conveying nuanced ideas?
20. Provide examples of complex sentences and discuss their role in expressing complex relationships between ideas.

About the Author

Elisha O. Ogbonna hails from Enugu in Igbo land, where Igbo is his mother tongue. His journey with the Igbo language began at the age of nine when he started on reading Igbo books and the Akwụkwọ Nsọ, aiming to assist his late parents who were unable to read or write in Igbo. This early exposure to language sparked his passion for teaching and translating English expressions into Igbo, a skill he honed throughout his high school years. Elisha's dedication and diligence is reflected in his outstanding performance in Igbo language in the West Africa Examination during his secondary education.

As he progressed through his academic journey, Elisha actively engaged in translation and interpretation work, contributing his expertise in both traditional and religious contexts. Even during his time as a teacher, he took on the responsibility of instructing adult learners in the intricacies of the Igbo language. His enthusasm for sharing his knowledge led him to establish a platform dedicated to aiding those interested in learning Igbo.

Looking ahead, Elisha is excited about his forthcoming book tailored for advanced learners, signaling his commitment to advancing the proficiency of Igbo language enthusiasts. With his wealth of experience and unwavering dedication, Elisha remains a beacon of support and guidance for anyone embarking on their journey to master the rich and vibrant Igbo language.

Other Books

Comprehensive Igbo Language: *A Contemporary Guide for Beginners And Intermediate Learners*

Comprehensive Igbo Language provides thorough and effective ways to learn and master the skills you need for Igbo communication, reading, and writing. Unlike every other Igbo language book, it contains a guide to pronunciation and a detailed explanation of pitch accent marking and syllable formation. Syllables are often considered the phonological "building blocks" of words. This book helps you in-depth guide on a unit of pronunciation and the formation of the whole or a part of a word.

It has a solid grounding in grammar basics and a progressive approach to learning Igbo in the manner in, which people naturally acquire language. You will be introduced to the most essential structures that will help you communicate in the Igbo language almost immediately, It uncovers the most common concepts that govern verbs and sentences used in everyday communication.

The comprehensive Igbo Language presents a unique and easy structure to master essential, grammar, verbs, and vocabulary. It contains words and names used for family, friends, people, plants, animals, foods, time, colors, days, nature, occupation, and so on. It also has exercises to help you test what you've learned and measure your progress.

Advanced Igbo Language: *A Simplified Guide to Igbo Orthography, Phonology, Morphology and Lexicology*

This straightforward and comprehensive book deals with encamping features of Igbo linguistics in a manner that is new, exciting, and revealing to both speakers and learners.

It is a well-organized and systematic material that started from the foundational principles of language study. This excellent book presents Igbo orthography, phonemes: phonemic analysis: phonetic transcription: place of articulation: prefixes: prosody: segmental phoneme: morphemes: class-changing: class-maintaining: word formation, lexeme, synonyms, antonyms, ambiguities, and solution to ambiguities in Igbo language.

This book should form a useful textbook for high and tertiary institutions: and private establishments where Igbo language is learned and taught.

Standard Igbo Language: *A Complete Guide to Learning and Speaking Igbo Language*

"Standard Igbo Language" is an expanded edition of "Comprehensive Igbo Language." It is comprehensive guide designed to empower learners to master the intricacies of standard Igbo language. It unlocks a deeper understanding of Igbo grammar. Starting with an exploration of the Igbo alphabet and pronunciation, readers are introduced to the foundational elements of the language, including vowels, consonants, and tonal accents. Through engaging exercises and practical examples, learners develop a strong foundation in Igbo phonetics and orthography.

The book takes readers on a journey through the essential components of the Igbo language. As readers progress through the chapters, they delve into a diverse array of topics, from common verb phrases and simple conversation to parts of speech, tenses, and punctuation. Each chapter offers insights into the nuances of Igbo grammar and syntax, accompanied by interactive exercises to reinforce learning.

Beyond language proficiency, "Standard Igbo Language" offers a holistic view of Igbo culture, with chapters dedicated to numerals, shapes, colors, nature, animals, and social institutions. Readers gain a deeper appreciation for the word usage and richness, as they explore the vocabulary and concepts that shape everyday life in Igbo society.

With its comprehensive and practical approach, "Standard Igbo Language" serves as an indispensable resource for learners of all levels, from beginners to advanced speakers. Whether you're seeking to reconnect with your Igbo heritage or embark on a journey of language learning, this book is your guide to mastering the language and embracing the vibrant spirit of Igbo culture.

Igbo Linguistics: *An Expanded Guide To Igbo Orthography, Phonology, Morphology & Lexicology*

"Igbo Linguistics: An Expanded Guide to Igbo Orthography, Phonology, Morphology, and Lexicology" offers a comprehensive exploration of the linguistic landscape of the Igbo language in an extensive form, providing readers with a deep understanding of its structure, sound system, word formation, and vocabulary.

The book starts with Igbo Orthography, tracing its development from traditional systems like Nsibidi to the standardized writing used today. Readers are introduced to the diverse Igbo orthography, including vowel and consonant sounds, spelling rules, and punctuation conventions.

It continued with Phonology and Phonetics, examining the sounds of Igbo and their articulation. From the classification of phonemes to the structure of syllables and the mechanics of speech production, readers explore the fundamental elements of Igbo phonology. Practical exercises reinforce learning, allowing readers to refine their pronunciation and phonetic transcription skills.

Further, the exploration extends to the Morphology of Igbo Linguistics, unraveling the structure and formation of words in the language. Readers delve into the nature of morphemes, the types of morphological processes, and the intricacies of word formation. In Lexicology, it examines the semantic relationships and lexical categories of words.

"Igbo Linguistics" serves as an indispensable resource for students, educators, and enthusiasts seeking to deepen their understanding of Igbo language. Through its accessible approach and comprehensive coverage, the book equips readers with the knowledge and skills to engage meaningfully with the linguistic heritage of the Igbo people. Whether you're a beginner embarking on your language learning journey or an advanced learner seeking to refine your skills, "Igbo Linguistics" is your guide to mastering the intricacies of this vibrant and dynamic language. Through detailed explanations and exercises, learners gain proficiency in reading and writing Igbo with accuracy and fluency.

Igbo Syntax: *The Structure And Rules That Govern Igbo Phrases And Well-Formed Sentences*

Igbo Syntax is a comprehensive guide that delves into the intricate workings of Igbo grammar, offering readers a deep understanding of how phrases and sentences are constructed in the language. From the foundational concepts of syntax to the advanced principles of transformational grammar, each chapter of the book provides a thorough exploration of the key elements that shape Igbo linguistic structure.

The beginning chapters introduce to readers the basic units of Igbo syntax, including words and clitics, laying the groundwork for a comprehensive understanding of the language's grammatical framework. It then proceeded with exploring word order typology and syntactic categories, gaining insight into the different types of word groups and the hierarchical structure of Igbo sentences. Through practical exercises, learners develop proficiency in identifying and analyzing the syntactic components of Igbo language.

The middle chapters focus on the lexicon and phrasal categories, examining the diverse range of noun phrases, adjective phrases, and prepositional phrases found in Igbo discourse. Readers learn how these phrasal categories contribute to the overall structure and meaning of sentences. Toward the end, readers delve into Igbo phrase structure rules, transformational grammar, and grammatical functions, gaining insight into the underlying principles that govern sentence formation and communication in Igbo.

Igbo Semantics: *A Comprehensive Exploration Of Simple And Complex Meanings In Igbo Language*

"Igbo Semantics" delves deep into the intricate world of meaning within the Igbo language, offering readers a comprehensive exploration of semantic structures and relationships. From the nuances of word meanings to the complexities of sentence interpretation, this book provides a thorough understanding of how meaning is conveyed and understood in Igbo communication.

Readers will embark on a journey through the semantic landscape of Igbo, uncovering the rich tapestry of meanings embedded within its vocabulary. Through detailed analyses and insightful explanations, the book examines the various semantic domains present in Igbo, including lexical semantics, compositional semantics, and discourse semantics.

Drawing on linguistic theory and empirical research, "Igbo Semantics" explores key topics such as semantic ambiguity, lexical relations, and semantic roles. Readers will gain valuable insights into how meaning is constructed through the interaction of words, phrases, and discourse contexts in Igbo language use.

Whether you are a student, researcher, or language enthusiast, "Igbo Semantics" offers a valuable resource for deepening your understanding of the intricacies of meaning in Igbo communication. With its accessible approach and comprehensive coverage, this book is an essential companion for anyone interested in exploring the fascinating world of Igbo semantics.

Index

Adjective Phrase **18, 164, 176**
Adjective Phrases **4, 92, 93**
Adjectives
    demonstrative adjectives 41, 49
Adjuncts
    Adjectival Adjuncts 88, 152, 160
    Adverbial Adjuncts 88, 152, 160
    Nominal Adjuncts 88, 153, 160
Adverb Phrase **18, 165, 176**
Adverbial
    Degree adverbial 145
    Manner Adverbial 144
    Place adverbial 141
    Time adverbial 139, 140
Adverbial Phrases **4, 92, 94**
Adverbials
    Distance Adverbials 143
    Duration Adverbials 140
    Frequency Adverbials 140
Adverbs
    Interrogative adverbs 42, 101
cleft constructions **6, 196, 197, 198, 199, 200, 201, 204**
cleft pronoun **6, 193, 195, 196, 197, 199, 204**
cleft sentence.**170, 191, 192, 193, 194, 195, 196, 197, 199, 200, 204**
Clefting Test **170, 176**
Clitics **3, 12, 15**
Clomplement
    Clausal complement 111
Collective Phrases **4, 92, 100, 101**
Colloquialisms **55**
Complement **5, 26, 27, 28, 29, 69, 70, 71, 72, 73, 77, 86, 105, 106, 136, 137, 138, 157**
complementizer **47, 72, 110, 111, 116, 198**
Complements
    subject complement ... 86, 136, 137, 151, 156, 157, 158, 200, 202
Conjunction **21, 45, 72, 123, 169, 182, 185**
Constituent structure **5, 161, 164, 175**
Construction
    Cleft constructions 192, 193
    Head-Modifier Construction 149
    Noun/Adjective construction 149, 150, 160
    Verb/Object construction 149, 160
Coordination Test **169, 176**
Copular clauses **6, 200, 202, 204**
Copular verb **198, 199**
Dative movement **117**
Deep structure **112, 118**
Demonstrative Phrases **4, 92, 99**
dependent clause **19, 154, 181, 182, 189, 214, 215**
Determiner
    Demonstrative determiner 44, 149, 150, 160
    Possessive determiner 43
direct object ... **18, 22, 23, 24, 25, 26, 27, 28, 32, 61, 62, 63, 64, 65, 66, 70, 86, 95, 97, 117, 119, 134, 135, 136, 137, 138, 151, 157, 158, 177**
Ellipsis Test **168, 169, 176**
Enclitics **3, 14**
Extraposition **120, 121**
Focus fronting **197**
focus marker **197, 198, 199**
Fragment Test **174**
Gender **46, 57, 58, 60, 150**
Gerund Phrase **4, 92, 97**
Grammar Rules
    Deep Structure 112, 113
    Surface Structure 112, 113
Grammatical functions **129, 147, 148, 222**
Identificational copular clause **202**
Idioms **54**
independent clause ... **18, 19, 153, 154, 178, 179, 180, 181, 182, 189, 212, 214, 215**
indirect object .**18, 24, 25, 26, 32, 37, 62, 97, 117, 135, 136**
Infinitive **38, 46, 49, 58, 59, 61, 85, 90, 95, 96, 98, 104, 186, 189**
Infinitive Phrase **4, 92, 95**
Insertion rules **126**
Interrogative Phrase **4, 92, 100**
Intonation Test **174, 175**
It-cleft **193, 198**
Lexicon **51, 52, 53, 56, 84, 90, 222**

Modifiers 5, 93, 101, 149, 156, 157, 158, 159
Mood 46, 47, 66, 134, 146, 147, 148, 181
Movement Test 166, 167, 168, 176
Negation 11, 46, 66, 86, 146, 147, 148
Neologisms 54
noun phrase 9, 10, 17, 35, 43, 61, 62, 63, 74, 86, 92, 93, 95, 97, 99, 101, 104, 106, 107, 108, 114, 116, 119, 122, 123, 124, 130, 134, 151, 155, 156, 162, 192, 207
Noun Phrase 4, 9, 18, 92, 106, 107, 110, 119, 122, 149, 151, 160, 161, 163, 164, 176
Nouns
    Abstract Noun 60
    Abstract Nouns 57
    Agent Nouns 58, 60
    Animate Nouns 58, 60
    Collective Noun 59
    Collective Nouns 57
    Common Noun 59
    Common Nouns 56
    Compound Noun 59
    Compound Nouns 57
    Concrete Noun 60
    Concrete Nouns 56
    Count Nouns 57, 60
    Countable Nouns 57
    Gender-specific Nouns 57, 60
    Inanimate Nouns 58, 60
    Material Nouns 59, 61
    Non-count Nouns 60
    Proper Noun 59
    Proper Nouns 56
    Uncountable Nouns 57
    Verbal Nouns 58, 61
Number Phrases 4, 92, 102
Passivization 119
Phrase
    Adjective phrase 10, 87, 93, 108
    Adverbial phrase 29, 94, 119
    Gerund phrase 97, 98
    Noun phrase 92, 93
    Number phrase 102
    Possessive phrase 102
    Prepositional phrase 10, 63, 70, 95, 108, 120, 203
Phrase Structure 4, 105, 162, 163, 176
Phrase structure tree 114
Phrase structure trees 115
Plurality 44
Possessive Phrases 4, 92, 101, 102
Predicate .. 19, 20, 61, 62, 72, 73, 74, 80, 87, 137, 148, 151, 153, 165, 177, 178, 179, 182, 202, 205, 207, 212, 213
Predicate Nominative 87, 137, 157

Predicational copular clause 202
Prepositional Phrase 4, 18, 63, 69, 72, 92, 95, 106, 110, 119, 165, 176
Proclitics 3, 13
Pronominalization Test 171, 172
Pronoun
    demonstrative pronoun 99
    Emphatic pronoun 37, 38
    impersonal pronoun 37, 126
    Personal Pronoun 36
    Reflexive Pronoun 37
    Subject Pronoun 36
Pronouns
    possessive pronouns 43, 102
Proverbs 54
Quantifier 43
Question Formation Test 172, 173
Relativization 123, 124, 199, 200
Sentence
    Complex sentences 21, 214, 215
    compound sentence 21, 213, 217
    Compound-complex sentence 215, 216
    Declarative sentences 207, 208
    Exclamatory sentences 210
    Imperative sentences 209, 210
    Interrogative sentences 208, 209
    Optative sentences 211
    Simple sentence 212
Slang 54, 55
Specificational copular clause 202
Subject-Verb-Adjective 28, 29, 30
Subject-Verb-Adverb 30, 31
Subject-Verb-Indirect Object-Direct Object 24
Subject-Verb-Object 8, 21, 22, 23, 24, 26, 27, 28, 63
Substitution Test 165, 166, 176
Surface structure 4, 112, 113, 118
syntactic category 21, 34, 42, 43, 49, 114
Syntactic function 35, 129
taxonomy 34, 49
Tense
    future tense 31, 46, 85
Topicalization 119, 173, 174
Transformational processes 113
Transformative grammar 117, 121, 128
Transformative Grammar
    deletion rules 122, 126, 128
Transitivity 63, 64, 66
Verb Construction
    Instrumental Serial Verb Construction 83, 90
    Locative Serial Verb Construction 84, 90
    Resultative Serial Verb Construction 81, 90

Sequential Serial Verb Construction 82, 90
Verb Phrase......18, 106, 108, 121, 122, 123, 163, 164, 176
Verbs. 3, 4, 34, 35, 38, 40, 46, 63, 64, 65, 66, 69, 70, 72, 73, 74, 75, 76, 77, 80, 84, 85, 91, 132, 134, 146
- +valency verbs 66, 67
- auxiliary verbs 38, 46, 85, 109
- Behavioral Process Verbs 80
- Bound Complement Verbs 69, 71, 77
- Ergative Complement Verb 73
- Existential Process Verbs 77, 78, 79
- General complement verbs..69
- Infinitive Verbs 38, 85
- Inherent complement verbs 70
- Intransitive verbs 64
- Linking Verbs...39, 85
- Material Process Verbs 75
- Mental Process Verb 75
- Modal verbs 39
- Phrasal Verbs 53
- Prepositional Complement Verbs............................... 72
- Relational Process Verbs 77
- Transitive verbs 64, 177
- Trivalent verbs 67
- Unaccusative verbs... 65
- Unergative verbs 65, 66
- -valency verbs... 66, 68
- Verbal Process Verbs 74, 76

Vocabulary 51, 52, 54, 90, 219, 220, 221, 222
Voice 46, 94, 120, 175, 206
VP hopping...121
Wh-cleft sentences..193
Wh-movement 118
word order. 7, 11, 14, 17, 18, 20, 21, 24, 32, 42, 91, 93, 94, 95, 97, 99, 100, 101, 102, 112, 113, 195, 222